AF711159

by JOHN WEIR PERRY

ROOTS OF RENEWAL IN MYTH AND MADNESS:
THE MEANING OF PSYCHOTIC EPISODES

THE FAR SIDE OF MADNESS

LORD OF THE FOUR QUARTERS:
MYTHS OF THE ROYAL FATHER

THE SELF IN PSYCHOTIC PROCESS

ROOTS OF RENEWAL IN MYTH AND MADNESS

The Meaning of Psychotic Episodes

John Weir Perry

ROOTS OF RENEWAL IN MYTH AND MADNESS

Jossey-Bass Publishers
San Francisco · Washington · London · 1976

ROOTS OF RENEWAL IN MYTH AND MADNESS
The Meaning of Psychotic Episodes
by John Weir Perry

Copyright © 1976 by: Jossey-Bass, Inc., Publishers
615 Montgomery Street
San Francisco, California 94111
&
Jossey-Bass Limited
44 Hatton Garden
London EC1N 8ER

Copyright under International, Pan American, and Universal Copyright Conventions. All rights reserved. No part of this book may be reproduced in any form—except for brief quotation (not to exceed 1,000 words) in a review or professional work—without permission in writing from the publishers.

Library of Congress Catalogue Card Number LC 76-19500

International Standard Book Number ISBN 0-87589-297-3

Manufactured in the United States of America

JACKET DESIGN BY WILLI BAUM

FIRST EDITION

Code 7617

The Jossey-Bass
Behavioral Science Series

Preface

In the psychotic state called acute schizophrenia, the symbolic concerns in which a person becomes engrossed belong to a subjective reality. Although these concerns are usually totally out of keeping with objective reality, they are meaningful and not merely random disorder. Such ideation may be suppressed by medication, producing a superficial appearance that normality has been restored. However, if the ideation is given full attention rather than being suppressed, the individual in the psychotic state has an altogether different experience of it that changes the very nature and phenomenology of the psychosis.

The retreat into disorder and insanity is a product of disturbed relationship and emotional connection with the social milieu. When the individual in this plight feels thus frighteningly isolated, his or her withdrawal deepens and the sense of disorder mounts. This becomes the occasion, in clinical practice, for high doses of medication. A self-aggravating cycle is set in motion, for this treatment removes the individual further again from the experience of the emotions and from the availability of the inner sources of psychic vitality. When medication is avoided and the imagery coming from psychic depth is heeded, it may be found that nature's own healing process is thereby allowed to do its work. The individual is relieved to know that he is in a legitimate altered state of consciousness in which certain processes tend to come into play for the reorganization of the self.

I am making the formulations of this reorganizational process on the basis of some thirty years of part-time psychotherapy with psychotic individuals, alongside my usual work as an analyst with "normal neurotics." During these decades I have found the symbolic imagery not only to be meaningful but even to follow the classical outlines of the renewal process that has parallels in ancient expressions of myth and ritual ceremonial.

In *Roots of Renewal in Myth and Madness* my intention is to demonstrate the reality of the renewal process. This process was prevalent in archaic phases of culture and follows its typical outlines in various parts of the ancient world; it also occurs in the contemporary psyche of our times in high arousal states—visionary states called psychosis. Such renewal is nature's own attempt to heal by way of the turmoil we know as psychosis.

In these chapters I therefore give a description of a method of psychotherapy for psychosis that makes such healing possible. I present a formulation of emotional development according to the Jungian model, and the dynamics of the self-image. An account is rendered of the difficulties that entrap persons in the chronically regressive state and the remedy that nature provides in the acute regression in the psychotic turmoil. There follow full historical studies of the components of the renewal process in the myth and ritual drama of ancient cultures, and with these, examples of their appearance in the modern psyche. The evolution of the messianic image is then traced. Finally, I outline the applicability of these concepts to clinical observations.

My book, then, is addressed to those who are interested in the problems of formulation and treatment of psychotic conditions, and in the phenomenology of altered states of consciousness. I hope it will also speak to those concerned with the question of the survival of myth and ritual forms in the present-day psyche.

San Francisco John Weir Perry
October 1976

Contents

Preface ix

Introduction: In Search of the Roots of Renewal 1

Chapter One. Healing Factors in the Psychotic Episode 11

Chapter Two. Emotional Development and the Self-Image 23

Chapter Three. The Chronically Regressive Personality 43

Chapter Four. The Acute Psychotic Regression 61

Chapter Five. The Ritual Drama of Renewal 79

1. The Center, 92

2. Death, 97

3. The Return to the Beginnings, 103

4. The Clash of Opposites, 111

5. The Reversal of Opposites, 122

6. Apotheosis, 127

7. The Union of Opposites, 138

8. New Birth, 144

9. The Renewed Society, 150

10. The Quadrated World, 159

Chapter Six. From Monarch to Messiah 165

Chapter Seven. The Renewal of the Center 193

Appendix: Case Protocols 201

Notes 223

Bibliography 245

Index 253

ROOTS OF RENEWAL IN MYTH AND MADNESS

The Meaning of Psychotic Episodes

Introduction: In Search of the Roots of Renewal

It is not wisdom to be only wise,
And on the inward vision close the eyes,
But it is wisdom to believe the heart

. . .

Our knowledge is a torch of smoky pine
That lights the pathway but one step ahead
Across a void of mystery and dread.

Santayana[1]

As I scan back over thirty years of work with schizophrenia, writing a number of articles and books on this and all the correlative topics that branch off from it in various directions, I realize that there was no point at which I made the decision to pursue this as my life task. From the beginning it was like a hidden plan that kept appearing in front of me and presenting itself to me. In this way it has become for me my main pathway of not only outer, but inner exploration.

As soon as I returned from my training and my analysis in Zurich, where I attended the C. G. Jung Institute, the first case I was assigned at McLean Hospital in 1949 was a young woman that I wrote up in my first book. She described herself as being "at the center," and in the most classical and vivid way imaginable, she hovered around that psychic midpoint for six weeks, working out her psychotic process in terms of drawings in color depicting the symbolic events happening at that dynamic focal center. I was staggered and bewildered that such a phenomenon was possible; I had never heard that that was what a psychotic process could do, and it fascinated me. Until that time, I had had no idea of doing any more with schizophrenia than what my residency would require. When I came to the West Coast that same year, I felt it would be intriguing to see if this train of events would appear in other people as well. I therefore volunteered to work mornings in hospital wards, to do psychotherapy with people undergoing acute episodes. Again and again, I found that similar cases revealed that same kind of process.

After twelve years of this part-time labor with acute episodes an opportunity came to review all this experience and gather it together. This opportunity was an invitation to present a paper in New York on the reconstitutive process that had been coming to light in these cases.[2] That year, 1960, was an extraordinary one for me, in that two other requests came along at the same time to write on topics related to this line of investigation. One request was from Alan Watts, to provide a volume on the mythology of the father figure. This volume became a study of all the original sources in the myth and ritual of centrality in societal form, that is, in the form of the sacral kingship, which I had recognized as the close parallel in cultural form to what I had been observing in individuals in their psychotic experiences.[3] The other request came from Arthur Burton, who was assembling a volume of the psychotherapy of the psychoses. This task moved me to formulate the therapeutic method that I had been developing along the way, and the manner in which the transference brought the process toward its resolution.[4]

By and large, most psychiatrists who deal with schizophrenia do so in their younger years and later move on to other concerns. Acute psychotic episodes of this kind occur in young adults, and a true affinity with people undergoing such episodes is most naturally felt when one is in that part of one's life cycle. I expected the same to be true for me. After writing those three expositions summing up what I had found, I thought, "That's enough. Now I can just sit back and be quiet and conduct a peaceful, sensible practice as a Jungian analyst and teacher."

However, I was pulled back onto my pathway only a few years later. My friend Julian Silverman telephoned from the National Institute of Mental Health (NIMH) with a quite intriguing proposal for a research project. I had a brief battle with this new thrust, to decide whether I actually wanted to pick up this whole undertaking again, not to overthrow a disorder, but to overcome our ignorance of these turbulent processes in psychic depth. I chose to do so, and, as it turned out, I thus got a second chance at a culture of youth more to my taste than my first round had provided, namely the era of the late sixties and the flowering of its counterculture. This new venture, called the Agnew Project, was a study, in a carefully designed experimental protocol, of the differential effects of personality style on the outcome of medication for schizophrenia. The question was: Who does well and who does badly with Thorazine medication for this condition? My task was to design the therapeutic milieu. It took me so much back into the thick of this labor again that I worked harder during these two or three years than I had since being a resident. It was fascinating and difficult—perhaps most valuable to me for learning on the negative side, discovering what does not work.

So little actually did work that I became unable to let the subject alone. Together with a colleague back in the late 1950s, I had thought of setting up a residence for handling the acute schizophrenic episode, after having experienced enough cases to realize that this environment would be the best for therapy. I dropped the idea, however, because of the magnitude of the undertaking, especially of the finances. I hoped someone else might pick up the idea and carry it ahead. In the early planning of the Agnew Project, we had intended to set up a residence in the countryside. This was not feasible, however, and instead we became housed in a state institution. In the course of time there, we learned that hospitals cannot provide the right setting in which to experience the acute episode. The staff undergoes conflict and frustration in such a setting because in many ways what a hospital does is geared in the wrong direction for persons who want to undergo the psychotic process in a nonsuppressive way. At the end of several years I was convinced, and this certainty was too great to ignore.

My friend and colleague, Howard Levene, and I began looking for funds to create the ideal setting that nature seemed to require. At the same time the Northeast Community Mental Health Service of the City and County of San Francisco, under a newly enlarged budget, found itself in need of an innovative program for the treatment of psychosis. An ideal marriage of needs and interests ensued, and our project was launched with full support and payroll under the city's mental health system.

This residence has now become Diabasis, a three-storied home for a community of young people, some of whom live in because they are in a psychotic episode, others who are on the payroll or are volunteering their time. We operate by a policy of establishing an atmosphere that is fully supportive to the psychotic mental space—not only accepting of it, but affirmative toward it. The imagery draws specific interest and attitudes, while the effect evokes real responses in a full range of spontaneous feeling from staff persons. Diabasis is a subculture, one might say, that is founded on the belief that no matter how great the turmoil a person may be in, something deep inside is happening that may be valid and worthwhile and easily listened to. Our staff were selected for a certain sensitive disposition—by nature their minds are tuned in to the subjective life and they have a specific kind of facility with psychic reality. Inasmuch as they are not professionally educated or professionally qualified, they have been able to enter fresh into the creation of this specific subculture without having to overcome the biases of the more traditional modes. Therefore, the paraprofessional people are doing the actual psychological work with the clients. Professionalism is not particularly appropriate and necessary here. Diabasis is the project of the paraprofessionals, and they do the significant work.

The atmosphere in Diabasis is harmonious and gentle most of the time, making it a lovely place in which to be and spend time. When one enters, all one sees is a group of young people in their twenties and thirties living and eating together. One cannot quite tell, a good deal of the time, who is psychotic and who is not. This absence of boundaries had been the ideal in our first vision of such a residence—that there should be no suggestion of a clinical arrangement that sets up a staff of "normals" watching over the poor "sick" people who are constantly in need of management and care; rather, that this should be a community of mutual concern and mutual healing. That is, the staff, as well as the clients, should pursue their own processes of growing and developing.

However, our expectations were surpassed in a very significant respect. We had anticipated that such a milieu as ours would pull people through their psychotic episodes within a matter of two or three weeks, with some periodic, horrendous crises and midnight turmoils, with nervous night calls to the consultants to ask for advice on what to do next and how to prevent the crazy activity from getting completely out of hand. What actually happened has been quite different. Though we have accepted persons mostly in the very acute episode—withdrawn, confused, living in their "delusional" mental space when they came in—within a matter of a day or two or three, these persons have come spontaneously out of their confusion and become entirely coherent. The longest time to reach this clarity was nine days. Medication has not been administered (except for one dose, and that for a behavior problem rather than a psychotic state, when we were temporarily understaffed). In other words, given a proper subculture for this state of mind, the so-called thought disorder may vanish of its own accord quite quickly and easily. Under these circumstances, such persons have been able to go in and out of the home with perfect freedom and without mishap.

All the while, the inner process keeps moving on. We have sometimes been distressed to observe that persons may emerge out of their psychotic state so readily that a new difficulty is created. They come out of it too quickly. There is a long job of work to be done by the inner process. Something wants to happen in depth, and being withdrawn and absorbed in that depth seems to be a requisite for good integrative work. When persons emerge rapidly out of such a high arousal state and quickly become rational once more, in an adaptive state, feeling like anyone else, they are apt to turn their back on their inner work. The traditional cultural norms tend to reemerge in the forefront, urging the individual to enjoy ordinary, rational "normality" once more. It feels so good to know that one can be sane once more that there is an inclination to stay away from the nonrational. Therefore, when persons are losing touch with their process, we sometimes want to make the paradoxical suggestion, "Please, stay with it, live with it for a while," as if to say, "Just be a little more psychotic for a time, please! Don't leave it too soon!"

I have recounted this personal history, and this description of Diabasis at its natural point of emergence into the present, as a background to explain the purpose of this book. Why should anyone be encouraged to remain mindful of a psychotic state and its contents? Indeed, a special kind of subculture is needed, to take such a position. And to hold to such a position needs a formulation of its views and values.

In this book I will be setting forth such a rationale and am describing what I have termed the *renewal process* as value factor that must be taken into account and followed conscientiously during the entire course of the high-arousal state, the psychotic episode. In my last book, *The Far Side of Madness,*[5] I gave glimpses, from many angles and points of reference, of this view of the altered state of consciousness that we have until recently been considering a disorder. In the present volume I will be considering in detail the healing factor, the psychodynamics of the center, and the mythological parallels. In other words, this book goes more deeply and thoroughly into matters of psychological theory and of the archetypal myth and ritual forms that bear on this particular process.

There are always workers in the field of psychotherapy who wonder how useful a study of symbolism is for the hard task of dealing with persons in emotional turmoils as tumultuous as acute psychotic episodes. When one is tussling with urgent life issues and heavy emotions and strenuous relationships, how can symbols bear much on the work at hand? Such persons may find this volume heavily weighted on the side of the imagery of myth and ritual as well as messianic visions. There is a trend in contemporary therapeutic methods to fasten on work with raw affect, to get it mobilized and experienced, at the cost of the attention due to the images that the psyche puts forward. I find, in consulting with staffs, that there are, as usual, two kinds of people.

Psychologies are forever dividing human beings into dichotomies. In Jungian psychological terms, we have introverts and extraverts, feelers and thinkers, and so forth. The psychophysiological study of attention styles shows these categories to overlap with these object-oriented and subject-oriented personality types. In working with psychosis another dichotomy impresses me again and again as vital to the way the staff relate to the clients. Some are inclined to focus on the play of symbolic images as representing the essential movement, where the real action is taking place, and that level is where they feel at home. Such staff members may reveal some shortcoming when sensitive perception of the emotions coming into play is needed; on the other hand, they may find that as soon as they see a symbolic expression they can seize on it as a kind of metaphorical statement of meaning about an emotion. The symbol thus gives them a grasp or handle on emotion.

Other staff members are just the opposite. They find themselves entirely at sea in the interplay of metaphor and image and symbol. Only when they get some strong and noisy emotion going back and forth, livening up the personal interchange, do they begin to feel that things are happening.

A good staff is made up of both kinds of people. They have a lot to give to each other of their perceptions of significant events taking place in a client's growth process. Not only does it balance the staff to have both kinds of orientation represented, but also the net effect is that each group learns from the other, with the result that eventually most experience an inner balancing within themselves.

I am therefore giving no small attention to work with emotion and work with imagery, both in the chapter on the healing factors and in the chapter on emotional development and the self-image.

The direction of exploration in this book is almost wholly an outcome of my own findings in psychotherapy with schizophrenic young adults and of my own investigations of the comparative symbolism in myth and ritual forms. My greatest debts are, of course, to C. G. Jung as represented in this respect in his *Symbols of Transformation,*[6] in which he made an exhaustive study of the symbolism of the hero journey, the Great Mother, and rebirth; also and equally to Anton Boisen and his *Exploration of the Inner World,*[7] which makes a full statistical analysis of the content of the psychotic process in 173 cases and which reveals Jungian inclinations. An unusual display of virtuosity in discussing symbolism is H. G. Baynes' *Mythology of the Soul,*[8] an account of two schizoid personalities and their inner processes.

Needless to say, much work has been done on such unconscious imagery from different standpoints. In mentioning this work and how my work relates to it, I would stress some overall trends as I see them. Up through the 1930s the psychoanalytic literature was occupied with an effort to understand unconscious, primary process content. Thereafter, for a decade or more into the mid-1950s, under the influence of the new ego psychology, attention shifted toward the uses of defensive mechanisms and maneuvers in psychosis. With the advent and growing prevalence of phenothiazine medications in the last two decades, there has been no more opportunity to explore unconscious productions unhampered by such drugs. One may read leading textbooks now that never even mention such common phenomena as the death and rebirth fantasies or world destruction and recreation fantasies occurring in the psychotic episode. Residents in training are customarily cautioned never to encourage such symbolic talk in their patients, and instead to do supportive therapy that avoids uncovering and bolsters the defenses so that the ego may cope with reality. Under these conditions, then, the focus on content falls mainly to the province of art therapy, whose journals continue to take an interest in the manifestations of psychotic image production, even though study is hampered by the usual medication regimen.

It is not the function of this book to review the vast literature representing many different theoretical frameworks and interpretations of the symbolic process in psychosis. A few comments, however, on comparisons and contrasts with some of the familiar work on these questions might be in order. I will limit these citations to the best-known interpretations of symbolic imagery, leaving aside the growing literature concerning ego psychology[9] and the formal aspects of schizophrenic thought disorder.[10]

What one makes of symbolic imagery in psychotic processes is a natural outcome of one's fundamental standpoint. Freud's famous analysis of the rich material in the Schreber case[11] focused on the love and hate in the relation with the father, and his formulation of the paranoid mechanism has become one of the pillars of psychoanalytic theory in this regard. Similar treatment of the world destruction and recreation fantasies rendered them in the perspective of object loss in the break with reality and the regression, and the restitution of object relations and the regaining of reality that followed. Other psychoanalytic writings have pursued these psychotic fantasies in much the same vein.[12] Salvations and rebirth experiences have been dealt with in terms of recapturing the oceanic feeling and *unio mystica* of the oral phase of infancy.[13]

All these efforts view the imagery on the level of what in Jungian psychology is called the *personal unconscious,* hence of the still-primitive object relations, parental bonds, and regression to infancy. However, once one enlarges the scope of the framework to give recognition to the dimensions of the myth and ritual forms concerning the governing and the evolution of cultures, then one has to take into account some fully adult issues. Culture change and its prophetic renditions of innovative probes into new values and meanings in the course of mankind's spiritual development and differentiation all make their appearance in visionary states that closely resemble psychotic episodes.

Somewhat the same may be said of a comparison with the work of Sullivan and his school. He paid very careful attention to the content of the inner process, yet the cases he reported very fully were ones that abounded in psychosexual concerns and security maneuvers,[14] so that his area of observation and comment differs from what I am dealing with in this book. Fromm-Reichmann entered into close relation with her patients' symbolic experiences and communications, in order to empathize and understand them, yet her focus in therapy was to interpret the defenses and not the imagery as such.[15] Arieti, in his monumental work on schizophrenia,[16] has elaborated a thorough theory of successive defensive positions in the regression toward archaic modalities that thereby casts the content of the unconscious imagery in a negative light; the resulting picture is that of a psyche becoming more and more closed into its untenable divorce from reality rather than one that is becoming wide open to the full reaches of its inner mythological experience.

On a more general level of the role of the image-forming process and its relation to affect, the work of Horowitz[17] is very congenial with the views represented in this book. I am dealing here, of course, more with the meanings of myth and ritual ideation than with the psychological properties of symbolization.

Three close affinities with the subject matter of this book deserve special mention here. Marguerite Sechehaye, in her *Symbolic Realization,*[18] makes a vital connection with the image process and provides a warmly caring relation to her patient, Renée, in ways that are quite in keeping with the therapy I am describing. However, Sechehaye focuses on the personal material to the exclusion of much of the mythological content, which is relegated to the appendix. A rich documentation, in a Laingian mode, of the inner psychotic experience is that of Mary Barnes and her therapist, Joe Burke,[19] at Kingsley Hall in England. The explorations of Stanislav Grof[20] into the processes of the unconscious as seen when activated by the psychotropic drugs show these processes to be roughly parallel to those encountered in the psychotic episode. Grof respects the meaningfulness of the more extreme dimensions of transpersonal experiences.

In the following pages I will be resorting to the psychiatric term "schizophrenia" to designate the psychotic process under discussion. This general usage is necessary for purposes of naming our subject, even though I intend to show that what occurs in this state is not mere psychopathology and hence deserves a better name. The *acute episode* is the phase of turbulence in which the lower centers are highly activated and mental contents that are usually unconscious take the place of reality. This high arousal state, sometimes called *hyperphrenia,* persists over a period of some six weeks and is entirely different in quality from what precedes and what follows it. The acute episode is preceded by a troubled condition of the psyche, the *prepsychotic* or *chronically regressive personality* (described in Chapter Three). The *acute psychotic regression* frequently follows the pattern of the renewal process (described in Chapter Four). The acute episode is followed either by a reorganized state of the self and thus by further growth and development, or, if the renewal process is unsuccessful, by a *chronic schizoid* condition in which the personality is handicapped by the effects of the acute episode.

In this book, after the opening chapter on the healing process, which draws on the experience of recent years at Diabasis, I will be presenting a study of the renewal process as found in history and in the persons with whom I was working directly in therapy during the 1950s. I have done so not only because I know those persons best, but also because the more recent material from the Diabasis experience is not yet worked out. That work belongs to the near future.

Chapter One

Healing Factors in the Psychotic Episode

The renewal process that I am exploring in this book consists essentially of a profound and powerful reorganization of the self. In the imagery that wells up from the depths of the psyche, the process is expressed as a dissolution and reconstruction of the affect image of the center, while in its emotional dimension it is experienced as a thoroughgoing transformation of one's feeling about oneself, one's self-worth and self-image. The historical parallels to this process indicate that it is the nature of the center to undergo periodic disintegration and reintegration, expressed as death and rebirth, world destruction and recreation, and cultural revivification.

Background of the Concept

There are several forebears to this concept of the power of the psychotic experience to do favorable work. As far back as 1914,

Jung[1] was beginning to suggest that the acute schizophrenic episode contained a healing potential that was discernible and describable. The productions from the unconscious could be recognized as compensations to the deficiencies of the conscious outlook, but they arrived in a form that was not acceptable to the ego, which found them threatening and which could not benefit from them without special therapeutic help.[2]

Sullivan, in the next decade,[3] found in the schizophrenic episode a process capable of "reorganizing whole masses of life experience." He was already grasping the point that the cataclysmic symbolic process was a vehicle for rearranging the very foundations of the life of the emotions and the instincts.

Again, another decade later, Anton Boisen[4] produced a very careful study of almost a hundred cases in Worcester State Hospital in Massachusetts. His own psychosis led him to enter the ministry and the chaplaincy of that asylum. In statistical form he established that there was a groundplan to the acute episode, with elements that not only occurred in case after case but that also gave good indications of the kind of outcome to be expected, many of which were favorable growth experiences.

A decade later, Margarite Sechehaye[5] expounded a therapeutic method for handling the deep psychotic regression that she called "symbolic realization." In this approach, the needs of the patient to experience certain emotions and gratifications would be given full attention and specific expression, especially those having to do with symbolic reenactment of the earliest suckling at the breast and even of the return to the womb for rebirth.

Laing, in the 1960s,[6] developed a vivid and popular argument that there is a benefit in allowing the acute turmoil in depth to have its way, and that the fruits of such turmoil should not be underrated. He was the first to put such a stand to the test by establishing a residence where persons could live communally and be free to let happen what will when the acute psychosis is given free rein.

More recently, Thomas Scheff has written a fine documentation of the labeling process.[7] He reveals the devastating effects of the societal concensus that disqualifies the individual in a psychotic state and uses diagnostic labels that express exclusion and extrusion. By certain experimental procedures, he demonstrates the part that such labeling can play in the precipitation of the psychotic episode itself.

There is agreement, therefore, among some of the pioneers in this work from decade to decade, that a healing potential, a reorganizational process, and a regularly occurring set of contents, make themselves known in the acute episode; and that what makes a natural process into insanity is found in the societal attitudes of labeling and disqualification.

External Factors in Healing

When we look into the factors that come into play to determine whether a psychotic episode is going to take a turn for the better or for the worse, the first and foremost concerns the cultural surroundings. Insanity is a category established according to cultural norms, a general and unassailable consensus. These norms determine what is acceptable and what is not, what can be included in, and what must be excluded from, the fabric of the society. This label of insanity is an image packed with a heavy emotional charge and it has an overbearing impact on the person receiving it. It is delivered in a manner that makes it into a directive: "If you are so crazy, this means you are going to do this and that; we fear you are about to break the place up, and we fear you are going to get out of hand and be violent unless we control you." These messages amount to telling the person concerned to do just what is thus expected, for that is how they are received by such an individual. It is urgently important for us to realize that this labeling becomes a component incorporated into the psychotic process itself, and built into its structure, determining its progress and its outcome. The societal attitude makes something into craziness that demonstrably does not have to be.

How are we to account for the vulnerability that allows such individuals to succumb to this impact? My observation has consistently been that in this altered state of consciousness, the ego identifies very easily with any emotionally laden image that appears on the stage of awareness. Thus, one may be momentarily convinced that one is a supreme ruler or a messianic hero, or a new Virgin Mary, or any other figure that presents itself from the archetypal depths of the psyche. These affect-charged images come up from inside and are very familiar to anyone observing persons in this state. However, we forget that the person may just as easily and vividly identify with any emotionally loaded image put onto him from outside; these are no less powerful. To identify with the Second Coming may blow one's mind, but it also blows one's mind to identify with Mr. Crazy. Any affect image that intrudes either from inside or from outside may lend itself to the weakened and vulnerable ego as a mantle to slip into and make into a self-definition.

Insanity has a long history in this regard, which Foucault has explicated beautifully.[8] In the Middle Ages, if a person in this state were not considered possessed in some holy or demonic way, he or she was put on the ship of fools and sent downriver for some other community to put on their health and care budget! What a dramatic demonstration of intolerance and extrusion! In the eighteenth century there was a theory abroad that to be insane was to be regressed, but in this case not to the state of infancy but to that of the beast. As animal-like creatures, such people were put in cages with straw on the floor, and indeed, they conformed and growled and barked and fouled up their setting just as expected, to such an extent that it was offered as entertainment to the public to come and see these brutish simpletons. A little later, the insane were regarded as perverse and were manacled in chains like criminals, and with this burden of guilt and unacceptability they were cast into a veritable inferno of shame and ignominy.

For the field of medicine to take over this task of the diagnosis and care of the insane was a great leap forward in human values out of this horror of previous centuries. However, the price was a system of psychopathology on the medical model, and while the disqualification of the insane was less horrendous, it only became more subtle. The medical psychiatric label creates for the individual an appalling sense of being different from the rest of humanity, from participation in the ordinary world, even outside the possibility of human, sympathetic understanding. I have seen cases in which there was a one-to-one relation between this kind of labeling and the way the individual felt. A person I know was dropping into such an altered state but was among intimate friends who were familiar with such subjective states and validated his experience. They affirmed him, telling him to stay with it, that it could be fruitful, and he consequently felt quite at ease with it, even though he was quite "spaced." However, when he was among his psychiatric friends, they would recoil in alarm and tell him he must get under cover and be medicated, that this would never do, going around in the open like this. He would thereupon not only feel crazy, but would enter what he experienced as an insane state. This could readily be rectified by his intimate friends, and he would feel restored.

The remedy to this trouble with labeling would be, of course, to achieve a different image of the psychotic state. If one can apprehend this process as it really is, as an archetypal process taking place in depth, then we could be more clear about what sort of label would be truly appropriate. If we can discern a sequence in affect images revolving about a center, the self, where powerful things happen at a locus of tremendous potency, transforming the self through death and rebirth, through the clash of opposites and their resolution and their union, and through visions of world destruction and creation and culture change, then we witness something that is too awesome to deserve the derogatory, depreciative label of a disorder or sickness.

We need new names for a fresh reevaluation of this state. If it can be accepted that this is a legitimate though entirely nonrational process, and that the nonrational state that goes along with it is pardonably offensive to the rational, conscious outlook, then the state can be tolerated as appropriate. The labeling process could be fundamentally altered and its effects be made benign rather than devastating.

Providing a protective sanctuary for persons in this state, with a firm subculture founded on these assumptions and deviating from the generally accepted, prevailing cultural outlook, becomes the critical factor that releases these people from their turmoil so quickly. This sanctuary requires an accepting atmosphere, free from prejudicial judgments, thus removing that very negative, difficult, and painful state of insanity that promises to be so unpredictably explosive.

Even more effective than acceptance, of course, is the general tenor that we can only call a loving atmosphere. The word love must be qualified to avoid any sentimental implications that it may convey.

Loving here means caring, being attentive, really wanting to understand, to reach the essential person behind the outer manifestations. It involves a kind of nurturant attitude, one that gives the energy that constitutes feeling. Such a staff responds to the full gamut of emotions that the client may put forward with an equally full range of their own. There is then no holding back of secret feelings that might let the client do all the suffering while the staff are free of it. The experience is shared in a mutual spirit.

I believe there is a mystique in this bearing toward persons that is little known and little understood, certainly in psychiatry and in psychology generally. One is reminded of the totally unexplained energies that seem to go back and forth between human beings and plant life that may bring vigor or wilting, according to the quality of interaction. At the negative extreme is the destructiveness between human beings that in its ultimate form is seen in the marasmus of infancy, where a neglectful parent leaves a child so much unloved and unnurtured that the whole organism withers and recedes into itself and its garbled chemistry, and melts away. The nurturant atmosphere I speak of is at the other pole. It seems visibly to energize, begetting good states of health and of feeling. I have the impression that this healing operates not merely at a level of overt feeling or understanding. Rather, it may work at the level of the tissues or cells, or of that basic flow of energy in the organism that we know so little about. One can watch the surge of life return to these persons who, on admission, appear so wiped out and their vitality so low, expecting so little to come to them from the outer world. When they begin to feel this flood of warm energy coming toward them, it is liberating and enlivening to them; their flesh soon takes on the glow of spirited vigor.

As a young resident psychiatrist, I used to be taught that a most reliable pathognomonic sign of schizophrenia was that there was an absence of the subtle awareness of being drawn on for connection with you. I now realize that that sign was reliable because persons in this state realized full well that if they tried, they would not receive the connection in mutual feeling and understanding that was craved. It is remarkable how strongly persons in the psychotic space draw on that empathetic feeling if given a chance; though it is invisibly and passively sought, it comes welling up in a staff member. When it reaches the individual, it has an immediate effect not only of appreciation but of enlivening.

Internal Factors in Healing

The subculture of the milieu that provides a surrounding in harmony with the altered state of consciousness is only half of the work of healing. The other is the inner process going on in the psychic depths, expressing itself in terms of images and emotions, a process that is new and unpredictable every time and yet that reveals some basic regularities.

It is said about the play of ideation throughout the psychotic episode that one should not be drawn into diversion by taking an interest in them. Symbols are said to be designed to "conceal as well as reveal," that they represent a defensive process to avoid and retreat from reality; psychosis is seen as a maneuver to defend against reality. Yet, when one watches the work these images are doing in the process, one finds them to be activating certain emotions. These affects have hithertofore been out of reach, important potential elements of the personality that have been missing up to this point and that have left the adaptation to the social setting inadequate in some noteworthy respects.

It soon becomes apparent that the individual needs a great deal of freedom to experience emotions that might be hard to handle both for him- or herself and for the others in the community. That is the principal reason they have been kept below the surface. Many of them become frank sexual advances, and many become outbursts of aggression or rage of one sort or another. In our American culture of recent decades, frank violence makes itself known to an unusual degree. These emotions are the most difficult, but there is an extensive range of others that are difficult to handle because they are unaccustomed and sometimes hard to comprehend at first, such as fears of as yet indiscernible things.

In this kind of work with emotions the aim is not catharsis or abreaction, as in so many popular therapies today, which succeed in "getting it all out," and "letting it all happen." Even "blowing out" is not the idea; this term originally derived from breathing practices in meditation but became converted into an expression for releasing a psychotic episode, for which one then needed protective "blowout centers." The objective is not just to unload, as if we had an organism filled with emotion that needs to overflow and pour out until the level gets a little lower, a little more manageable.

A different model is needed for the play of affect. It is in the nature of emotion to want to be conveyed to somebody, to be rendered to someone who will receive and acknowledge it. This communication requires a person in whom one has confidence, to whom these sensitively difficult emotions may be entrusted. Moreover, the person in the therapeutic role should understand the essential meaning of the emotion. It is not enough merely to have a display of the outburst; it also must be meaningful both to the giver and the receiver of the affect.

How different is this kind of experience from that in hospitals! With the staff I am describing, an outburst of rage may be delivered to someone and be validated and understood and allowed to come into full play in order to make this charge of precious affect available to the personality for fuller development. In a hospital, such a person is considered a threat to the control of the ward and its quiet, and therefore is usually put into a seclusion room behind a closed and locked door, alone, with a little window to be observed by staff who peer in at intervals to see how things are going; the person is in a bare and isolated space, being told that such an emotion is not acceptable in the human community.

These ward policies can go on even though the staff are quite aware that the problem of the psychosis is that the affect is first withdrawn and later dulled and finally deadened. These emotions are the elements one is trying to reach in the psychotic episode, and are vital to the growth of the personality. I have just mentioned that the nature of emotion, as I see it, is not something that one should be rid of by getting it out like a noxious substance, but rather to be communicated and conveyed to a person. The corollary of this view is that it is a painful experience to have to hold an emotion back, because it is forbidden or misunderstood for some reason.

The play of imagery occurs together with the emotion. I have always preferred to call the archetypal components in the psyche *affect images,* inasmuch as this term describes how such components really reveal themselves. The term *archetypes* gives the appearance of belonging to the realm of philosophy and larger meanings, and hence seems to be particularly difficult for American psychiatrists to accept with any comfort. When working with the everyday experiences of ordinary therapy, I find that to speak of *affect images* brings the archetypes into the here and now. The implication is that each emotion has its image to represent it and convey its meaning. The image can conduct an emotional issue through a process and transform it for development. The emotion, correspondingly, has its constant relation to that image and gives it its dynamic power, its energetic potency.

A major aim of the symbolic play of images seems to be, as I have mentioned, the activation of emotions that have not been reached before, and that have been lying dormant in the psychic depths, as potential only, and therefore unconscious. Once they are activated, they arrive in the arena of expression in a very crude, primitive form. One then may observe the images transforming them into a form that can take part in the integrative process. Thus the image represents, activates, and transforms the emotion in the integrative process. The emotions that are brought into the process of integrating the total personality constitute the experiential aspect of the individuation process. When profound psychic depths are dealt with, the emotional life, as well as the life of meanings and world outlook, is being integrated.

Among the various images and emotions, the self-image seems to be the component most in need of transformation in the psychotic process. People undergoing psychotic episodes usually have looked down on themselves as somehow faulty and not as worthy as other people, and perhaps somehow unloveable, even guilty. The self-image, in other words, involves a whole cluster of emotional issues concerning oneself.

I would like to offer an instance of this kind of imagery, produced by one of the clients at Diabasis. A young woman went through a nightmarish experience, for two days, of believing she was watched by space vehicles manned by aliens. They were using her eyes as television cameras, so that every time she looked at a friend she was endangering them and betraying them. This sent her into a constant flight from place to place and friend to friend.

The world picture she had at the time was that the world was divided into factions, of north and south. The northern powers were bearing down on the southern from their cold regions; they were materialistic, power-dominated computer cultures, very collective, technological, and heartless. In their advance, they were compressing all the humanness, the animal and snake life, and the heat down toward the south pole. As this pressure was applied from the north, it made a compaction, an intensity of those powers in the south that would become so hot and so intense that the world would blow up in consequence.

Such world-destruction fantasies have received much comment in psychiatric literature. In the Jungian model, the world image represents the psychic totality. The fantasy in this case implies that unless these opposites are brought into balance, the psyche would fragment into smithereens—a very threatening picture indeed, causing justifiable fright. It is this fright with which the unconscious process deals.

This patient felt specially called to save the world from this disaster by reaching the northern powers and their computer culture leaders, to point out to them that they were defeating their own ends. For if they continued to do as they were doing, the entire world would be destroyed. She found, however, a force field around the equator which she was unable to break through. Yet she did get a little glimpse for a moment of the "clear light of God," off to one side. This, she knew, would make the communication to the northern powers possible and thus remedy the urgent crisis.

One might find it at first hard to read the significance of this kind of imagery, but two other parallel items in her case show very clearly what was transpiring. The first item was in the form of a a couple of paintings she had made in her first week at Diabasis. One was of a male head, in blue—a little like her husband, like her father, and like a generalized male figure—with a smooth dome on top but trailing off into dribbles below. Her husband had a beard like this, but the image suggested more that all the features were amorphous at the lower end. A second picture showed a woman pointing to her pelvis, an almost verbal statement that her problem lay in her womanly and sexual instincts.

The second clarifying item came in the comments from the staff as they discussed their impressions of her. They were saying, "You know, with her you can't reach her feeling because she seems to be so cerebral most of the time. She is too rationalistic about her experience. She's trying to conceptualize it all, and talks about wanting to know more about psychiatry and psychology and read about symbolism so that she can explain herself, and she isn't coming across with her own real feeling."

It now becomes apparent how parallel these three expressions are: the world image, the paintings, and her behavior. The staff saw her as being too technological and rationalistic, leaving the feeling out of account. This behavior was being thrown onto the world stage as a metaphor, in which the north represented her overly cerebral outlook, while the south represented her womanly instincts and emotions. In the paintings the dome of the masculine head was the north; the pelvis of the woman was the south. As a result of these expressions, troubled relations with both her husband and her father came to light.

The center made its appearance also in a self-image that was very eloquent. She had a fantasy in which she was looking through her own rear end, her rectum. This she saw as a repulsive and nasty part of the body, full of disgusting flesh and wormlike or snakelike organs. These were in rings that kept opening up layer by layer, until way down inside there opened up to view an image of herself at the age of thirteen, looking pretty and fresh and pristine.

This was not at all the kind of image of herself that she held later on, but appeared here as she might have if she had been able to maintain her good feeling about herself, which she lost at that time. At that age, the beginning of her puberty, her mother began to bear down upon her as being sexually loose and prone to trouble making. This was the mother's fantasy and it was beginning at that juncture to make the daughter feel guilty about her womanly feeling. This was the principal factor that had led her to disassociate herself from her natural loving instincts.

These experiences afford us a glimpse of the nature of the imagery in an altered state of consciousness. The imagery might appear at first glance as "crazy, mixed-up" ideas, sounding wild and nightmarish, out of the personal world altogether. Yet with careful attention one finds that these images are instead quite accurately descriptive of what is transpiring in the emotional psyche, her feelings about herself, the way she presents herself to people, and the way she relates. Down inside the midst of her organism, in the center of circular forms, is her own favorable self-image, still buried at the age level at which it became lost to her, but ready now to be reactivated from that dormancy.

This is an example of the image providing the way to the affect. It is not enough to suggest to such a person that she should be free with her feelings and should release her emotions and socialize. Instead, she must take a long detour through the play of imagery and let the psyche do its natural work. The psyche has its own strange capacities for healing, and it accomplishes healing through its own particular kind of affect-image process. The therapist must be receptive and attentive to the psychic process, but the psyche does the work of healing.

In conclusion, the milieu is that part of the therapy that deals with the label of insanity, by means of a particular kind of subculture and of community relationships. The psychotherapy is a second part of the work, and deals with the inner journey and the renewal process, by means of the psyche's work through image and emotion and individual relationship. In either case, loving, caring, and attentiveness appear to be the factors that allow the healing to reach its goal.

Chapter Two

Emotional Development and the Self-Image

In order to grasp the nature of the healing reorganization in psychosis, especially in nature's own renewal process, we need to have an adequate concept of the processes that govern the development of an effective consciousness. In the broad picture of evolutionary development, whatever its future may be, the crowning achievement of the development of the human psyche is the emergence of a well-rounded consciousness and a clear-cut ego. The qualities that characterize this level of the individual self are the fruits of the integrative work of the entire psyche throughout its years since conception.

The Ego

If one starts from a premise that the human being is fundamentally a biological animal possessed of superior powers of mastery over his* environment, then the ego is the psychic organ for perception, intellection, and motility all serving the purpose of adaptation to external reality. The ego's primary concerns are, then, object relations handled with objective realism, that is, a well-developed capacity for reality testing. To achieve this capacity, such an ego must defend itself against the power of the instinctual drives and serve instead the aims of a good adjustment to the social milieu and its demands.

If, however, one's premise is that we have become primarily psychological beings, whose basic drive is the growth and development of our awareness of ourself and of the meaning of our life, then the ego takes on a different appearance. Structuring and broadening the ego consciousness becomes the aim and objective of many complex inner processes. These processes strive to round out my awareness of the meanings of the inner psychic world and of the outer objective world, and to single out my individuality from all the various influences, pressures, and identifications that have impinged on me since birth. For the ego is in this case the carrier of the sense of identity, the *me*-ness of me that takes a lifetime to realize to the full, and the *my*-ness of my world view that is the substantive expression of my nature. The quest for meaning that unfolds year by year is the same as the effort to become the person that I am; for meaningfulness involves both my understanding and appreciation of my existence and my nature, and also my understanding of the world.

Emotion

When the inner psyche is regarded in this light, it appears less as a mass of drives seeking gratification, and more as an immensely dynamic matrix pushing forward its contents into the arena of life to get them into consciousness. All through the decades of a lifetime these contents are projected into the field of emotional experi-

*The traditional use of the pronouns *he* and *his* has not yet been superseded by convenient, generally accepted pronouns that mean either *he* or *she* or *his* or *her*. Therefore, the author will continue to use *he* and *his*, and hereby takes the opportunity to acknowledge the inherent inequity of the traditional preference for masculine pronouns.

ence one by one, to be confronted by the subject and, hopefully, assimilated.[1]

For instance, a young man may grow through his youth highly motivated to accomplish and to excell, highly interested in his work and competitive in his activities, but having no particular sense for personal relatedness. The trouble with girls, he might say, is that they are always being so subjective and their interests are so limited to personal things. Then he falls in love with a young woman who seems to personify everything that is beautiful about woman. Lo and behold, he finds himself delighting in spending long hours talking with her all about the most intensely and sensitively personal things about his life and her life, and even about their families and friends. A new aspect of the world unfolds itself to him, and he becomes somewhat transformed, along with his outlook on people. What has happened is that the image of the feminine, of the essence of woman,[2] has been projected on someone who could carry it well, and it has created for the young man a powerful motivation for involvement in relationships of a new kind for him. That is, the autonomous psyche[3] has activated this image at a fitting time for his development, and pushed it out into his emotional field, there to be encountered by him. A new content has arrived in his experience and into his consciousness through his emotional life, a new potential that brings to his ego consciousness an appetite for intimate, personal, subjective relating and mutual understanding.

This example shows how the groundplan of development is elaborated. New dimensions of development arrive on the scene in our emotional fields, and our egos are offered the opportunity to engage or to avoid, to accept or to reject these new elements, to make them conscious or to leave them in the limbo of fixated emotional problems. The emotional life is the stage upon which the new images and new issues arrive, and the emotional psyche, the unconscious or autonomous psyche, is the source from which they emanate.[4]

To get a clear picture of how these new elements are made we need a model, only provided we do not become so entranced with the theoretical structure that it eventually seems to have a reality apart from the observed experience itself. The model I am using grew out of Jung's painstaking and detailed work of experimentation with the Word Association Test, which revealed measurable disturbances of response when emotional components were activated.[5] This model visualizes the entire unconscious as structured in complexes, each of which operates as an emotional entity with a certain amount of inner cohesion and consistency. Each complex is a grouping of psychological associations around a nucleus that gives it its affect; that is, both its qualitative feeling tone and its quantitative energic charge.[6] In the case of the young man and his love, his image of the ideal woman is a complex, which when projected onto the young woman, causes him to become intensely enthralled with her.

This complex, called in Jungian terminology the *anima*[7], is founded on an image that is universal; let us say, for instance, that it would appear in his dreams as a princess, and would be blond and generally tinged with golden attributes. This sort of image is what in Jungian terms is an *archetypal image,*[8] recognizable by its fairytale or mythological or archaic cast, and by its royal attributes. An archetype is defined as an innate propensity to experience and to represent a universal human emotional experience in a universal way.[9] When for the first time activated in some emotional interchange, this propensity becomes manifest in the form of an image and an emotion and becomes the "affective foundation" of a complex.[10] It combines with the image of the other person in that emotional interaction to form the nucleus of the complex. Thus the nucleus, the innermost core of the complex, is the archetypal image and emotion combined with the representation of the first "object" to evoke it.[11] Since we are dealing with emotional encounters, this "object" will not be the conscious aspect of the other person, but one belonging to his or her emotional psyche, or *non-ego.*[12] Doubtless, in our example, some aspect of the mother's unconscious makeup, or perhaps of the father in his anima aspect, or of the sister, as persons who may have been first objects, might be involved in the formation of the nucleus of the anima complex. Around this nucleus would then cluster any other presentations belonging to the same affect.

In terms of actual experience, we see the complex making itself evident whenever a person is under the spell of an emotion. The play of an emotion is the activity of a complex.[13] If the young man of our example were in an interview, as long as he would be speaking out of his ardor and giving vent to the heat of his infatuation, we would be hearing the contents of the complex; associations would flow freely and we would be told about emotional impressions of the parents or siblings that belonged to this specific kind of experience, and then perhaps about early loves in elementary school years. Then there might be a hiatus of many years, in which this young man might as a boy have turned away from girls and given his full interest to things of the boys' world. It might be the case that we would see in his dreams the activation of the anima image before it appeared in projection on a young woman, and we would have to ask, Is it really the young woman herself that he loves, or the dream woman? If all goes well, he would eventually discover the young woman's reality emerging from behind the projected image.

A complex acts with a certain inner cohesion and may act quite autonomously with respect to the ego. It amounts to a partial personality, with its own views, values, and habits of expression that might be very different from the ego's.[14] The complex personifies itself in dream or fantasy; that is, it speaks and acts in the form of a person.[15] A complex may be encountered in the projected form, seeming to be embodied in another person closely enough to correspond to the dream image. Or the complex may appear in the field of awareness of the subject, in the form of a certain state of mind or mood or emotional spell, in which case not the ego but the complex is producing the speech and behavior. Thus it is seen either in projection, or in a dream image, or in a state of mind. The more unconscious such a complex is, the more autonomous it is and the more arrested in its development.[16] The complex is essentially an energic phenomenon: the stronger the affective stress, the more it gathers contents to itself, thereby gaining further in size and energic load.[17]

I will be speaking of the *unconscious* as being the *autonomous psyche* or the *emotional psyche*. What enters the field of awareness may be conscious if it is directed by the ego, but autonomous, and hence unconscious, if it is not. Strictly speaking, unconsciousness does not imply that the subject is unaware of such and such a problematic emotion, but that such an emotion is autonomous, acting independently of the ego's intentions and even in opposition to its values.

It is characteristic of these unconscious components that they come into play to compensate the biases or deficiencies of the ego's stance in regard to any issue.[18]

This autonomous psyche, then, is composed or structured of complexes, some old and derived from childhood, some new and still developing. At the level of the clusters of personal associations, we speak of the *personal unconscious,* and at the level of the archetypal imagery, the *collective unconscious.*[19] These levels should not be thought of as being distinct and separate, but only as suggesting that the archetypes come into action as the innate images at the root of the complexes, located in the deepest and most dynamic foundations of our being. For this reason, I prefer for ordinary usage to use the term *affect image* to designate what is technically defined by Jungians as *archetypal image.*[20]

A negative mother complex thus may be founded on the earliest apperception of the annihilative aspect of the mother. The apperception is in terms of an affect image—perhaps of the witch image. If this hurtful interchange becomes a major problem for the child, it gains a strong emotional stress, becomes a complex swollen up with more and more associations, and thus is ever more easily projected. The complex may keep on being reencountered afresh in relations with various women, even to the extent of dominating the person's entire emotional life and overclouding all the experiences of woman.

An axiomatic statement we may make about the subliminal psyche is that any of its contents that are activated are first encountered in projection onto the persons and objects of the outer world.[21] These images create our emotional ties, negative or positive, with our world. It is therefore important to bear in mind that we encounter and become involved with our own psychic depths out in this external emotional field; we usually seek out the further reaches of our psychic life not so much down inside us as out around us, if we are following the ordinary way of nature.[22] Only by special techniques of analysis, active imagination, creative activity, meditation, or drug trips do we get directly into contact with these contents. Equally important to realize is that when new components are activated and are pushing toward consciousness for assimilation, they appear in the external emotional field, in the form of projective involvement with someone or something.

The emotional life, then, is the activity of the unconscious psyche, and becomes the vehicle by which new psychic contents come to consciousness. The autonomous complexes are thus not merely our "problems"—they are, in their favorable aspect, equally our "components of development."[23] The emotions make up the reservoir from which we draw to keep our consciousness nourished, vitalized, and quickened with increase.

Nowhere is this principle of more momentous import than in the plight of the prepsychotic schizoid personality. This principle is, in a sense, what the whole problem of such personalities is about, as we shall see shortly. First, however, we should examine what the psyche does to convert its old, habitual problems, in the form of arrested autonomous complexes, into these auspicious components of development.

The Self-Image

We noted, at the beginning of the discussion of emotion, that if the psyche is regarded in the framework of a developmental psychology, then the question of identity becomes the crucial issue. This statement is not a mere value judgment that identity is more worthwhile than instinct. Rather, it is a statement derived from observation of the actual phenomena of emotional processes.

Let us return to the example of the young man's first experience of a great love. After being so stirred in his depths, the young man becomes a somewhat different kind of person, more sensitive to the meaningfulness of personal relations. In his state of being in love, he is not only experiencing his first profound exposure to the image of woman, the princess figure, the affect image known as the *anima;* he is also, at the same time, stepping into the role of a corresponding affect image, perhaps that of the young prince and courtly lover. The emotional heat of the passionate episode is generated by the interplay of these two affect images,[24] prince and princess, and the two young people as ego personalities are being swept up into a drama whose course has been established over hundreds of generations and over most of the world. It is a programed experience that runs its course as long as the projections remain operative. He not only projects the princess image on her, but also projects the prince on himself.

This drama is a very normal experience. Now let us consider another one that is common enough but not so normal: a young man repeatedly finds himself involved with women whom he finds strong and dominant, and with whom he feels obligated to live up to some standard that he senses they may be setting up for him. In contrast to the anima experience we just recounted, this experience is an old complex that has been involving the second young man in habitual and difficult emotional patterns. Here, a mother complex is being projected again and again on teachers, older women, and, indeed, on young women who may not even fit the configuration. What is the factor that keeps this kind of complex so autonomous and so easily projected despite the young man's better judgment?

We do not have to seek far to recognize what is operating. The young man's tendency to put himself into the role of son to a dominant mother, and thus into a filial relation to any such woman, keeps the problem always fresh. He may habitually see himself as obligated, and thus as being without free choice, because somehow the woman always seems to capture the initiative from him.

However, the mother complex contains that very assertive initiative that his ego lacks and needs. The autonomous complex contains and holds what the ego stands in need of, but what it does not grant itself. The attitude of the ego keeps a complex banished from the arena of the conscious makeup; the autonomy or unconsciousness of the complex remains as long as this renunciation continues. This form of resistance is motivated by a self-image,[25] which in this case is dominated by the filial role. If this young man regards himself—that is, harbors an inner feeling about himself—as only a boy in relation to such a woman, when in fact he is in his twenties, then he is making a projection on himself. This projection is as compelling, and as autonomous and beyond his intention, as his projection of the dominating mother image on his young women friends. Or the projection might be an image of powerlessness rather than age, making him see the parent figure as withholding from him all the effective will that he feels himself to lack.

In such circumstances, the only remedy for such a habitual emotional pattern is a change in the self-image. If the young man could achieve a feeling of strength of will or of adulthood, the parent complex would automatically become less alien and undesirable—he could feel a kinship rather than an antipathy to the parent image. The self-image, which determines the autonomy of the complexes, thus needs to be understood in two respects: the first, retrospective—how the self-image came into being—and the second, prospective—how it might change and grow.

THE GENESIS OF THE SELF-IMAGE

In the earliest years the child has little formed ego and little discriminating consciousness, a situation in which the slimmest boundaries between subject and object exist. He experiences his world in the more archaic, archetypal modalities of the psyche, which later fall back into unconsciousness. The earliest activations (projections) of these archaic affect images begin to form the roots of the most basic complexes in the following ways.

First, complexes are rooted in emotional apperception.[26] If, for example, the mother appears hostile at some moment, she may stir in the child the emotion of dread and be perceived in the image of the witch; if this perception occurs repeatedly, it may form a disturbing complex composed of all such fearful impressions of the mother. But such emotional states of the mother are the play of her autonomous complex, and thus are unconscious, even though they appear in the field of awareness. Her complex therefore constellates a complex in the child.

Second, at this archaic level the child lives in a state of emotional participation *(participation mystique)* with the psyches around him, as if immersed in an emotional continuum where subject and object are indistinguishable.[27] This unconscious emotional atmosphere plays a part in the formation of the complexes. The child takes on the complexes of the parents, and their unacknowledged and unresolved problems give the child his problems.[28] The child is most emotionally impressed by and most deeply immersed in these parental problems, and hence the least able to handle them effectively. From this point of view, the so-called traumata of this early age are not isolated and unforeseen catastrophic events, but rather are sudden, explicit dramatizations of chronic painful problems between parent and child from birth on.[29] They are crucial junctures at which complexes are welded into their abiding form in the intense heat of painful and exciting emotion.

Thus the complex is formed in part by the child's psyche itself, and in part by a complex that belongs to the parent. The child's complex represents a conditioning of an innate, universal configuration in the child's psyche by his own specific emotional responses to the parents, and by the peculiarities of the typical affective events transpiring between parent and child at this autonomous level. It is to be stressed that the mother problem of any child rarely derives from the mother as an ego personality, but rather from the various autonomous complexes in her, as though she appeared as many different persons to her child, each evoking different attitudes and emotional reactions.

THE EARLY BOND WITH THE MOTHER

In this early state of emotional participation, of nondifferentiation from the psyche of the mother, the child is embroiled especially with her unconscious—partly hidden in the shadow of her conflicts, partly effaced in the brightness of her ideals. Because the young offspring's selfhood is thus mainly an adjunct to the psychic life of the mother, this stage is represented by the archetype of the Divine Child in the arms of the Great Mother. Many characteristics of this psychological phase correspond to the analogous archaic levels of cultural development in which the same archetype dominated both mythology and social forms.[30]

Under these conditions the child is open to every possible injury that the mother's psyche unconsciously tends to inflict. The mothers of schizoid personalities are usually found to be subtly quite destructive, yet regard themselves as conscientious, dutiful, and dedicated to molding the child into a well-disciplined character. This appears to be a paradox, but may be partly clarified by the limited knowledge we now have of the psychology of such maternal attitudes.

This knowledge again rests on the understanding of the complexes and the difference between the feelings that come from quite different quarters in the mother's psyche.[31] Instead of relating to what is actually going on in the child at any moment and responding appropriately to it, she may find herself passing a judgment that says, "What my child is right now is unacceptable—he should be different, the sort of child I have in mind for him to become." She might have the best intentions imaginable. Yet the difference in feelings is crucial—in one mode she relates to the child as he really is at the moment, while in the other she relates only to the ideal child in her mind and rejects the actual child.

These different responses come from quite different aspects of the mother's psyche. The first response comes from herself as a woman, if the ego relates personally to the child's reality of the moment. The other way does not so relate, but instead interjects an idea. This latter comes from the mother's *animus,*[32] that side of her nature that abstracts from experience and has a preference for ideals, opinions, moralistic judgments, categorical absolutes, and other nonpersonal concerns. Empirically, it is found that this judgmental aspect of woman's nature is a masculine component, usually mingled with her father complex. The animus may be motivated by the concerns of right principles, yet it is always close to the will to power, too easily aggressive and authoritarian, and often frighteningly guilt-producing and annihilative. A woman's animus, if it is not sufficiently developed and brought to consciousness, has a will of its own, and may tend to distrust any manifestation of the world or of human nature that is not controlled. In contradistinction to the ego, which is clear and realistic, such an animus may create an atmosphere that is charged with emotional force. A sense of the uncanny is produced when this charge is half-hidden and unaccountable and when subtle and powerful authoritative pronouncements of judgment appear that seem incontrovertible and that one cannot deal with effectively.

The tragic consequence is that just in those interchanges in which the mother feels most correct and righteous, she is actually being the most rejective and damaging.

However, this interaction is only one among the many taking place on an unconscious level. A natural companionpiece to it is another projection that gives even more substance to the rebuff implied by the animus judgment. Inasmuch as the child's nature is still unformed, its vagueness and ambiguity leave the field open for all sorts of projections on the child.[33] When the mother at some moment finds her offspring unacceptable, her feeling may well rest on her misperception of him through a negative complex in her own unconscious. This complex is detectable by certain signs: the situations in which it occurs are colored by considerable emotion, and her responses are frequent, repetitive, and stereotyped; on close scrutiny, they are found to be at least somewhat inappropriate, if not frankly off the mark.

Such projections or expectations encourage the child, very subtly, to live out the complex image for the mother. It becomes an unwanted burden delegated by the mother to the child to carry for her. She can at one and the same time lay the expectation on the child and also condemn the child for fulfilling it under the dictates of heavy animus judgments. This conflict may engender a load of guilt that the child may be powerless to withstand. For example, if the mother resists her own feminine erotic nature, she may delegate the feminine image to the daughter to live out for her—yet her own animus judgment may moralistically condemn this erotic quality in the child. Her animus is then judging the child by the same pronouncements by which it scorns and deprecates her own feminine qualities. The child would then pick up both complexes from the mother, a view of herself as instinctive, and a judgment toward herself from the animus that considers this eroticism a weak and inferior trait. It is my impression that the "double bind" described by Bateson[34] as the source of acute trouble in the schizoid personality may also be derived from such conflicts.

The complexes overshadowing the child may not only derive from the mother's psyche but also may be reinforced by the rest of the family group. It is in the nature of the complex that, as an emotional phenomenon, it is highly contagious. The typical picture is that the whole family shares the same complex patterns to greater or lesser degrees. These patterns form a strong but hardly perceptible organic network, all subliminal. Thus a projection on the child, though starting with the mother, may become a binding role assigned to him by the entire family group and enforced with relentless but invisible tyranny.[35]

The identities and roles assigned to a child may form along the lines of any strong, unconscious images from the psyche of either parent. These images have always been designated in Jungian psychology by the term *parental expectations.*[36] The main problematic identification of the child is not with the visible parent as such, as a manifest ego personality, but rather with some autonomous complex or archetypal image in the parent, whether hero or princess, rebel or witch, hermaphrodite, and so on. Often exactly opposite projections will fall on a couple of siblings, whereby the one becomes the golden boy, the other the black sheep; in such a case one often hears the symbolism of day and night, light and dark, expressed quite succinctly by the parent. It is not hard to locate the place of the mother's brothers or father or uncles at the source of these complexes. Locating these sources should be the real function of the so-called family history in psychiatry. There seems little doubt that the nature of the differing pathology in the various siblings is determined in large part by the question of which expectation or projection falls on which child.

A most instructive illustration of this kind of unconscious activity occurred in a young man in his mid-twenties. He told me a dream that superficially appeared to distance his problem by rendering it in such fairytale style that it promised to baffle us both. Yet on the other hand, when its context of associations was filled in, the dream showed itself admirably expressive of the exact remedy to the patient's plight. In the dream, he is a captive of a black king. The king tells him he may have his freedom if he kills the white king and brings him his head. A young voice nearby says, "And Mammon, too?" He wakes unsure whether or not to carry out this task. This symbolic way of expressing the problem at first may seem so far removed from life that one might well turn away from it as useless. This apparent remoteness exactly parallels the difficulty with schizophrenic content of delusion and preoccupation: these mythological and religious symbolisms appear too far away, and appear, on the surface, to be defensive evasions of the tough issues of life. I am not implying that this young man was schizophrenic; he was not, and only was experiencing the kind of symbolic activity that goes on at the level of the affect images whenever the unconscious psyche is activated in depth. If he had thought these kings were actual people in the outer world, then he would have been psychotic.

His first associations ran in the direction hinted by the allusion to Mammon, and he wondered if to be captive of the black king referred to his involvement with dialectical materialism in the theory of Marx and Engels, an area of philosophic thinking that had been a skill of his and that he had taught for some time. Since this involvement represented a form of rebellion against his Christian parents, the association seemed to be a good lead. Seen thus, the murder of the white king would have been a crime against the spirit on behalf of the worldly power figure, the black king. The young man felt both danger and guilt in this possibility. On the other hand, these associations did not seem to him to touch the emotional core of the dream, for he was not moved by these reflections, which seemed instead to belong still to the intellectual level.

A few days went by, and then, as he was making drawings of the dream story in an effort to get to its meaning, he noticed that he was associating Greek columns with the white king. That insight called up associations about his mother, who had a predilection for Greek philosophy and had a graduate degree in that field; she had set up for this son high expectations of becoming a kind of specially gifted philosopher and man of the spirit. In the same vein of associations, the image of the black king called up the way the young man had felt all his life in respect to his father's expectations; this parent had habitually looked down on this son as an unpromising weakling, and had given him a feeling about himself that he would never be like other men. These associations did have the affective punch to them that conveyed the feeling of conviction. The black king's hold over him represented the experience of being unfree and constricted in his negative relation to himself. The remedy was to perform a sacrificial killing of the white king, representing the mother's equally binding bright expectation of him.

There is much to learn from this imagery. This young man had foisted upon him, so to speak, a self-image from each parent, a projection on him on their part. The problems that enter the unconscious of a child and form complexes, coming as they do from the unconscious of the parents, may be recognized as the problems left unresolved in the parents.

In this case the mother had delegated to the son a calling that she herself had dropped in her life, an involvement with philosophy that had not yet done its work and that left her with the feeling that there was something important to be accomplished in this area. She left the unfinished business to her son to carry out for her. As a boy, he became thus burdened with a weighty expectation that belonged to an adult mind.

The father, on his part, had delegated a different sort of thing to his son. He had felt himself to be a weak and ineffectual young man during all his early years, until the experience of World War I had put some starch into his character and enabled him to get under way with his education in a professional calling. However, the image of the weakling had remained pushed below the surface to dog him through the years with the constant threat of losing the ground he had gained. Being too uncomfortable with this sort of possibility to grant it full recognition, he had found it more convenient, all unaware, to unload his fear onto his son to carry for him.

The father's expectation became as overly negative as the mother's had been overly positive, and equally burdensome. Each expectation became a self-image for the son, and he found himself always sustaining these two deeply contradictory views of himself: dark and depressive on the one hand, bright and exhilarating on the other. His attempt at rebellion by teaching dialectical materialism as a philosophy had been a compromise, never sufficiently effective to win his place in the society of worldly men.

We have not yet explained why the abstract symbolism of kings appeared to express the conflict. Why could this not have been expressed more lucidly in terms of the parents themselves? Is the dream a device to reveal and conceal at the same time, and to protect the ego from the disturbing truth? I think there is a much more obvious way to account for this imagery, if one considers the comparative symbolism of these motifs. When we examine the symbolism and imagery of the royal figure, we find it comes into play when the processes for reforming and reorganizing the self are activated. It is age-old, having become part of the fabric of man's psychic life some five millenia ago. The ritual sacrifice of the king for rejuvenation and renewal is an essential part of the meaning of the image. The fact that a male royal figure could represent the mother's expectation here is no obstacle, since it is the mother's masculine component, her animus, that is involved in this projection. I do not see the significance of the kings as images of the parents themselves, since it is not the manifest, unitary parents as ego personalities that give rise to the complexes of the child. Rather, it is the emotional interrelations with the parents, and the embroilment with their complexes in their autonomous psyches, that cause the difficulties. The kings thus represent the affect images of the self, the archetypal self-images, positive and negative.

These particular experiences of the parents, and all they signified for their son's self-image, had not yet come to light before this dream in this person's analysis, but one might say they were ready to. He had gotten to the point where he was prepared to look at his experiences and his parents in this way. The dream, however, not only put the finger on the problem, but also offered a remedy. It suggested: "Now it is time to make the hardest sacrifice, the killing off of the thing that has been of highest value till now, your investment in the high expectations that were laid on you by your mother." The dream then carried out this possibility in the form of the primordial rite of the killing of the king. The fact that the psyche not only describes, but also prescribes, indicates that the healing power lies within.

THE TRANSFORMATION OF THE SELF-IMAGE

It is characteristic of the archetypal images that they concern the self and the formation of a self-image. They also provide the initiative and the wherewithal to undo an unsatisfactory self-image, one that is no longer serviceable to the psyche under its current conditions, and then to synthesize a new one that can meet the needs of the coming phase of the personality's development. The therapist does best to follow the lead of the patient's own autonomous psyche in this respect. The healing and integrative process does not come from the therapist's knowledge, through the patient's ego and so down on the unruly psyche, but rather starts from the patient's unconscious processes. Patient and therapist work together to cooperate with the psyche in its own efforts at healing and growth.

The model of the psyche that results from such observations requires two levels of integrative work. The ego is conceived as a center of consciousness that organizes its contents by understanding and insight. It is a complex like any other, and like the others is rooted in an archetypal affect image. This latter is the archetype of the self or, as I prefer to call it because of its own way of representing itself, the *central archetype;*[37] it is a governing center for the psyche as a whole, conscious as well as unconscious.[38] This affect image takes the form of a ruling center and a periphery, and tends to structure itself as a squared or otherwise quadrated circle (a morphology described in Chapter Five, section 10).[39]

The affect image designating the center of the psyche's totality, the "self," is basically composed of opposites, notably of the archetypal parents in the form of the images of the sacral king and queen, who in their ceremonial significance personify the Sky Father and Earth Mother deities.[40] At this most fundamental level, the parent images are not so much the introjected representations of the external parents as they are the archetypal images of the self, which become projected on the parents. Because the ego in its early development has its source in this affect image, the ego can be seen to arise out of the archetypal parent images as its internal matrix, just as it differentiates out of the emotional bonds with the actual parents as its external matrix.

The emotional representation of the central archetype is found to take a new form for each of the major phases of psychic life, and the transitions from one to another are critical turning points in the morphology of the self.[41]

At the beginning the image is that of the young child god in the arms of the Great Mother, who at first is sky and earth, father and mother.

At the famous Oedipal phase, the characteristic image is that of the young son and lover of the Great Mother, the youthful hero who is always possessed by her and at regular intervals submits to cyclic death and birth in her. In adolescence, the image is that of the young hero, whose task is to overcome the Great Mother by violence and win the symbol of selfhood from her, and who affiliates himself with the Sky Father, to whom he now owes his first allegiance. At this stage, qualifying in the social group of fellow initiates is all-important. A little later, when falling deeply in love begins to occur, at the heart of the experience is the image of the Prince and Princess, or the Royal Brother and Sister Pair. The image of the Divine King and Queen is the full-blown form in the adult participant in society. Each image is the archetypal representation of the self appropriate to its own phase of life's development. However, this schema is a rough and incomplete approximation. Much observation, revision, and checking with experience is yet needed to refine it.

Each transition from stage to stage is a rite of passage,[42] with an image sequence of death and new birth, and thus each is an emotional cataclysm with more or less upheaval and distress. It should be noted that, in the symbolism described, the ritual location of such sacrifices, deaths, descents, and new life is characteristically at a locus designated as the center or navel of the world, often as the cosmic axis which joins the midpoints of the sky worlds, earth, and underworld. This locus thus represents the central archetype.

It will be observed that each of the early stages of the evolution of the archetype involves a love bond:

Outer Relation	*Inner Relation*
Mother-Baby	Madonna and Child
Mother-Boy	Great Mother and Son Lover
Father-Son	Sky Father and Hero
Group-Youth	Secret Society and Initiate
Lovers	Royal Brother and Sister Pair
Adult Couple	King and Queen: Sky God and Earth Goddess

The step into each is by way of a relationship in which the affect image is projected, because an archetype, if it is to come into emotional experience at all, must be encountered in projection. Most especially, the archetype of the self appears in the containing bond of an emotional relationship with the person who carries the projection. It is the dynamic core of that love bond. In equal measure, the step out of each phase into the next must involve a sacrifice of the form of the bond that has been prevailing and highly valued, in order to yield place to the new one. This sacrifice occurs in the symbolism of combat and death, and is accompanied by emotions of antipathy. Love and antipathy are integral essentials in the steps of the growth of the self from point to point, as one is drawn into the next stage and repelled by the previous stage.

The early formation of the central archetype and the way it is experienced emotionally from the start is crucial in the genesis of the prepsychotic personality. At each of the major stages of the evolution of this central affect image, if there is a failure of the love bond from a lack of mutuality, the projection is disappointed. Then the affective experience and its image both become distorted. When this distortion occurs, the central archetype of the self is prevented from achieving its fulfillment at that stage. The distortion that occurs instead takes the form of a painful complex. For this phenomenon I have suggested the term *central injury.*[43]

Much of the phenomenology of the acute schizophrenic episode becomes understandable when one watches for the play of imagery around this motif of the central archetype. One can only conclude that the psychotic process is one of renewal and reorganization of the self-image, a process that has become so powerfully charged with energy that it overruns the ego consciousness completely, and takes over the whole field of attention and awareness while the process is running its course.

Chapter Three

The Chronically Regressive Personality

In the psychotherapeutic handling of the nonparanoid schizophrenic conditions, it is almost self-evident that the prospect for a successful outcome depends entirely on the quality of the ego. Insight and consequent growth toward integration develop only through the assimilation of components until now left in a state of unconsciousness, whether they be repressed emotions and conflicts, or unrealized potential and factors necessary for a full development of the personality. Such development requires an ego capable of such assimilation.

The acute schizophrenic episode tends to develop in the opposite direction—the ego is swept back into a state in which it is dominated by the unconscious, and even frankly identifies with the various contents of the deepest layers of the psyche. In this acute process, the components needed for growth present themselves and intrude into the field of awareness, often coming up in the discussions in therapeutic interviews. Yet, however much they make their appearance, it is difficult for a personality undergoing the episode to make use of and benefit by them. While some individuals succeed in doing so, these elements tend to slide back obstinately into unconsciousness, leaving the personality prey to the same repetitive sequences of events so damaging to its growth and survival.

To approach an understanding of this problem, the nature of the prepsychotic ego needs to be studied. This type of ego usually appears in a person who has been hurt early in infancy and is left with a fragile self-esteem and damaged self-image. Since closeness threatens renewed disappointment and hurt, he tends to lose his connection with his affects, which are either dulled or repressed or remain so unconscious as to function in a distressingly autonomous fashion. A combination of circumstances leads to a self-defeating situation in which this individual finds himself entrapped in a chronically regressive state, well-nigh powerless to extract himself from it without a major upheaval of the entire psychic economy. Thus the acute psychotic process, as distinct from the chronic prepsychotic state, may be construed as an attempt to effect just such a turbulent overhauling of the self-structure. The acute regression, nature's attempt at healing, contrasts strongly with the preceding chronic regressiveness.

My experience with my clients leads me to agree with the trend in the literature, in finding that, in the schizoid history, the damaging projections and negative expectations originate with the mother, very early in childhood, and do so for a reason that is consistent with the whole concept of development in our model. In infancy, the mother is the supreme figure in the emotional life, which signifies above all that the central archetype, the self, is carried by her. The Great Mother with the Divine Child is the affect image that is the dynamic core and containing circle of the initial relation with the mother. Any hurtful projections on her part distort this early growth of the self-image, and leave the child more vulnerable to any later projections and complexes of the mother.

By the same token, the father figure in early infancy is still contained in the mother bond[1]—her own masculine component, her animus, is then a more powerful father figure than the actual father himself. One might call this image the *pseudofather.* In later years, whatever the actual father might be in himself, it is not hard to see that he is usually emotionally perceived by the child through the mother's eyes; therefore the mother's projection on him becomes a more powerful image of him than the one derived from the actual experience of him himself. Since the father is usually found to be as unassuming, passive, and uninvolved as the mother is forward, aggressive, and controlling, there is every encouragement for her animus to become the more active father figure in the life of the family.

Thus, when the parent imposes on the child images and values that do not belong to his own nature, the child is not given a chance to feel his real native identity affirmed. Rather, he grows to feel depreciated, unrecognized, unloved, or worse—guilty of some hazy fault that leads him to sense that he should in some way be other than he is. Schizoid personalities usually reveal the scars of this kind of destructive relation with the mother. Such damage involving the self-image I prefer to call *central injuries*,[2] as distinct from the lesser difficulties visited on the more peripheral parts of the personality, so to speak (inasmuch as both ego and self are represented in the psyche's own imagery as centers).

The consequences of such injuries are manifold, but fall into a pattern that characterizes the individual who is caught in the unconscious bond with the mother on the one hand, and with the mother complex and archetype on the other.

Consequences of Central Injuries

First and foremost, the individual withholds his or her feelings. (In the Jungian model of the psyche the term *feeling* is used to designate one of the functions of ego-consciousness, a rational function of valuing. Feelings differ from emotions, which occur through the activation of complexes and their affect-images and are autonomous in respect to the ego.) Again and again hurt by the mother's way of response, the feelings are only timidly brought forward, since people are expected to respond by denying the validity of the child's feelings as the mother once did. To relate is to be hurt again, and so the whole potential for relatedness is abandoned. Considerable resentment builds up over this anticipation of painfulness in relationship, but this resentment must again be withheld for fear of its alienating even further. Finally, the feelings become withdrawn and even repressed, to the point where the individual is not even aware of the problem, and new promises of warm feeling are fought with a surprising involuntary hostility.

The chief damage that arises out of the withdrawal of feeling is that the ego becomes weak and poorly structured.[3] Feeling[4] is vital to the sense of reality and relatedness. When feeling is inhibited or repressed, the people and things of the outer world hold little conscious meaning and value, either positively or negatively, and their apparent loss of importance renders them vague and unconvincing. Another way of putting this idea is that feeling disposes libido in a form that is experienced as interest, either positive or negative.[5] As this feeling or interest drops away from objective concerns, it naturally falls back on the contents of the inner life of imagery, which gains impressiveness to the same extent that the outer world loses it.

The ensuing state, in which the unconscious becomes to some extent predominant over ego consciousness, is both childlike and archaic. Its modes of thought and feeling are overwhelmingly governed by the forms of the personal complexes on the one hand, and of the archetypal mentality on the other.

THE COMPOUNDING OF THE MOTHER-BOUND STATE

The identity of the child having become overclouded with the parental projections and thus damaged, he is left in later years knowing no alternative other than this negative relation to himself and to parents or parent figures. Nor, given the lack of the feeling function, is there the capacity to recognize the hurt for what it is. He longs for acceptance, yet at one and the same time he expects and disbelieves a rebuff. It is sometimes astonishing to watch this kind of personality gravitate back to the most destructive emotional bonds, as if they were powerful magnets with a fateful inevitability in their capacity to overwhelm all resistance. At bottom, the ego is remaining obstinately attached to the unloving aspect of the mother and the complex that represents her. (A negative fascination such as this is not wholly without sense, for complexes habitually reassert their patterns until resolved.)

At the same time, the central archetype of the self remains in the form of the image of the Divine Child in the arms of the Great Mother, that is, the image of the as yet unfulfilled, still potential, affirmative relation to the mother. Such an individual looks on the world as if it were all a beneficent, surrounding mother who should be yielding love and nurturance, but who instead is found ever and again to disappoint the expectation—inevitably, since the world does not relish the role.

This mother-bound state is further encouraged by another characteristic set of phenomena. When the state is severe, certain features conspire to hold the ego imprisoned in the grip of its chronic regressiveness, creating a spell under which it is unable to see the way out. In describing each of these features, I will stress the parallels between the personal and archaic psychological patterns, that is, the patterns of the complexes and those of the archetypes.

THE LOWERING OF THE LEVEL OF CONSCIOUSNESS

The chief principle that operates to keep the ego enclosed in this schizoid state has been described by Jung as the *abaissement du niveau mental,* a term borrowed from Janet to designate a lowering of the level of consciousness.[6] This concept implies that a quantum of libido that drops out of ego consciousness appears in the unconscious. The more active and affectively toned the complexes become, the more they make their appearance in the projections and misperceptions and inappropriate responses in the day-to-day emotional life of the individual. This development leads to an increasingly stereotyped set of emotional situations following the blueprint laid down by the complexes. Such a personality keeps encountering destructive mothers and unreliable fathers at every turn, and if he does not find them ready-made according to specifications, he molds them into the familiar shape by subtle emotional maneuvering. The complexes become thus strengthened by repetition. Each new instance in which they are found operative somehow confirms the illusion that this is really the way things are. The more these complexes are strengthened and confirmed, the less possible does it become to have wholly new and different experiences of relationship; that is, new complexes are not readily formed. The old complexes, becoming stronger through further experiences, gather more and more fresh associations around them, which in turn add to their energic, and hence affective, strength. Thus, the world comes fairly to bristle with parent and sibling figures. On the archetypal level, the images of the Great Mother and Great Father also predominate.

THE WEAKNESS OF THE EGO

The most significant feature arising from the lowered level of consciousness is the weakness of the ego, which then lacks will and determination, and passively tends to let things slide along without the active hand of mastery to give them shape. The ego shows a prevailing inertia or ineffectiveness, with a proneness to rumination. Such an ego is not free to create a satisfactory world for itself according to its best interests. The prevailing stance, on the contrary, is one of passive expectancy when the world is looked on as an all-embracing mother, asked to be attentive as a mother should. Since the world is bound to fail this hope, the world appears to behave as did the actual mother who was found ungiving. This disappointment freshens the old wound at every turn, and keeps the ego demoralized and thus further inclined toward passive waiting for rescue.

A weakness of the ego brings in its company uncomfortable uncertainties regarding one's masculinity or femininity. For, as the energy potential of consciousness is lowered and that of the unconscious is heightened, inevitably the contrasexual components become activated and even stronger than the ego; that is, the anima in a man and the animus in a woman begin to threaten the soundness of the personality as man or as woman. In the man, his passivity tends to become thereby augmented and the assertion of his masculine initiative undermined. In the woman, the animus breeds a kind of autonomous aggressiveness that occurs without her deliberate intention, making her fearful of its unpredictable appearances and thus of assertiveness in general; her feminine ego grows more passive than ever. As archetypes, the man's anima tends to remain the regnant mother image; the woman's animus remains part of this mother image as a rather magical *daimon.* In either case, the proper role of the anima or animus, as a *function-complex* mediating the contents of the unconscious to the ego,[7] becomes distorted, or even reversed, tending rather to suppress the ego and draw the ego toward entanglement with the archetypal images and processes.

THE WITHDRAWAL OF FEELING

The withdrawal of feeling already mentioned accompanies the abandonment of the potential for relationship and produces several regressive effects.

One result of the withdrawal of feeling and its falling out of the arena of the conscious relations to the outer world, is that the libido that might have belonged to feeling reappears in the activation of the unconscious components. This transfer is conceived in energic terms as an autonomous shift.[8] At the personal level, this shift is the principal factor in the loss of the reality sense and in the corresponding illusion that one's subjective impressions are somehow more real than the object; the involution sets up the trap of discouraging any evaluations of new experiences as such, and fosters stereotyped reactions in terms of the old, familiar complexes. This pattern perpetuates the family constellation indefinitely, as if it were the vast hand of some determined sculptor thumping the world, like clay, into his preconceived plan. All the while, the deficiency in feeling prevents the ego from recognizing and evaluating the hurtful emotions in these episodes; either these emotions are not perceived where they are operative, or are perceived where not operative. On the archetypal level, meaning shifts from the disappointing and uninteresting world now devoid of feeling, to the more ideally delineated and apparently reliable world seen in terms of the great universals—a cosmos whose broad outlines are made clear and impressive by the primordial images that appear in complicated philosophical or religious preoccupations. Here are great and timeless meanings, in contrast to which the mundane actualities are seen as insufficient, mistaken, or tawdry. Thus the withdrawal is compounded by this shift of interest.

A second result of the withdrawal of feeling is a prevailing ambivalence. Consciousness of the feeling function means an ability to know one's feelings and to make them known; one likes or dislikes, chooses or rejects, appreciates or depreciates, and sustains a more or less consistent attitude accordingly. When feelings are unconscious, the affects now conveyed solely in the complexes are both love and hate, attraction and repulsion, in a bewilderingly simultaneous array. At a deeper level, the archetypes are by nature correspondingly split in dualities (God and Devil, heaven and underworld, Christ and Antichrist, Aphrodite Ourania and Pandaemonia—the heavenly and spiritual as distinct from the earthy and instinctual); the sharply contrasting images and emotions emanating from them tend to neutralize all evaluations of the person's concerns. He or she no sooner sees things one way than the other way presents itself as equally true, and so there can be no point of view and no convinced decisions. This neutralizing of valuations tends to hold the libido suspended at dead center between the polarities. Progressive movement and development are out of the question under such circumstances.

A third result is that, having lost the service of the feelings, the one most necessary agent of liberation from the harmful mother bond is lacking: that is, anger. The proper function of anger is to rise up and protest against the annihilative aspect of the mother. The anger itself tends toward this function, to give vent to the long-accumulated emotions of resentment and thus to introduce some saving consciousness into the relationship with the mother. On the archetypal level the anger appears as the aggressive fight of the hero (the prototype of the ego's self-assertion, whether in men or women) against the Terrible Mother monster;[9] his aim is to force her to yield up the vital treasure she hoards, the symbol of the self, that is, to grant him his first experience of selfhood, which she has willfully denied him up to this point. This struggle for selfhood would mean a liberation from the mother in the sense that the bonds of dependency on her favors would be cut. Hostility is the great separator or differentiating agent, just as its opposite, love, tends to make all things one. Anger is withheld in the mother-bound personality, as I have just mentioned, because the individual fears alienating people and earning the already too much feared condemnation of being found hateful. The assertion of this aggression, on the other hand, would supply the necessary ingredients for an active ego and stronger will, determination, and assertiveness.

It should be emphasized that I am speaking here of feelings as distinct from emotions. I am not trying to say that there is no anger in the schizoid—quite the contrary—but that the anger is renounced, and hence too autonomous, undirected, and explosive. Hence, whereas the feeling function would have given aim and sense to anger, even providing a consistent intent to throw off the mother bond, this autonomous form of rage appears to both the subject and the object of the emotion to be senseless, accidental, and certainly ineffectual.

EROS AND POWER

When the self-image is debased and the ego weakened because of the factors being outlined here, and when the feeling necessary for relatedness is withdrawn, the inevitable outcome is that a power problem prevails.[10]

Logos and *Eros* are the terms used in Jungian psychology to designate the two general modalities in which we experience our world. The Logos mode abstracts out of experience and discriminates, with the aim of understanding; this mode may not only perceive order but may motivate to impose it, thus leading into a power drive. The Eros mode, however, relates and interweaves, with the aim of entangling us in living experience; it may not only deal with relatedness and love, but may motivate to crave it and be felt as desire.

The proper role of the hero archetype is to motivate the ego to carry out a life task, that of liberation from the mother. When the ego is too demoralized to take on this responsibility, and settles into its weakness as a way of life, playing the part of the sick or handicapped personality, then the only outlet for the hero image is in compensatory fantasy. That is, all the potential of self-assertion and self-reliance drops back into the unconscious and accumulates in the image of the hero. Its effect then is experienced by the individual as a sort of hidden secret, a greatness in him that is not recognized by anyone and that might someday break forth and transform him in the eyes of the world. The modicum of expression actually allowed this image from day to day usually takes the form of an urge to impress or to win some little prestige, over against the otherwise miserable feelings about himself. As Jung has often pointed out, where love drops away, power takes over.[11] But this urge is self-defeating, because prestige is just as lonely as debasement; prestige has nothing to do with the principle of mutual relatedness, but instead is manipulative toward others, appealing only to their competitive impulses, not to their warmth. Even more self-defeating is the result that, in contrast to this secret sense of great "specialness," the ego only finds itself the more worthless when it fails to live up to the stringent demands of an awesome prestige fantasy.

The predominance I am giving to the power problem raises the question, What about psychosexual components here? While there is plenty to say about the sexual difficulties in this kind of personality, I still do not find them following consistent lines except insofar as in this area, too, feeling is strikingly left out. At bottom, the sexual problem is really a love problem; Eros and power turn out upon close scrutiny to be opposite principles.[12] The syndrome under discussion is founded on the dynamics of the self-image and the power drives that grow out of it, while the sexual maladjustment appears to be a more secondary outcome and symptom of those disturbances. In other syndromes, such as hysteria, there is no doubt that the dynamics form along sexual lines, and that the various mental contents become sexualized.

Individuals prone to catatonic schizophrenia usually seem to be potentially capable of more than usual lovingness. The one factor holding this potential under lock and key seems to be the threat of hurt felt by an overly sensitive nature. Such individuals resort involuntarily to power rather than to relatedness, as a way of interacting with other people. No matter how much the sexuality does or does not develop, a lack of feeling leaves it relatively meaningless; there is little relatedness or reaching out to partners. Instead, the feeling remains attached to the inner components of experience—to the instinct itself, or to the imagery of union, often on a lofty plane; when thus inwardly directed, the feeling is fully autoerotic, that is, directed toward the subject rather than an object.

THINKING

Thus the weakness of the ego and the withdrawal of feeling tend to perpetuate the mother bond in the schizoid personality.

Another feature of the syndrome occurs in terms of thinking[13] that corresponds to what has been said of feeling, and that also may be considered a kind of withdrawal.

The falling away of libido from consciousness leaves a lack of zest for doing one's own thinking, that is, for formulating one's own concepts for understanding one's world, according to the data of real experience. On the personal level, ideas are borrowed from those same figures who have created the strongest complexes—"everything turns out to be just as mother (or father) said." On the archetypal level, something happens akin to the sense of meaningfulness that I have just mentioned in connection with feeling. The cosmos as seen in terms of the great universals becomes far more convincing than its poor rival, the weak conscious outlook. Understanding then comes in flashes that are often entirely inappropriate and uncorrected by a discriminating conscious mind. Further regression is involved in the peculiar circumstance that at this level all knowledge is foreknowledge; such an individual believes himself already to know and comprehend the meaning of all things, without having to learn it by the harder method of shaping one's thoughts through the mistakes one makes and the discoveries one encounters. Nothing new is wanted because it does not seem needed.

We have been discussing the weakness of the ego and the withdrawal of feeling and thinking as two factors holding the individual in his chronic regressiveness. There are two other features of this mentality that are even more strongly operative in creating this state of imprisonment: the sense of guilt and the sense of timelessness.

GUILT

The guilt inculcated by the parents' judgments and injunctions is usually referred to by the familiar term *superego.* While Jungians might borrow this term from time to time for colloquial purposes, it does not properly fit into the Jungian schema of the psyche, which has no great triad of ego, superego, and id.[14] We see in this guilt not one complex but many.

The guilt with which parents endow their child is most hurtful when it damages and severely distorts both the personal and archetypal self-image, that is, the self-image of the ego and of the central archetype, thus creating a strong sense of unwholeness and inner strife.

On the personal level, the chief instigator of guilt in this mother-bound personality is the mother's capacity for moralistic judgments, which resides in her animus. If it were healthy, this component would endow her with the motivation toward the masculine (Logos) properties of discrimination and reflection, also of mastery and will.[15] In the mother in question, however, we find a sinister habit of thinking in terms of how things should be or ought to have been, in contrast to the way a more conscious and feminine disposition would relate to things as they are. To take the child as he is, means to respond to what is his reality, to what at any moment he is actually thinking, feeling, doing, or being. Maternal feeling tends to respond in this way. The animus cuts across any such relationship with habitual judgments, that what is there in the child at such a moment is not what it should be, that it ought to be better or different. Such an animus is antagonistic and suppressive toward anything that is too naturally spontaneous and uncontrolled. In schizophrenic histories one finds this criticism touching very basic matters, such as the child's bodily, natural, emotional, and instinctive makeup. The animus has an incredible capacity to make the child feel unworthy and wrongheaded, for it operates with all the force of an unconsciously directed function, willfully commandeering all the weight of tradition and authority to back it up.

On the archetypal level, guilt is based on a less familiar principle, belonging to the ways of the archaic mind and not so easily recognizable to our modern consciousness. Yet I find it as prevalent in the problem of the schizoid personality as any other archaisms. This kind of guilt is analogous to the primordial view found in tribal societies, that only acts performed according to the prescribed ways of the ancestors are right, meaningful, and endowed with truth; other, more random acts are considered liable to error, meaninglessness, and untruth.[16] To paraphrase, only the archetypal ways, which underlie all tradition and are considered sacred, are capable of rightness. Perhaps the old usage of the word *righteous* best describes this attitude, because it implies an entire way of life both ritually and ethically in traditional cultures. The other, profane ways are those initiated by the individual ego, which, unlike adherence to the strict sanctions of the collectivity and of the ancestral tradition, assumes the privilege of making its own choices, according to its personal needs and views. From the point of view of the archetypal mind, this act of the ego is an infringement and a *hubris*. In the myth of paradise, this arrogation of choice by the first man was from the point of view of the deity a sin and a fall from wholeness and grace, yet from the point of view of man it was the absolute necessity, if any individual consciousness was to be born in him. Guilt, according to Jung, is the emotion felt when one falls out of the state of wholeness, whether it be out of the collectivity and its preordained ways, or out of one's inner integrity.[17]

For the mother-bound personality, these guilts are very binding. From the point of view of the mother figure, either the personal mother with her demanding animus, or the primordial Great Mother, who holds all order and wisdom in herself, guilt is inevitable if the ego chooses to act on its own, according to its own lights. There must be no change. Such an ego grows to be mortally afraid of action that might lead to error and to making mistakes, which threaten to bring down shame; such an ego has an inordinate need for absolute rightness. On the other hand, another kind of guilt ensues if the ego does not find freedom from the mother and does not learn to act on its own.

THE SENSE OF TIME

Hand in hand with this tendency to feel guilt goes an aversion to the sense of time. Awareness of time seems to be proportional to the degree to which consciousness is differentiated. For our consciousness, time is a linear sequence of events and constantly brings new experiences and new learning. Archaic time, on the other hand, is cyclical, in which there is nothing new under the sun and the most meaningful events are only repetitions of things that have been since the heroic age, as first experienced by the ancestors, closely bound up with the flow of life and death, of passing and renewal in the cycles of nature.[18]

When, in the mother-bound personality, libido falls away from consciousness, this cyclical sense of temporal relativity arises from the psychic hinterland and pervades the general orientation. In the more personal sphere, time holds little reality because the all-pervading complexes resist change; things seem perpetually to remain as they have been, inasmuch as the events of the emotional life are mostly repetitious. This atmosphere of timelessness blinds the person to the meaning of the years passing, so that there is no vivid realization of what it means to reach adult years, and what it means to be reacting to the world in the same terms at the age of twenty-five as at five. The hallmarks of the psychology of the *puer aeternus,* the eternal child,[19] are the arrest of time and a provisional life, holding things off to an imaginary future that never arrives.

I have been enumerating the powerful factors that mesh to hold the individual in the archaic mentality and the infantile complexes, that is, in the mother-bound state, which is colored by its "matriarchal level" of consciousness, to use Neumann's term.[20] When severe, this state is unstable and anxiety ridden. The ego finds itself further and further trapped in the complexes, which are now overgrown in size and potency, and feels itself in increasing danger of being overridden by the overwhelming force of an archetypal invasion.[21]

A Case of a Prepsychotic Personality

As an example of such a prepsychotic personality, I will describe the case of a young women whom I first knew during her acute schizophrenic episode. (See Case 4 in the appendix to this book.)

This was a young, single Irish Catholic woman of twenty-three in an acute catatonic schizophrenic episode, her second, the other being seven years previously. She entered the hospital with a chief complaint of confused talk and behavior, of two days' duration. On admission she presented the characteristic picture of a hyperactive young catatonic, carrying on a stream of "bizarre" and disconnected talk, posturing, dancing, and pausing at intervals to listen to voices.

Her history was notable for a remarkably destructive relation to her mother, who herself had paranoid and depressive tendencies, and who developed a psychotic depression a few months before the daughter's break. The mother, although she had regarded her daughter as a pretty baby girl, had always found fault with her daughter since she was a child; she had undermined her self-esteem in such a variety of ways that one could only call them as ingenious as they were appalling. The father, on the other hand, doted on her. Being alcoholic, he was weak and passive, and the daughter was unable to get any emotional support from him to speak of; on the contrary, she found herself having to be somewhat maternal toward him, even handling him authoritatively during his bouts of drinking. There were younger twin siblings, a boy who became neurotic and ineffectual, and a girl who retired from the world to take the veil.

During school years, this young woman was unable to do her work at her own capacity. She also had difficulty with her relationships because her mother would insult her friends to such an extent that she would be ashamed to invite anyone home with her. This was especially the case with boyfriends, for whom she could only hold silent infatuations, at a distance.

Her first break came at sixteen, a not very severe episode characterized by religious visions. After a year without somatic therapy, she was released from the hospital and took some business courses, also some night school courses in Catholic philosophy and psychology. She found congenial work, and for the year before her break had a job she really liked, one that took her traveling by air.

She showed in her personality makeup most of the qualities enumerated above as characteristic of chronic regressiveness.

She was likeable, and one could sense with appreciation her struggle to make something of her life. She kept herself, however, in a position of weakness in regard to handling her relation to the world, by keeping herself wandering and traveling, always meeting new people on superficial terms and never needing to settle into deeper and abiding relationships in a stable situation. Her money kept slipping away as fast as it came in, so that she could not achieve any further education, which she badly needed in order to put her capable mind to work. Rather, wherever she was, she made it her chief concern to seek a kind of acknowledgment as favorite daughter, with special appreciation and privileges, an aim that usually eventually defeated itself. Her passive role in this regard led her into letting herself be used by people, especially by men who would take her up easily and drop her deftly, in rather meaningless sexual encounters.

This young woman, though attractive in appearance and carrying a gay and feminine demeanor, could not accept her role in relation to men, and tended to shun such involvements. Under the condemning judgment of the mother's animus against feminine nature, she achieved little realization of what her womanhood meant, and lingered at the emotional level of a preadolescent in this respect. Her few sexual encounters only proved damaging and frightening, leaving her more confused than enlightened about erotic matters.

Her animus was not overly assertive, as her mother's was. It tended rather to behave as it did in relation to her mother, baiting in furtive little ways to aggravate and arouse impatience in the other person, leaving her wondering why she drew other people's disfavor. More open manipulative aggression seldom came into play; she could have profited by more. Chiefly, the animus functioned in the opposite aspect, in the capacity for religious reflection, enticing her away from the practical world. This animus was projected onto a certain priest whom she held in high regard as mentor.

The withdrawal of feeling, which ensued on her constant hurt in the destructive relation with her mother, was expressed chiefly by a flight into chatty garrulousness, light and amusing, but superficial and circumstantial—and endless. At first glance one might be struck with this apparently extraverted drive, but on a closer look one found that she rarely let any real feelings show through this lively, skittery concealment, and that this outwardly-directed drive occurred only when she was under the pressure of some difficult emotions. She felt herself to be of little worth and feared ridicule, and learned to resort to that device so common among schizoid persons to conceal their sensitiveness: playing the clown. (Another, equally frequent expression of this withdrawn state is feeling like a ghost, an insubstantial and invisible spirit creature, dead to the outer community.) There was no sharp line of demarcation between what she knew herself to be and what she expected others to take her so negatively to be.

This withdrawal of feeling resulted in her perpetuating the family constellation indefinitely. She had repeated encounters with dominating mother figures, unreliable men, and sibling rivals. It seemed to her that she could never trust men and had better steer clear of them. She found more gratification in the luminous world of religious speculation and rumination. Her feelings toward people were flighty and ambivalent, fear of being let down following hard on her need for vital contact, and resentment over her fate coloring her optimistic bids for approval. Her ideals were lofty and spiritual, yet undermined by a disillusioned awareness of the evil in people's natures and her own. She could not put her anger to effective use, but rather sought to spare her mother the sort of hurt that she felt moved to inflict on her, and that she so constantly received at her mother's hands. She thus could not bring herself to confront her mother with any of their mutual difficulties, in order to try to work them out and resolve them to whatever extent might prove possible. This passivity kept her in a state of weakness and defenselessness.

As to her capacity to think, she was intelligent and had an alert mind. She should have had it educated and disciplined, but despite her occasional intentions to do so, she never made education possible for herself. The inevitable direction her thinking took was that of quoting what other people said. Her own thinking remained largely within the Roman Catholic structure. Her flair, whenever she did any special studying or reading, was in the field of the Catholic philosophy and psychology.

She was generally guilt ridden, in the sense that she had been made to consider herself a person of no worth or promise. Thus, when her ego acted for itself, it did so with the conviction of failure. She was especially guilt bound in the sense that her strong erotic needs and preoccupations were under the ban both of her mother's negative judgment against such matters, and also of her church's anticarnal mores. To be a woman seemed to mean only to be a wanton temptress. She could take some initiative in setting up her life in other ways, so long as it did not involve this issue; when it did, she could only bow to the taboos set up for her. It seemed to her, therefore, that her only fulfillment as a woman could be in the archetypal role of the spiritual vessel of grace, not the carnal vessel of the marital union and childbearing. In the latter matters she maintained an obstinate innocence that refused the fruit of the tree of knowledge.

In respect to the sense of time, she remained in these several ways always the young girl, flanked at every turn by the overbearing mother and the unreliable father. The future that her fantasy kept insisting on for her was a career as a great mystic; but this career was to be a recreation of a certain famous historical personage described to her by her mentor, the priest. Thus her life, someday in this imaginary future, was to be no new phenomenon, but the repetition of what had happened before, and had become part of the hoary heritage of her church.

It will be observed that I am, in this particular context of the regressive personality, presenting a picture of the unconscious in a very negative light, almost as a crippling and threatening mechanism. The point needs this simple clarification, that the unconscious mentality is so generally negative in its effects only when it becomes a prison for the undeveloped individual. Ordinarily the symbols and processes of the archaic psyche are found to endow life with more and deeper meaning than consciousness is usually able to find in its own proper modalities. The archetypal affect images are found to act as determinants, and their images as forerunners, in the healthy mind, of the insights, new discoveries and experiences, and progressive steps of consciousness. A balanced relation to the unconscious psyche is essential, enabling it to do its work by forming symbols for the promotion of consciousness. The healthy mind derives from the productions of the unconscious psyche those life-giving intimations of meaning and value that evolve into the more sharply delineated concepts and feelings of the conscious functions.

Chapter Four

The Acute Psychotic Regression

It is my impression that when the regressive mother-bound state is firmly ensnaring an individual's ego, and when there is, nevertheless, a strong potential for development, nature can spontaneously intervene to provide a way out. This intervention is the cataclysmic turmoil of psychosis, which is designed to enforce developmental changes. It would be preferable to avert this upheaval through psychotherapy. The therapist's aim should be not only to gain insight into the emotions of the complexes, thus developing the feelings, but also and more especially to release and assimilate the blocked Eros potential now residing in the unconscious. The therapist would hope that the consequent strengthening of the ego would avert the psychosis. However, nature's own remedy remains otherwise a profound reorganization of the self through the turbulent psychotic experience.

In the schizophrenic episode, the central and most dynamic issue concerns the self-image. The self-image involves two interrelated systems: the ego's severely damaged view of itself, and the ego's basic affect image, the self, which tends to compensate the debasement with an exalted play of fantasy imagery full of its lost potential. Since I use the term *self-image* regularly in discussing this problem, I wish to avoid confusion of terms and call the former (the ego's self-image) the *personal self-image,* and the latter (the self) the *central archetype.* The affect image of the central archetype is here conceived as making its appearance at all phases of life and in all kinds of states of integration and disintegration, and thus is not always associated with the conscious experience of selfhood, in the sense of being an achievement requiring the long and arduous work of spiritual or psychological development designated by Jung as the *individuation process.*

The prepsychotic state characteristically shows an anxiety-laden contrast between a debased personal self-image and a compensatorily exalted archetypal one. An acute demoralization of the ego usually seems to be the factor that upsets the balance in tension between the two self-images. The acute catatonic process appears to manifest two contrary trends resulting from a central injury. One trend is the identification of the ego with the central archetype, thus creating a gross inflation, involving delusions of being a deity or hero of world dimensions. The other trend is the balancing movement directed against this central identification, involving delusional fears of people and social insurrections hostile to the inflated subject. The guilt-ridden, inadequate, and withdrawn personality becomes overwhelmed by an eruption of archetypal contents, whose affect images describe more or less regular processes of death and dismemberment of the old debased self caught in the mother-child bond, and of renewal and reconstitution with a more viable form of the self. This latter process, of renewal, carries the potential of the next stage of development.

To illustrate the concepts just outlined, I will continue with the experience of the same young woman whose prepsychotic state has been described in Chapter Three.

The events leading to the psychotic break concerned two close relationships, one with a girl companion and another with a boy-friend, both of which went badly and became rejective.

On admission to the hospital and for a few weeks after, the young woman showed a typical picture of catatonic schizophrenia in a hyperactive phase: she was disheveled and denudative, talked incessantly, danced and chanted ritualistically, made seductive motions and gestures, and expressed fears of poison and communist uprisings. She was thus at first quite out of contact with external reality, but within a few weeks, on a course of insulin therapy in subcoma doses, she regained a good deal of her ego standpoint and sense of reality. I should perhaps say here that in the hospital concerned there was a time limit of six months in which to handle the acute psychosis before discharge. As for the medication, there are two advantages to subcoma doses of insulin: it interferes least of any somatic therapy with the psychotherapeutic interviews and process, and it helps to correct the physiological aspect of the psychotic process (especially the havoc raised by the chronic alarm reaction of anxiety and its consequent pituitary and other changes).

Interviews were held three times a week through all these conditions. When she regained more contact with the outer world, she was inclined to revert to her chatty, gossipy talk about her relationships of the past year, but it came in a flighty, circumstantial series of scattered anecdotes in which the affect was strikingly missing. I therefore indicated my doubt about the validity of these communications and asked her whether there were not perhaps other concerns that were more pressing and significant to her. After considerable misgivings about entrusting me with such confidences, she gave me the following account of what had really been going on during those weeks.

The Delusional System

She felt that there was a cosmic struggle. The Devil was hatching a plot to destroy the world by an explosion of radioactive substances with which he was experimenting. Opposing him was Christ, who was struggling against him to save the world. Each had followers, thus dividing the world into two camps: the communists, in league with the Devil, aimed at bringing about the final disintegration of everything, and the democracies, under the banner of Christ, aimed at keeping the world intact. She said she also felt these camps to be two sides of her own nature, masculine and feminine sides in conflict. In another polarity, both the Devil and God were constantly speaking with conflicting voices in her ear. God's voice was always hilariously funny, cracking jokes and laughing. The Pope was possessed by the Devil, just as she was, and was in hell, as she was. The Pope's hat (the threefold tiara) was torn into little triangular bits of paper that were scattered about the earth, and at the same time the Holy Trinity was separated on earth in the same way, so work had to be done to reunite the Pope's hat and thus the Trinity.

Then she felt herself to be going through a whole drama of her own. She was in hell, which was a crazy place or a jail; it was a single room like those in the hospital. Around her were various friends, wearing huge masks of animal's heads. She had a severe task to perform as a test: to crawl through a skeleton from bottom to top without breaking it, and come out of the mouth. This she achieved successfully. The Devil was in her bones, and she had to turn these around one by one, reversing all but the head and neck back to front. The hands, meanwhile, became claws. At the same time, another trial she had to perform was to repeat creation and evolution again. She was under the sea for a long time, in the presence of primordial monsters. Then she came on land and saw the age of reptiles. Finally she lived among primitives and took part in their rituals and dances and chants. Also, she had to return to her own beginning, that is, her own birth, and repeat her childhood and growth to her present age; in this repetition of her life everything had to be done precisely and without error, otherwise she had to go back to the beginning and start over each time. She only reached the age of sixteen in this performance.

Now the central drama running through all this conflict and resolving it concerned the birth of a divine child. She felt herself to be in the middle between the Devil's and Christ's sides in the struggle to destroy or save the world. She was to give birth to a baby as an outcome of having intercourse with God every night, God appearing either in the form of her father or of the man of her infatuation. This baby was to be a saviour child, like Christ, but in a new form, with a special function in saving the world from the conflict described. This birth made of her a kind of Virgin Mother. Now, it was to the interests of the communists to steal this child and do away with it, and there was a critical question of how to rescue it. The solution lay in a certain patient on the ward, a motherly sort of woman who reminded her of a neighbor who had been as warm to her as her own mother had been cold. This woman appeared in the drama as Queen of the Sea, who had magical ways of protecting the life of the child and thus saved it from destruction.

Along the way through this fantasy drama occurred a few impressive visions that the patient found deeply stirring. One was of the world as a mountain, with a plane circling around it going to four planets, which were called God, Mercury, Mars, and Venus. On another occasion she and a lover stood each on a globe, with another couple looking on from two other globes. The spheres were planets, and her lover and she were King and Queen of the Universe, and were also twin brother and sister or Prince and Princess. They adopted foster parents, the kindly mother who lived near her as a child, and that mother's husband. Finally, and most fraught with meaning, was the vision of a pair of gold rings flanking a vertical gold staff, which she understood as a symbol of marriage; to the right was the standing figure of Christ. The Virgin appeared to her to give her a message of import to the world, that the women of the world were not keeping their marriage vows and the sacrament of marriage was not being respected; this message was given to her to correct this evil.

AMPLIFICATION OF THE DELUSIONS

The delusional form is mainly Christian, but there are indications of a more archaic type of expression in Mesopotamian myth and ritual, that bring into play the same chief elements of cosmic conflict, regression in time, marriage with the god, and the divine child, features regularly found in the seasonal festivals of renewal in archaic times. The Babylonian New Year (Akitu) Festival was one such ritual that was clearly recorded and derived from very early roots.[1]

Ritually, the setting for this renewal festival was centered on the cosmic axis, the world mountain, and the time was reversed to the world's beginning. The creation myth (Enuma Elish) was recited and enacted in ritual drama in the form of a cosmic battle between the forces of light and those of darkness. The manner in which this drama was depicted is obscure in the records, and there are conflicting opinions about it. The king was the representative of the god of light, Bel-Marduk, "Son of the Sun," in defending the gods against the onslaught of darkness and chaos in the person of the water-monster and primordial mother, Tiamat. The prevailing opinion seems to be that the ritual form was "a foot-race between Zu and Ninurta, in which Zu is defeated and afterwards, apparently, slain".[2] (Other, parallel forms of the ritual pattern of the Near East represent the powers of chaos in the form of the king's terrestrial enemies of the surrounding hostile kingdoms.) In the myth, Marduk was for a time held captive in the realm of the dead, that is, in a chamber in the mountain, and, correspondingly, the king in the ritual was humiliated, stripped of his regalia, and struck, in the stage tower. This interval while darkness held the upper hand was a kind of Saturnalia, the society's laws being suspended, social positions reversed, and disorder rife—an enactment of chaos as a general "topsy-turvydom." Liberation from death and disintegration came at the hands of Marduk's son, Nebo, accompanied by other gods summoned by the lamentations of Marduk's consort, Beltis. The final rite was that of the sacred marriage, in which the king and priestess, as god and goddess (Marduk and Sarpanitum), by their union brought new life and fertility to the earth and to man and vigor to the people. There are indications[3] that initiations of youths may also have taken place at this time, judging by the practices at the other similar festivals in that part of the world; these initiations were a ritual death and rebirth of the neophytes in conjunction with and probably in identification with those of the king and the god. Texts describe the neophytes passing through an artificial representation of the underworld, where they were shown "the altars amid the waters" and other ritual objects of veneration.[4]

GENERAL COMPARISON OF DELUSIONS AND MYTHS

In these ancient customs are inescapable parallels to the symbolic productions of the psychotic individual's psyche, which put forth the same main elements of the drama of renewal in the form of: the return to the beginnings and the repetition of creation; the primordial flood; the cosmic battle between the forces of order and those of disorder, or light and dark, or democracies against communist powers; the humiliation of the king in the person of the sovereign of the Catholic world, namely the Vicar of Christ, the Pope; the world center as a mountain, and the captivity within it, in the underworld; the salvation in the form of the divine child and the intervention of the goddess; and the sacred marriage in nightly intercourse with God. It seems to be well in accord with our expectations, and a natural occurrence, that the practices of archaic times should concur even in detail with the productions of the archaic psyche in the present day.

Interpretation

Thus the symbolism of the young woman's delusions is found to be generally recognizable by amplification, but interpretation must go further in constantly interrelating this archaic level of experience with the personal, in order to make these contents meaningful and acceptable to the ego, as already mentioned. The schema I would draw to express this procedure is that the archetypal image, the only factor that has the transforming power necessary to make profound changes in the psyche, acts as a vehicle for all that must happen on the personal level. This archetypal image is made up of a driving force or affect and a meaning conveyed by its image, which is the form that the energy takes. A complex derived from personal experience clusters about the archetype. The archetypal image brings to light the significance for development that the contents of a complex might have. In dealing with the archetypal forms, then, the prospective understanding and constructive interpretation must be brought to the forefront, while the associations constellated around them need careful and extensive analytic handling. Thus the image either shows what *should* be happening on the personal level of the individual's emotional life, or it shows the meaning of what *is* happening here that otherwise goes unrecognized or remains perplexing.

I feel this relation of archetype and personal life must be emphasized. Particularly in schizophrenia, many affects essential to liberating the ego are lost to consciousness and appear only in faraway imagery, on the one hand, and in inappropriate acting out of projections, on the other. The great puzzle is how to reclaim these affects. In my experience, reclaiming them necessitates extracting the personal meanings in the imagery without making a reductive interpretation of collective contents. Reclamation may require bringing to light once more the original situations in which the affects were first repressed, but it more especially involves locating the actual but hidden role of these affects in the present psychological field, inasmuch as these emotional components are to be regarded as essential ingredients of potential psychic maturity.

I will attempt, therefore, a rough indication of the kind of connections between archetypal images and personal life issues that I see as important.

THE CENTRAL ARCHETYPE AND THE MOTHER'S ANIMUS

In the case being discussed, the ego had identified with the central archetype in various forms, most notably as the mother goddess in giving birth to the divine child, and as the queen of the universe, a member of a divine, royal, brother and sister pair. In the prepsychotic personality there had been, compensating the young women's sense of unworthiness, a fantasy of becoming a world-famous mystic. This fantasy now expanded and activated the archetype underlying the woman's ego. The archetype was so charged with libido, while the ego was so weak, that it could not help but engulf the ego, and inflation was inevitable. She became the great mother about to give birth to the divine child, but now a new kind of infant, not passive as her infantile nature had been, but superbly active, and not the victim of hard fate but its master, not entrapped in conflict but superordinating and reconciling the opposites.

The identification with the central archetype also led into another turning point. Whereas this young woman had been entrapped in the judgments and attitudes and mores imposed on her by her mother and had been kept an innocent and unpromising child, she now was brought into the process that forces a release from the mother, namely initiation. She identified, as do initiates generally, with the archetype of the royal divinity, whose fate it is to suffer, descend into death, and be renewed again at the center. In this sense she was undergoing a classic rite of passage, which is preceded by fasting and deprivations, and other such expressions of the phase of mortification.[5] These expressions may well spring from the same instinctive basis as the habitual refusal of persons to eat and sleep on entering the psychotic episode. Just as the Babylonian initiates were passed through a representation of the underworld, so this young woman found herself in a room designated as hell, and had to pass through a skeleton as an ordeal or test of fortitude; we may assume that this test dramatized the passage through death and out through the mouth, the devouring organ. This ordeal is, of course, reminiscent of more primitive usages in puberty rites, as in New Guinea, in which the neophyte is passed through the jaws of a monster into a chamber within it, where he is considered dead until his eviction from it.[6] The animal masks also belong to this symbolism.

The king may be said to be the archetype of the governing structure of values (in the feelings) and meanings (in the concepts) of the personality. The old king (the Pope) would then personify that heretofore dominant structure of Catholic values that for her can no longer promote life and further development. This system of values and meanings had been taken over from the mother's animus.

The patient produced confirmatory evidence for the thesis just presented. One day she perceived another woman on the ward, who had a witchlike nose and chin, as both saintly and evil, and she found her to resemble the present Pope so closely that she decided it must be he. This resemblance confirmed my impression that the figure of the old king, as the Pope, represented the witch mother or mother's animus, which had undermined the patient's self-evaluation by criticizing her from the standpoint of her rigid Christian ideals and finding her always somehow guilty by contrast. This whole animus-derived structure was what was undergoing the death and renewal.

This old structure has to be dissolved and yield to a new individual attitude as soon as the old one is unfit to withstand the impact of other possibilities not included in it, that is, the impact of the opposites. The archetypal or archaic expression of this crisis is the sacred combat, which is a test of strength for the old king, leading either to renewal or to overthrow. In the case of the renewal process, with which we are concerned, the divine child and royal prince is the image of a new outlook, the potential of a structure of values and meanings embracing other possibilities or other opposites, to supersede the old king and what he stood for. This process implies the discovery of the daughter's own individual views, apart from the mother's, and of an individual standpoint as opposed to that of the collective.

Individual values cannot be established adequately by conscious calculation, but only by their spontaneous emergence from the unconscious matrix. By this process they receive the stamp of the individual's own unique disposition. Thus, while the old king might be regarded as infantile in origin, his successor, the new king, is nothing of the kind,[7] but rather is this young woman's own inner potential of selfhood, the opposite of the collectively determined animus.

THE COSMIC CONFLICT

We now come to the patient's idea of a cosmic conflict. In the delusional story, the young lady saw the world as a rather classic mandala formation: a central mountain, with a plane defining four points in its circular flight around the mountain, in a pattern that is analogous to a ritual circumambulation. It is an astonishingly archaic conception, in which the sun stands as one of four planets around the earth, and the world is not a globe but a mountain, just as in Babylonia "the earth was a sort of hemispherical dome-shaped mountain rising from the cosmic ocean."[8] This world was divided in strife between opposing forces, corresponding to the universal ritual of the sacred combat in the renewal process. The two chief figures in the combat or *agon,*[9] protagonist and antagonist, were Christ and the Devil.

The Pope possesses the chief attributes of the sacral kingship,[10] and stands in the same relation to Christ as the Babylonian king to Marduk; as an image, what the Pope personifies is the body of ritual and doctrine of Catholic Christendom. The young lady was closely linked with the Pope by suffering the same fate as he, in the possession by the Devil and the descent into hell, just as the neophytes in the initiations accompanying the New Year festivals of the ancient world underwent death and rebirth in close relation to those of the king. This thinking means that in this phase of the process she felt moved by the Devil image and its rebellious influences. The significant point about him was that he was seen here as wholly evil and destructive, and thus the affects that came under his domain—both sexuality and aggression, according to her various associations—were unacceptable.

For her the twofold archetype had the net effect of irreconcilable opposites. Correspondingly, she had compensated her sense of personal inadequacy and unworthiness by fantasies of having some special calling of a religious nature, perhaps being a great mystic or saint. Briefly, when being made to feel that she was the worst and least of all girls, she was moved to be the best and the greatest. But this compensatory fantasy ruled out all aggression and sexual feelings, which now burst in on her cataclysmically.

The communist powers in the delusional story, the henchmen of the Devil, are best understood by comparison with the role of foreign powers in the ritual pattern of the Near East, such as the Jerusalem New Year Festival, in which the enemies of the king were agents of the chaotic abyss in the struggle to overcome him and drag him down into the underworld.[11]

Dismemberment is the archetypal representation of the schizophrenic turmoil, a time of psychic chaos and disorder in which the lower instinctive contents and drives run rife without central control. In this young woman's delusions, the dismemberment was depicted as the fragmentation of the Pope's (threefold) tiara (that is, the king's crown), corresponding on the human plane to the fragmentation of the Trinity on the divine plane. The Pope, as in Babylonia the king, was dethroned and humiliated. To translate the imagery directly, one may say that the higher pole of the central archetype was dismantled by the lower and reabsorbed into it for a while, there to be reconstituted. This process required tearing down the regnant structure, the collective Christian animus, and then commingling that structure with its opposite, the temptations from the non-Christian nature. This nature was symbolized, perhaps quite aptly, by communism, which is anti-Christian, materialistic, and deterministic, and pushes revolution from below, that is, from the collective lower strata of society, the masses.

PERSONAL ASPECTS OF THE COSMIC CONFLICT

All through this young woman's life there had been a painful tension, characteristic of schizophrenic persons, between expectations set up by the mother's animus and what the individual felt herself to be experiencing or wanting to experience spontaneously. Guilt accumulated and was compounded as more random acts, unapproved by this sanction, came into play. The discrepancy between what one should be and do, collectively, and what one is and does, individually, was the cause of her guilt and anxiety. The only possible resolution in such a situation is in the process of dismemberment of the whole guilt-ridden, conflictful structure of values and meanings.

Just as on the mythological level in the psychotic productions time regressed to the beginnings of creation, so on the personal level, it regressed to infancy, in order that the young woman could rediscover the ingredients of wholeness formerly left out of development in the unfavorable bond with the mother. The ego must be reconstituted from its inception. Her symbolism could not have been more explicit about the interrelatedness of these regressions on the archaic (cosmic) and the personal (infantile) levels, and about the parallel recapitulation of the evolution of the world and of her personality.[12] She let herself act out, in the interviews and on the ward, these feelings of being one and two years old, telling me as she crawled about on the floor by my knees that she was one year old and that I was like her father. Her descent into the primordial waters of the beginnings was her journey through the maternal deeps, on the way to her own rebirth along with that of the world, that is, the recreation of her ego through the activity of her central archetype. This voyage in the depths was comparable to the mythological motif of the "night sea journey" about which Jung wrote in his early work on archetypal imagery, *Symbols of Transformation.*

The meaning of the communist powers and the dark phase, in respect to her personal psychology, therefore seems to be that these agencies would dissolve her identification with the image of the superior Christian being. This archetype was also entangled with the whole complex of rejection, since both have to do with outsideness, that is, with being beyond the pale, whether of a society or of a family.

Turning back to the archaic forms found in ancient cultures, the imagery of the dark powers shows them to be both below and outside the order of the kingdom—underneath the center and beyond the periphery, where only the ghosts and demons dwell.[13] Outsiders are equated with demons in the thinking of such cultures.[14] There is a natural affinity between such archaic modes of feeling about outsideness and this young lady's early rejective experiences with her mother. In these experiences, she was probably made to feel an outsider to what should ideally have been the love and acceptance and harmony of her family circle, her first world, to feel as one that could not belong to the organism of the family relationships. More accurately, inasmuch as she might conform to the pattern of the mother's animus expectations, she was acceptable and inside; but whatever in her was individual and essentially herself remained, in excommunication, outside. With such powerful archetypal roots, it is no wonder that rejection is accompanied by feelings of death, dismemberment, and annihilation.

THE PARANOID ANXIETY

It has been observed, that the paranoid voices in schizophrenia make pronouncements and threats that can be traced to the unloving aspect of the parents in the schizophrenic's early life.[15] But the voices also spring from the archetypal parental images, the terrible mother and terrible father and their cohorts, all of whom threaten the ego when it is in a state of identification with the central archetype.

The discrepancy between what to this young person seemed to be acceptable and what not acceptable, gave rise to a deep cleavage in her self-image—to fears of the guilt of being herself, which left her outside, and to fantasies of the bliss of being a superior Christian spirit, which might redeem her. For her, the archetype of the former was the demon people; of the latter, the Madonna. The violent archetypal process in such cases comes into play when the ego is standing in an unbalanced relation to the central archetype, unbalanced because of the compelling pressure of the unconscious and the passivity of the ego in the mother-bound state. Only by allowing the archetype to do its work—that is, by allowing the deeply cloven self-image to be dissolved and recreated on a more favorable basis—can any healing and development take place. Paranoid fears, in my experience, prove to be exactly the terror of letting this dissolution happen, and lead to the stubborn projection of the threat on to the outer world in order to keep free of the apparent desecration that such a disintegrative and reintegrative process seems to forebode. Acceptance of the threat in this person would entail a sacrifice of her secret but precious fantasy of being a special personage, and would thus entail an acknowledgement of her ordinariness, of herself as a natural woman with the same emotions and instincts and faults as any in the crowd. The communist powers are in this sense the symbol of the levelers, allowing no one to claim individual specialness. However, only by taking this leveling as her starting point could she hope to substantiate and make meaningful her true uniqueness.

The paranoid process tends to clothe itself in political attire: witness the inflation in the magnificence of high office, the debasement in the threat of attack by a foreign power or subversive party. The natural language of paranoia is in the terms of the power drive. I am now becoming convinced that the paranoid system is based on those archetypal drives that have to do with rule, in the sense of ordering, governing, controlling, manipulating, separating in anger, and other such means by which the structuring of the psychic field of the subject is handled. I feel it might enhance our clarity about the basis of this general category of drives if we called them the *mastery* drives, as well as *power* drives, and if we consider them to be derived from the Logos principle.

The close affinity between paranoid tendencies and homosexuality in men is well known. I find it to be most marked where the phallic imagery is most compelling, and where the anima is not leading the man into erotic entanglements; mastery over the love object is one of the strong motivations in such cases. Only in the acute turmoil are the compensating Eros drives released and brought into play. The characteristic symbolism, as in the present case, tells of the humiliation and dissolution of the heretofore rigid and isolated rule of the governing figure (the Pope, dedicated to celibacy and deriving from the mother's antierotic animus), and portrays the promotion of the archetypes of the feminine and of marital union. What could be more fitting to such a transition than the symbolism of fertility and the renewal of the king!

INDICATIONS OF RESOLUTION

This discussion now brings us to the images indicating resolution of the process. The child to whom the young woman was to give birth was very clearly depicted as the divine child, who was to redeem the world from the cosmic conflict between the forces of light and darkness. He corresponds to what in the archaic ritual is the symbol of the renewed life of the king, the personification of the new order, new time, and new year cleared of its guilt.[16] The child is the renewed central archetype, in an image that has the capacity to reconcile the antagonism of the high and low opposites of its older form. Just as the symbolism of the cosmic regression of time back to the beginnings of creation had its counterpart in the personal regression back to her own conception and infancy, so similarly the birth of the divine child seemed to be the archetypal basis for the healing of the personal self-image. Because the old image was torn between deflation and inflation by the problem of her earliest relationships, the libido now had to go back over that early development of the self, and experience anew its growth in the more favorable conditions of a truly affirmative relationship.

The occasion for this young person's psychotic break was love experiences both with a man and with a woman. In my experience, such encounters often precipitate an acute turbulent psychotic episode in an otherwise borderline schizoid personality. It might seem paradoxical that the undermined ego should quit the field just at the point when acceptance promises most, unless one looks at the situation as a juncture at which the deepest emotions are stirred and the most powerful archetypes activated. The central archetype usually is seen to come into play in love relationships, as it also does in therapeutic transference relationships. This arousal of the archetype is entirely natural, inasmuch as love not only stirs our emotional and archetypal depths in general, but also, and more specifically, presents us with a new occasion for intense mutual affirmation of the self, and for its further realization in both partners. The delusional story tells us that both of the young woman's loves played a part in the evolution of the central archetype.

First, a close woman friend had taken on the aspect of her mother in certain ways, thus stirring up the mother complex and its archetypal roots. In the ensuing delusions, the divine child was protected from destruction by the Queen of the Sea, a figure constellated by the kindly woman on the hospital ward who so resembled a loving and protective neighbor of her childhood, the only positive mother figure she had had. This person's womanly warmth contrasted with the negative mother figure on the ward, the witch-like animus creature who appeared as the Pope. That the Queen of the Sea set her protective arts against the work of the communists signified that a loving acceptance of the emergent self defended it against the fate that had so damaged it before, that of rejective annihilation. Consequently, the emergence of the renewed archetypal self was actually accompanied by a recapitulation experience of the childhood personal self, since she in fact did let herself act like a young child, both on the ward and in the interviews with me.

Her love for a close man friend, on the other hand, stirred the father complex and a more forward-moving direction of the libido, toward the union of male and female. The most compelling and impressive of her delusions was the message of the Virgin Mother about marriage vows, and her fantasy of being nightly united in coitus with God. Now the deity appeared as her father, and she said that I also seemed just like her father. Thus I as therapist was also constellating the kindly father figure, and the transference was bringing the healing images of the self into play. Here, the basic healing image, the divine child, was the fruit of this fantasized sexual union, which had a most powerful archetypal foundation. The *hieros gamos,* the marriage of the gods, is the model of all earthly marriages, a psychological fact that is borne out in the widespread customs of crowning the bridal couple "King and Queen for a Day".

It will be recalled that this *hieros gamos* was the culmination of the renewal rites; it was accompanied by feasting and merrymaking, the *hilaria.* Not even this element was missing in this young woman's experiences: the mood of her union with God was "hilarious." Just as the depressive mood of the catatonic cycles is based on the mortification phase of the process, so the euphoric mood is founded on this phase of the erotic union and new life. These phases have been traced from the ritual pattern into the dramatic forms of tragedy and comedy.[17]

In this young woman's delusional imagery there were two sacred marriages. The first, the union of father and daughter, brought the recapitulative experience into play along with the emergence of the renewed self. The second marriage led the emergence of self forward, in that she saw herself and her lover as twin brother and sister and universal monarchs: the "royal brother-sister pair" that constitutes the pure archetype of marriage.[18] It is noteworthy that both these unions are incestuous and both are representations of the central archetype.

In the young woman's hallucinatory experience at her window, the Virgin's message about marriage vows was a verbal accompaniment to the vision of the gold staff flanked by two rings, which she felt was symbolizing what was being said. The imagery is puzzling but the configuration suggests the very ancient emblem of the mother goddess as found in Mesopotamian seals.[19] This ringed staff and the Christ beside it would then represent the archetypal wedded couple, *sponsus* and *sponsa.*[20]

This allusion to the central archetype brings me to a final comment on the general species of symbolism found in this process. It has been particularly striking to me that political symbolism predominates in almost every case of acute catatonic schizophrenia I have been treating. I have elsewhere stated an opinion that the political symbolism served to emphasize the collective nature of the conflict.[21] However, I now feel that explanation to be inadequate, for I had not then fully realized the tremendous significance that the ritual of kingship has had in the evolution of these archetypes of renewal. Just as, on the one hand, kingship and government play a large role in the ritual and teachings of the great religions and philosophies of former times—Taoism, Confucianism, Hinduism, Buddhism, Judaism, Christianity, and Alchemy, and so on—so in the archaic psyche of today as we observe it analytically, this symbolism is the foremost expression of the central archetype.

The therapeutic implications of these unconscious productions, then, may be summarized in this manner. The young woman's task is to relinquish both aspects of her split self-image, her view of herself as worthless and the compensating view that she harbors an extraordinary future. This task entails recapitulating her experience of growing up in order to discover her true individuality, which was ruled out heretofore. To expedite the change requires a reexamination of her guilt-forming, governing structure of values and meanings derived from her infantile relation to her mother's animus. This reexamination involves a free play of aggression and other separative emotional agencies. Only then would she be free to take the culminative step, entering her maturity and taking responsibility for her erotic nature and her woman's role. This step requires letting herself become aware of her sexual passions and of her deep craving for loving union, heretofore among the forbidden opposites.

Chapter Five

The Ritual Drama of Renewal

As one goes through the experience of first becoming acquainted with myths, they usually give the appearance of being somewhat divorced from life. One gets the sense of embarking upon a play world of fantasies of endless shapes, sometimes lovely and admirable, sometimes horrific and loathsome. Myths tend to give the impression that the possibilities are without limit and that their selection and arrangement are somewhat arbitrary. However, soon one finds oneself in the same process of discovery that scholars have experienced over the last eighty years, that the myth's relation to its context in life lends it an altogether different appearance. This means, first and foremost, the relation of myth to ritual, and beyond that, to the entire pattern of the culture to which the myth belongs.

At the end of the last century, Robinson Smith, in his studies of the culture of the Semites,[1] was the first to make the observation that not only did myth and ritual belong together but that in all probability ritual was primary. He found ritual to be the more conservative, stable phenomenon, while myth tended over the generations to be modified and altered, finally becoming a rather free literary expression. Jane Harrison, in her researches into early Greek religion,[2] felt that myths and rituals were the "expression of collective emotion" in the dual aspects of "things done" and "things spoken," amalgamated into ritual drama with action and script. Many scholars have taken up this "myth and ritual" thesis and demonstrated its validity, most notably perhaps Theodore Gaster in his "Thespis,"[3] a detailed documentation of the ritual drama forms in various cultures of the ancient Near East.

Two features attest to the importance of any myth for the culture that produced it. The great ritual drama to which the myth belongs is staged for the participation of the entire corporate body of the community. Also, the proper accomplishment of the drama is considered necessary to the proper functioning of the community and of nature—that is, to the sustaining of the sacral king's power both to give life and fertility to all living things, and to give order and justice to the social body.

On this account I do not pass lightly over the statement, which persons typically make during their psychotic episode, that they are taking part in some dramatic performance that has been already written and prepared beforehand. That statement conveys the subjective sense that one gets when in the grip of archetypal processes—nothing about them feels arbitrary or "made up," but rather they seem to follow well-established configurations.

To indicate how frequently this feeling occurs and how vividly it is expressed, I will cite examples of such statements. The case numbers refer to the twelve case protocols given in the appendix to this book.

Case 3. This young man had the idea that things were going on that looked like the acting of a play, and that there were people on the ward helping him who were movie actors from Hollywood.

Case 4. This young woman participated in what she felt to be primitive rituals and dances and chants, which she carried out with energy in her room almost constantly during the first hyperactive phase of her episode. She felt herself under compulsion to carry out certain assignments as ordeals or trials: to crawl through a skeleton and out of its mouth as part of a primitive ceremony in which her friends wore masks; to return to the beginnings of creation and repeat the history of evolution; and to return to the beginnings of her own life and repeat the stages of her own growing up to the present.

Case 6. She felt herself to be reliving the story of a drama in the movie, "Not as a Stranger," and to be among her friends, the movie stars of Hollywood, in enacting this. This fantasy had to do with her conviction that she was Queen of the Aztecs, and explained why she was not ruling as a woman but as a doctor. She tore up her hospital gowns to make them into Aztec costumes for the drama.

Case 9. This young man felt some connection between himself and performances on television.

Case 10. While she did not say that everything going on during her episode was the enacting of a play, this young woman did narrate two occasions when there was a distinct conviction of a ritual drama taking place. At Christmas time she looked out on the stone grotto behind the hospital and had a vision of a performance of the Nativity story. On another occasion, she saw herself and the others sitting at table together as Christ and his twelve disciples in an enactment of the Last Supper, which was being broadcast on television to the entire world for its edification.

Case 11. This young woman felt herself implicated in dramas taking place on television.

Case 12. This young woman felt that having to enter into the interaction with the frivolous emotions and concerns of ordinary people was like the son of God's submission to the humiliation of incarnation and crucifixion. She called this humiliation "the folly of the cross," saying "we all have parts to play in this act"—which seemed to her "just a game."

Although many ritual dramas from various parts of the world might be said to belong to the archetypal process under discussion here, I am selecting those parallels to the acute schizophrenic process that belong strictly to the background of our own cultural and historical tradition. That is, I could provide parallels and comparative material from India, China, and the early Central and South American civilizations, and from the Norse, Irish, Iranian, or other Indoeuropean traditions. Much of this material I have briefly reviewed elsewhere.[4] For reasons of brevity, and particularly of clarity, however, I feel that here it is enough to trace the Judeo-Christian tradition from its sources in Egypt on the one hand, and in Mesopotamia on the other, thence through Canaan to Israel. These origins in the ancient Near East are the roots of our religious tradition and thus of our psychic makeup. In all these sources we will find ceremonies for rejuvenation of the year and of the king and kingdom, being therefore New Year festivals and at the same time enthronement festivals of the sacral king. These ceremonies were the great public religious rites of the corporate body of the people in those ancient communities. They were also at the root of later religious forms. Various specific rites familiar to us today differentiated out from them: marriage and the ordination of priests, possibly initiation, and such observances as the celebration of the death and resurrection of the deity, and "holy wars."[5]

The components of the inner journey in the psychotic form that I have found so regularly repeated in one individual after another I have designated as follows:

1. Establishing a world center as the locus.
2. Undergoing death.
3. Return to the beginnings of time and the creation.
4. Cosmic conflict as a clash of opposites.
5. Threat of the reversal of opposites.
6. Apotheosis as king or messianic hero.
7. Sacred marriage as a union of opposites.
8. New birth as a reconciliation of opposites.
9. New society of the prophetic vision.
10. Quadrated world forms.

For the sake of clarity in drawing the parallels in the historical forms, I will enumerate and describe the components in myth and ritual order by the same designations.

Egypt

In Egypt the exact order of the proceedings of the enthronement festival can only be reconstructed from unclear accounts, so that it is not certain exactly how they went. Also there were several different New Years, one at the start of each of three seasons, each involving an enthronement. There were the Sacred Marriage of Edfu, the Summer Festival of Minh, and the Sed Festival or thirty-year jubilee of the king's renewal. It is believed that the latter was the main enthronement and New Year rite of the earliest dynasties, that is, the early third millennium B.C.[6] The time was the beginning of spring and of the subsiding of the Nile flood or inundation.

1. *Establishing a world center as the locus.* The place was the city of Memphis, the center of the "union of the two lands," that is, of Upper and Lower Egypt and thus of the ordered world.[7] The throne was placed on a raised podium that represented the Primeval Hill, the first land to appear at the creation, and the center of the world, charged with vital power that radiated out into the whole kingdom.[8] On the eve of the ceremony, the king made a circumambulation around the white walls of the city.

2. *Undergoing death.* In the last few days of the Season of Inundation occurred the ceremony of the Raising of the Djed Pillar, a column of bound stalks resembling a tree trunk, and there was enacted the burial, in the column, of the Dead King, Osiris, drowned by his brother Seth in the flood of the Nile. The theme of death prevails at this turning of the year, when the powers of chaos gain the upper hand and when there is a temporary disruption of the union of the two lands and of the normal order of the realm.[9] The dead king, father of the living king, becomes Osiris through a ritual purification and transfiguration and rebirth into a new life in the Beyond as Lord of the Kingdom of the Dead, and his son is enthroned as the Sky God, Horus, Lord of the Kingdom of the Living.[10] The vital force that gives life to the kingdom is transmitted from the ancestral realm of the dead, through Osiris in his embrace of his son, the living king, and thus into the realm.[11] After the funerary rites and on the first day of spring, the king is crowned as the living embodiment of Horus.

3. *Return to the beginnings of time and the creation.* The ritual time is the moment of the creation. As the king stands high over the land on his dais, he is personifying the first divine king and creator, Atum, standing on the Primeval Hill as it arose from the waters of Chaos (represented as the Goddess Nun).[12] These waters were the source of the life-giving subsoil waters of the abyss and of death and of the Nile flood, while the hill was the place of the creation, and of rebirth and resurrection.[13] The king was put through baptismal lustrations and purifications in these waters and dressed in brilliant vestments representing the first sunrise and first shining forth of the light over the newly risen land.

4. *Cosmic conflict as a clash of opposites.* As the myth tells of Horus avenging the death of his father Osiris by doing battle with his uncle,

Seth, the ritual represents the Sacred Combat as a mock fight between the men of two cities of the Delta, designating the forces of death as against those of the living.[14] Seth personifies the King's Enemy, in the form of a boar, as the pretender to the throne against the legitimate heir.

5. *Threat of the reversal of opposites.* For a while death and the enemy hold the upper hand, and there is a period of chaos in which there is a suspension of the normal order of the realm (it is not clear how this phase was dramatized).

6. *Apotheosis as king or messianic hero.* The coronation and investiture of the king as the Living Horus extols him as victor, as one with the first king god, Atum, and as partaking of the nature of the sun god, Re, ruling over the entire ordered world.[15] There takes place first a procession of the gods in the form of their standards and emblems, and then a Dedication of the Land, in which the king performs a dance circumambulating a field that represents the realm, holding in his hand the will that assures his legitimate claim to the throne of Horus.

7. *Sacred marriage as a union of opposites.* The occurrence of a sacred marriage is not certain in this particular ceremony, but at the other New Year festivals there are well-documented marital rites. Notably, at Edfu there was a summer harvest festival at which the effigy of Horus was brought to the temple of his mother and consort, Hathor, to cohabit with her for two weeks; a sacred combat and funerary rites for the ancestors were also performed.[16]

8. *New birth as a reconciliation of opposites.* The motif of rebirth and resurrection runs through the entire series of rituals as a dominant theme; it primarily concerns the transfiguration of the dead king, Osiris. On the one hand the Goddess of the Night Sky, Nut, is represented as his mother, through whom he is reborn, and she is ritually identified with the sarcophagus or coffin as the body of the mother.[17] On the other hand, the Djed Pillar is also a representation of the mother of Osiris as Hathor, as the tree pregnant with the king Osiris, surrounded by the wings of Nut.[18]

9. *New society of the prophetic vision.* The coronation rite signals the creation of a new epoch, after the dangers of the interruption by death and chaos, a new time of harmony between society and nature, yet partaking of the qualities of the original time of crea-

tion.[19] In his achievements the king only makes manifest what has been potentially present in the plan of creation. The world order, as established at the beginnings of time, remains the normative order, whose champion is the king; he maintains justice as the representative of Re, the sun god.

10. *Quadrated world forms.* The representation of the quadrated world recurs throughout the rites. In his baptismal purification rites at the start, the king is given water by the four gods of the cardinal directions, conveying their life and power to him. At the enthronement he is seated four times on four thrones, in the cardinal directions, conveying their life and power to him, and he is proclaimed to each of the quarters of the world as an arrow is shot by him into each one.[20]

Mesopotamia

The other mainstream of tradition came out of ancient Sumer in southern Mesopotamia and was passed through the hands of a sequence of successors to that culture: Akkad, Babylonia, Assyria, and Chaldea. Here the program of the New Year (Akitu) festival has survived word for word in tablets,[21] at least in its late form, from which earlier forms of the third millenium B.C., have been deduced. Also the myth of the creation, the so-called Enuma Elish,[22] telling of Marduk's election to kingship, his battle with the water monster Tiamat, and his creation of the world from her body, was the spoken myth that accompanied the ritual drama.

The time of the festival was a period of twelve days at the beginning of the autumnal month of the new year, and the place was the temple compound, in which the scene is dominated by the Ziggurat, the pyramidal stage tower representing the world mountain.

1. *Establishing a world center as the locus.* At Nippur, the original Sumerian holy city of the king god, the locus of the rite was defined as the world center and cosmic axis by the term "Bond of Heaven and Earth" (Dur-Anki),[23] and the Ziggurat was conceived as reaching the sky and equally distant downwards, the watery abyss.[24]

2. *Undergoing death.* The first four days are given to preparations and purifications and sacrifices, for danger prevails as the order of nature is threatened by the disappearance of the king god

into the realm of death.[25] The fifth day is a day of atonement for the king, in which he is humiliated and degraded in the likeness of the suffering of the king god in death. The populace carries on wailings and lamentations, and "descends" in procession to the suffering god below. There is commotion throughout the city as the "search" goes on for the lost king god, on the model of Ishtar's search for her consort, Tammuz, in the underworld.[26]

3. *Return to the beginnings of time and the creation.* The ritual time is that of the creation, when as the Sumerians told it, the storm god Enlil separated his primordial parents from their fusion together as the world mountain, and threw the father upwards to become sky and his mother to become earth, whom he then mounted to impregnate.[27] As the Babylonians rendered the creation, the sun god Marduk has replaced Enlil and splits the Mother Monster, Tiamat, into sky and earth; the ritual enactment of this phase is the throwing of a dove into the air and splitting it into two halves.[28]

4. *Cosmic conflict as a clash of opposites.* On the seventh day Marduk's son, who has arrived by barge on the river the day before, takes up the heroic task as avenger of his father, and liberates him by force from "his mountain grave" of the netherworld (this act in Sumer had been performed by the hero Nunurta, to free his father, Enlil). In the Sacred Combat the King's Enemy is represented as a boar that must be killed, also as a sheep that is sacrificed, and the rescuing hero is personified by the king.[29] The monster Tiamat is the primordial waters of chaos, the mother of the deeps who fashions all things, the source of all life. On the ninth day a triumphal procession of the gods, in effigy, and of the populace makes its way to the festival temple (Bit Akitu), enacting the part of the king and his hosts. The procession represents the joyous participation of the community in the victory over the King's Enemy, which is taking place in nature and in Marduk's destruction of Chaos and creation of the world.

5. *Threat of the reversal of opposites.* In the first five days, the power of vitality, in both nature and king alike, is at its lowest ebb, and chaos tends to prevail. The normal order of society is suspended, roles are reversed, and servants rule their masters.[30]

6. *Apotheosis as king or messianic hero.* The gods gather in their assembly and bestow on Marduk their combined powers, thus granting him as king god a "destiny beyond compare"; which also implies

the reinstatement of the king as his earthly representative.[31] This drama is the First Determination of Destiny, on the eighth day. On the tenth day the king god celebrates his victory with the gods of the upper and lower worlds at a banquet, which is enacted by the king and his retinue.

The kings at Sumer and of Akkad rarely considered themselves frankly as gods, as the Egyptian Pharaohs did; in a period of eight hundred years, only twenty claimed such divinity.[32] However, the office was divine, for "kingship was lowered from heaven" as a gift from the sky god, Anu.[33] The kings called themselves Lugal, Great Man, and entitled themselves King of the Land, or Lord of the Four Quarters, or King of the Universe. This supreme title represented the concept that each city of that world had its ruling god, who in the assembly of the gods elected Marduk to govern over them all as king god of the ruling city.

7. *Sacred marriage as a union of opposites.* On the evening of the tenth day, Marduk returns to Babylon itself, to perform the sacred marriage that night. The scene of this rite is a hut of greenery atop the Ziggurat, and the partners are the king in the role of Tammuz, "Great Lord of Heaven," in sexual union with a consort representing the Goddess of the Evening Star, Ishtar.[34] The ritual reflects the change in nature, and is designed magically to induce prosperity and abundance, specifically perhaps the rains. It appears that the king depends on the initiative of the goddess, for the texts relate that she chooses him to be her consort, yet this choice is also the basis for the claim to supreme deification of certain kings, that they have been the ones so chosen by her.[35]

8. *New birth as a reconciliation of opposites.* It is in the role of Tammuz also that the motif of the king's rebirth enters into the myth and ritual; in death Tammuz is called Feeble One, and in resuscitation called Strong One or Manly One.[36] Likewise, the kings claiming to have been selected by the Goddess as her consort, that is, as her Tammuz, present themselves in the texts as the offspring of gods, chosen from the womb; they are apparently given a ritual birth and suckled at the breast of the Goddess, thus as both her son and her lover and consort.[37]

9. *New society of the prophetic vision.* The condition of, and outlook for, the society for the ensuing year is now assessed in the Second Determination of Destiny (eleventh day). Man's concern with

the will of the gods arises from the need to keep in harmony with nature and its powers residing in the gods, which in the Near East means an unstable concord requiring special ritual devices to strengthen and restore it. The rite is intended to deflect the consequences of any errors and defilements of the year and to ensure a prosperous year ahead.[38]

10. *Quadrated world forms.* Finally, the image of the world as quadrated is mentioned often in the texts,[39] and even more convincingly portrayed in a stone relief representing Babylon at the center of the circle of the world with points extending in the cardinal directions.

Canaan

Now both the Egyptian and Mesopotamian traditions passed into the Canaanite area, where it is presumed that in the second millennium B.C., similar New Year festivals were enacted, corresponding to the myth forms that have in recent decades been unearthed at Ras Shamra, concerning the king god, Baal. However, no rubrics or itinerary have been preserved to indicate how the drama was enacted, and the ritual forms can only be conjectured.[40]

Israel

When Israel became heir to the Canaanite urban culture and began to establish its own first city life, it took over Canaanite myth and ritual forms and incorporated them into its own ancient tradition, at about the year 1000 B.C.[41] Therefore David and his successors were sacral kings in much the same manner as others of the Near East of that time, and at Jerusalem the New Year festival was correspondingly akin to others in that the kingship was renewed.[42] Its practice degenerated in a short while, but its ideology kept evolving and found its way into the image of the Messiah as propounded by the prophets, and thence into the image of Christ the King as portrayed and formulated in the gospels.[43]

Israel's New Year festival was grafted on an autumnal agricultural rite of the land, the Feast of Ingathering: the Israelites, after all, had arrived as a desert nomad people, who became urbanized very gradually after their arrival in the country of the Canaanites,[44] and took over from them the rituals belonging to an agricultural economy. With urbanization came the sacral kingship in the manner of the entire Near East of that time, and David was the great innovator and founder of a cult based on what he took over, together with the city of Jerusalem, from its previous masters, the Jebusites.[45] The former Canaanite forms were readapted to the new context in Israel's faith in Yahweh. This deity took on many of the attributes of Canaan's pantheon, especially of Baal in his aspect of Storm and Warrior God, and of El in his aspect of God of the High Sky, namely as El Elyon, "God Most High."[46] The sacral king, called "David" as a generic name for David's successors, was regarded as having divine attributes as an "Elohim," that is, of the nature of an angel or lesser divinity, and an extension of the divine personality of Yahweh as his representative and his "son by adoption."[47] In the enthronement rites he was transformed into a state that was both human and yet more than human, in which his person was considered sacrosanct and inviolate.[48]

The New Year festival was a celebration of the renewal of the year and of creation, and an enthronement rite to reestablish Israel's kingship and hence its covenant with its god.[49] Yahweh was Israel's real king, and the Davidic king only his delegate. The celebration was at the time of the autumnal full moon, and was called the Feast of Tabernacles (or of Booths), Sukkoth. It was a ritual drama enacted in the royal temple, a "ritual performance or acted 'picture'"; as the psalm puts it, "we have pictured Thy devotion in the midst of Thy Temple."[50] One should visualize the setting as the royal temple, as the visible representation of Yahweh's Holy Mount, the protagonist as the priest king, whose actions depict the experience of the nation and of its king god, and the participants as the populace, who take part in lamentations, jubilations, and triumphal processions.

1. *Establishing the world center as the locus.* The locus of the rite, on the mythological level, represents Yahweh's enthronement on his Holy Mount of Zion, whose zenith is the sky and whose nadir is the abyss of the cosmic waters. This sacred mountain therefore establishes a cosmic axis and world center.[51]

2. *Undergoing death.* Here there takes place a ritual humiliation of the king at the hands of his enemies; he is forsaken by his Father

in Heaven, who abandons his covenant with him, and he is allowed to sink into the abyss and the waters of death.[52]

3. *Return to the beginnings of time and the creation.* Time becomes now the mythical time of the beginnings of creation and of Yahweh's heroic fight with the dragon of the waters of chaos or of death; the seven days of the festival are equated to the seven days of creation, whose events are retold in the liturgy.[53] In this context the king is the Primordial Man, Adam, as First Ancestor and First King, the Gardener of God, Keeper of the Garden of the Mountain of God.[54]

4. *Cosmic conflict as a clash of opposites.* A Sacred Combat or Cosmic Conflict is dramatized, with the king as Yahweh's suffering servant in opposition to Yahweh's enemy. This formidable antagonist is a composite image of darkness and chaos, the waters of the abyss, and death, which are embodied then in the Kings of the Nations, the foreign goyim who dwell in the outside wastes and who represent on the earthly plane the rebellious and unrighteous lesser gods of the divine assembly over which Yahweh presides.[55] The king succumbs temporarily, and there are lamentations on the part of the attending populace.

5. *Threat of the reversal of opposites.* For a while death and chaos have the upper hand, the normal order of things is suspended, and the covenant with Yahweh seems to be abandoned; the king is humiliated as his enemy mocks him and lifts up his heel against him.[56] (It is an open question whether what Gaster calls "topsy-turvydom,"[57] the reversal of roles and general upsetting of the social order, was expressed ritually, as it was in some other cultures).

6. *Apotheosis as king or messianic hero.* But now Yahweh manifests himself as savior at dawn, and the cry goes up: "Wake!" and "Yahweh lives!"[58] He lifts the king from the abyss and death. With the rising of the sun, a triumphal procession forms at "Israel's Spring," Gihon, where perhaps the cosmic waters issue forth and where the king undergoes a ceremony like baptism in—and taking a cup of—these waters.[59] The joyful columns bearing the Ark of the Covenant, representing the assurance of God's presence and blessing, proceed with music and dancing, carrying festal boughs; the dance is led by the king in an ecstatic state. They pass around the temple on the Holy Mount. Yahweh is enthroned as Victor in splendor "over the flood," and seated overlooking the world from Zaphon's heights.

The king is similarly anointed, invested, appointed priest forever, and promised universal rule over all the kings and nations of the earth for all time.

7. *Sacred marriage as a union of opposites.* Very possibly a sacred marriage is performed, in association with the festal booths of greenery, and representing the production of the fertilizing rains.[60]

8. *New birth as a reconciliation of opposites.* The king is now undergoing a new birth, "born from the womb of Dawn," the Goddess;[61] he is transformed into a new creature, an Elohim with divine attributes, and is adopted by Yahweh as his son and his firstborn.

9. *New society of the prophetic vision.* A reign is promised, full of righteousness and justice and peace, with life-giving abundance and fertile rains, and the covenant with Yahweh is reestablished and reaffirmed.[62]

10. *Quadrated world forms.* The image is that of the first Paradise ruled over by the Primordial Man and King, enthroned on the World Mountain at the center with its four rivers issuing forth toward the further reaches of the circle of the world.[63]

Of great import for this discussion of the renewal process is the element of initiation in the Babylonian festival. The initiation of young men may have taken place at the time of these various ceremonials and in relation to them.[64] The neophytes underwent a death and rebirth in conjunction with and probably in identification with the passage of the king and of the god through death. Various texts of the time indicate that the neophyte passed through a ritual in a dramatic setting representing the underworld, where were revealed to them "the altars amid the waters, the treasures of Bel (Marduk), Anu, and Ea, the tablets of the gods, the delivery of the oracle of heaven and earth, and the cedar tree, beloved of the gods."[65] The element that in the opinion of scholars ties this rite in with the New Year festival is the mention of the tablets and oracles.

From these accounts it is clear that the mythological parallels to psychic productions from the unconscious represent no mere pretty tales decorating the literary imagination. These ceremonies and myths consist of the earnest actions of people to keep their societies vital and their productiveness vigorous, and are concerned with the handling of government, ethics, and the moral order, and the spreading of cultures by conquest. The history points to the same conclusion as does the psychological approach to the topic of myth. Myth is composed of affect images, and takes ritual as its natural expression of emotional involvement. Affect images tend toward active expression in dramatic form. Just as myth has its "Sitz im Leben," its place in the life setting, in ritual drama,[66] so the affect images in the individual psyche have their rightful context in the emotional environment of the subject in life. In examining the psychotic experience, one looks for this relationship. A person's life of involved concern acts as a dramatic form in which the affect images come into play and motivate the person to progressive activity in a developing psychic life.

In the ensuing sections I will discuss in more detail the individual elements of the ritual drama. To convey the feeling experience of these elements, I will first present the deeply poetic rendering of each in Israel's Royal Psalms, since these cultural forms are in the mainstream of our Judeo-Christian heritage. The Royal Psalms are those found by scholars to date back to pre-exilic times (before the Babylonian Captivity) and to show the characteristics of ritual texts, probably therefore used in the ceremonial dramas of the New Year festival in what is called the "Jerusalem Cultus."[67] Then, to amplify the imagery, I will trace in each the background of these ritual motifs in the more ancient Near East. Finally, I will give, for each element, some selections from the inward journey of my clients undergoing this renewal process, to exemplify the individual experience of these symbolic themes.

This presentation of ritual forms thus parallels my treatment of the corresponding myth forms in my volume, *Lord of the Four Quarters*,[68] to which the reader may refer for a fuller picture of the background and context of the following accounts.

1. THE CENTER

The motif of the center comes into play throughout the psychotic process in this particular form of schizophrenic episode that I call the renewal process. Indeed, this motif appears to provide the locus or framework in which all the other movements in the process take place: it is where the death may occur, and then whence the new birth may issue forth; it may be where the infant is encompassed in the mother's embrace; it is the point at which the opposites may clash, and then resolve themselves, and where creation may occur; or it may be where the sacred marriage is performed. In the ancient ceremonial form the same is true, that the mythical locus for the phases and episodes of the drama is the world center or cosmic axis.

The Center in Israelite Myth and Ritual Form

The myth and ritual of Israel borrowed from Canaan, and hence from the older traditions, the image of the holy mountain as world center. By virtue of his victory over the monster of the deeps, Yahweh as Israel's true king is enthroned over the waters of the abyss on the sacred mount, Zion or Zaphon. This world was shaped as a mound with Mt. Zion as its highest and central point:

Great is Yahweh and greatly to be praised
In the city of our God [or *in our divine city*]*!*
His holy mountain is beautiful in elevation,
The joy of all the earth
Mount Zion, the heights of Zaphon,
The city of the mighty King!
God in the palaces thereof
Hath shown Himself a stronghold.[1]

Zion is also the temple in Jerusalem on the earthly sacred mount, where the ritual drama takes place, for the psalm continues:

For, lo, the kings assembled,

. . .

They saw, they were startled,

. . .

Trembling they laid hold of them there,

. . .

As we have heard, so have we seen
In the city of Yahweh of Hosts,
In the city of our God [or *in our divine city*],
Which God maintaineth for ever.
O God we have [*pictured*] *Thy devotion*
In the midst of Thy Temple.[2]

The word "pictured" here refers to the portrayal in the form of drama.[3] The sacred mount is to be visualized as reaching into the sky itself:

For He hath looked down
From the height of his sanctuary;
From Heaven did the Lord behold the earth.[4]

Equally does it reach into the abyss below, for a stream was thought to issue from the cosmic waters below the temple of the god of the high sky, El Elyon: "As for 'The River,' its streams make glad the city of God, / The most sacred abode of the Most High."[5]

BACKGROUND OF THE IMAGE

We have observed that the Egyptian king's throne was set upon a raised platform designating the Primeval Hill, as the cosmic center from which the creation of the world had its inception. The first royal city, Memphis, was defined from the earliest dynasty as constituting the midpoint between the opposing halves of the Egyptian world, the Upper and Lower Kingdoms, and thus at the point of balance of all the elaborate opposites and at the center of the entire ordered world.[6]

In Mesopotamia we have noted that the temple compound as the site of the enthronement and rejuvenation festival was dominated by the Ziggurat stage tower, representing the world mountain and the axial "Bond of Heaven and Earth" at which the renewal rites of death, combat, victory, creation, and marriage could be effective. This tower reached as far into the abyss downwards as into the sky upwards.[7]

Canaanite sources described a center at which the king god, by his victory over his antagonist, was established as master over the waters of the abyss; from this palace on the heights of Mount Zaphon he could dispense the life-giving waters to the realm in their due season. Later, the same holy mount was assigned to Yahweh when Israel took over these cities and some of their myth and ritual forms.[8]

The Center in Psychic Form

Sometimes in the psychotic process the allusions to the center may be only vaguely implied, but often the theme is made as graphic and explicit as can be. The person may state quite concretely that "I am" at the center of everything, a midpoint between opposing forces, or more indirectly, that at such a point in the midst of things a world movement is about to be inaugurated under "my" leadership. At other times one may only discern, in the symbolic expressions, the traditional associations of centrality that have belonged to it over the centuries, as for instance when the image of the World Mountain, the Garden of Eden, or the New Jerusalem are invoked.

I will illustrate this motif with a case that has already been published and discussed at length,[9] but that bears further attention since it exemplifies so clearly the role of the center in this syndrome. What it brings out more than usually vividly is that the individual is most psychotic when identified with the center, and least psychotic when not so identified.

This is a young married woman (Case 1 of Appendix) who, in the first interview, told me that she felt herself to be at the center of millions of ideas. Sensing that she might well be experiencing the psychic center, I asked her to draw what it felt like to be at the center. While we sat together in the interview she constructed a complex mandala composed of these elements: concentric circles, lotus petals, dots indicating a rotary movement, and, containing the whole, an outer square with gates. She endowed the center with godlike significance, and there represented herself, in two halves, her "light" or "gay" and her "dark" or "quiet" personalities, and around herself the two halves of the world, the mother's and the father's. She explained that her being at the center came from her being a self-centered child; "Because I love me," she declared. She "had godlike powers from being the center of attraction at home," and was in a position of supreme rule over the world. This world was divided over an election contest of opposite political parties, and she was tying up the election while they were all waiting for her to make up her mind, since she held the deciding vote. The paranoid state was indicated by the presence of sixteen policemen watching her, balanced by four detectives guarding her. There was in the diagram not only a dimension of position but also one of a sequence of events or states of mind: this dimensionality gave the drawing the essential features of the category called "space-time diagrams." The concentric circles were her progress from ward to ward during her psychotic experience of the first three weeks, each designating a degree of mild or severe disturbance. The six petals of the lotus represented all her "mixed-up ideas." The diagram had many dimensions of meaning: a divided self and a divided world in conflict, a child cuddled in the parental adulation, a godling at the center of the world, a psychotic state of mind and a political state of the world, and a shape of the hospital and a shape of the world.

Her second drawing also emphasized her being the center of attraction and being in a divided state. It exemplifies beautifully how many levels of experience can be condensed into one form. The drawing is essentially another squared circle comprising a space-time diagram, having both personal and cosmic dimensions. As she drew, she was narrating the story of her two most significant friendships and the rivalry involved: in the jealousy, the essence of the experience was the question of her self-valuation or worth. The drawing emerged as a plant whose four fronds were the friends (one reduplicated to show her closeness to either friend), and whose blossom was the sun and whose base the moon. The world of this life was a circle, but the world of the afterlife was a square in four opposing colors. This person drew many images of the center, from among which I will select only one more to illustrate a particular point.

Her sixth drawing represented her movement away from the godlike position of supreme rule at the center. It was Easter time and she was filled with excitement over an insight, realizing that for her and other Christians it was Christ who dies and rises again and who exists in us all. Up to this time she had believed that she had died and was resurrected and living in an afterlife state in a godlike relation to the rest of mankind, supreme over them; now she knew that only Christ can do and be all that. Therefore she put Christ at the center of everything now, in vibrant red to indicate the loving principle: those closest to the center were the ones that could "give more," that is, be more loving, like Christ, and appeared in more intense red.

She put herself out toward the periphery, as being "only a little bit," that is, just plain human. She was at this time in a perfectly clear-headed state, back in her customary ego, in contrast to the deranged state when identified with the center and the god.

This young woman's work on the form and fate of the center was her effort to differentiate and synthesize the central archetype as a prelude to development of her ego personality along the lines indicated in the imagery: the development of her many facets and the alignment of her life along the directions of the Eros principle of relating (no longer the directions of the tyrannical young child wanting to be surrounded always by a parental and protective world).

The myth and ritual center, or likewise the center that becomes such a preoccupation in the psychotic process, is a representation customarily and habitually endowed with an immense powerfulness. Even greater than its supreme rule over the world is its effectiveness as the locus of the major organizing and reorganizing processes: creation, death and renewal, the clash and resolution of the opposites, the union of male and female or sky and earth, and point from which the renewed world reaches into the four cardinal directions. All these aspects are descriptive of the psychic entity that occupies this position of centrality and dominance. This central archetype is the affect image that lies at the root of the ego complex and gives it both its dynamic and its lead in the developmental process. Just as in the myth and ritual form, in the psychic structure the central archetype is the locus of the great processes of formation and transformation of the self, giving form both to the self-image and at the same time to one's outlook, world view, and way of life.

2. *DEATH*

It is striking to anyone listening to the preoccupations and delusions of persons in an acute schizophrenic episode how often the initial ideation has to do with the theme of death. It would seem that when a person enters on a psychotic break of this type, the affect image representing the transition over the borderline is that of dying, being killed, or entering into the realm of death. The corresponding affect image, characterizing the state of mind when the ego has surrendered its position and the unconscious prevails over the whole field of awareness, is the afterlife.

The rites we are reviewing were designed to effect renewal, and in these processes there is no renewal without death, no new start without the cessation of the old. Undergoing death and dealing with death in symbolic form are misunderstood items of human experience in the hands of the psychological professions. There is a safe corrective: to pay special heed to the data of observation, in this case, to the expressions of the meaning of death as they have occurred in the myth and ritual, the religious and mystical, forms over the generations.

Death in Israelite Myth and Ritual

In the Royal Psalms of Israel are vivid descriptions of the experience of death undergone by Davidic kings in the corresponding rites. Since Israel removed the goddess from her earlier place in the cult, the bringer of life and resuscitation was Yahweh himself. As in the Mesopotamian form, so here the theme of the king's death is mingled with that of humiliation and temporary nullification of his kingly status:

Yet Thou hast spurned and rejected,
Thou hast been wroth with [*Thine Anointed*].
Thou hast repudiated the covenant with Thy Servant;
Thou hast brought his crown to pollution in the dust.
Thou hast broken down all his walls;
Thou hast laid his defences in ruins.
All the passers-by have despoiled him;
He hath become a mockery to his neighbors.
Thou hast raised on high the right hand of his foes;
Thou hast made glad all his enemies

. . .

Thou hast made an end of his splendour [or *Thou hast destroyed 'his illustrious sceptre'*]
And Thou hast hurled his throne to the ground.
Thou hast shortened the days of his prime;
Thou hast wrapped him about with shame.[1]

That death is equated with the dark waters of the cosmic sea, with the underworld (Sheol), and with the king's enemies, is made clear. Calling for Yahweh to be delivered from his enemies, the king cries:

> *I call for Yahweh, the subject of my praise,*
> *And I am delivered from mine enemies.*
> *Death's breakers engulfed me,*
> *And the evil torrents o'erwhelmed me.*
> *Sheol's cords were round about me;*
> *Death's snares confronted me.*
> *In my distress I called for Yahweh,*
> *And unto my God I appealed for help.*[2]

In a psalm of later date, the king's lamentation and grievous suffering of death and oppression find powerfully poetic expression. The reference to going "with a multitude that kept holiday" points to the same festival rite of renewal:[3]

> *As the hart panteth after the water brooks,*
> *so panteth my soul after thee, O God.*
>
> . . .
>
> *My soul thirsteth for God, for the living God:*
> *when shall I come and appear before God?*
> *My tears have been my meat day and night,*
> *while they continually say unto me, Where is thy God?*
> *When I remember these things, I pour out my soul in me:*
> *for I had gone with the multitude, I went with them to the house of God,*
> *with the voice of joy and praise, with a multitude that kept holyday.*
> *Why art thou cast down, O my soul?*
> *and why art thou disquieted in me?*
> *Hope thou in God:*
> *for I shall yet praise him for the help of his countenance.*[4]
>
> *Deep calleth unto deep at the noise of thy waterspouts:*
> *all thy waves and thy billows are gone over me.*
> *I will say unto God my rock, Why hast thou forgotten me?*
> *why go I mourning because of the oppression of my enemy?*

As with a sword in my bones, mine enemies reproach me;
while they say daily unto me, Where is thy God?[5]

BACKGROUND OF THE IMAGE

In Egypt, death was a motif constantly in the foreground of the ceremonial life. The kingship was dual, in that it provided rulership not only over a world divided into opposing halves, of the Upper and Lower Kingdoms, but also over the two worlds, of the living and the dead. Horus was the Pharaoh as Lord of the Living, Osiris the most recently deceased king as Lord of the Dead.[6] In the enthronement festival at New Year, the death and resurrection of Osiris was enacted in ritual and recited in myth as the prelude to the reestablishment of the living king in his renewed rule. Osiris' myth[7] tells of his being tricked into his death by drowning by his wicked brother and enemy, Seth (represented by the boar), and being carried away by the waters of the Nile encased in a sarcophagus made of the trunk of a cedar. His sister Isis retrieved his body and resuscitated him. He reigned then as chief of the ancestors and King of the Underworld, and from him the life force was conveyed from the realm of the dead through his son Horus to the realm of the living. In later times, any soul aspiring to a continued existence in the afterlife had to "become an Osiris" as the vehicle for such existence, and still later, any soul striving for spiritual renewal in this life had to identify with Osiris as the agency of such transformation.[8]

The corresponding figure in Mesopotamia of the dying god who carried the life principle was not a father of fathers but a youth, the young Tammuz, brother or son and lover of the goddess Ishtar. In the early Sumerian kingdoms the young king or king god underwent death by first submitting and then being rescued by the life-giving power of the goddess; a cylinder seal has been found that represents the king in the mountain grave, being sought and resuscitated by her.[9] A little later, as the kingship increased in its patriarchal and aggressive qualities, the king in his "Tammuz role" underwent a brief submission to death and overcame it. The later cylinder seals then depict the battle of the heroic king god's champion against the representative of death or chaos or darkness, that is, the storm bird or dragon.[10]

The Canaanite king god, Baal, derived many of his attributes from this ancient tradition of Mesopotamia. He performed several heroic deeds, but the one that cost him most dearly was his battle with the god who personified Death, Mot.[11] Baal succumbed to the power of Mot for a seven-year period, then to be victorious and in secure power for an alternate seven years. The myth relates that his sister, the fair Anat, goddess of love and of war, frantically sought his body when he lay in death and brought him back that he might have life again.

It is noteworthy that in the case of all three dying gods, the goddess (either his sister or his mother) sets out to retrieve the body and bring him back to life. During the period of the demise of the god, the women of the community, in sympathy with the experience of the goddess, performed ritual lamentations. The purpose was more than the mere expression of grief, however, for the shedding of tears on the ground was an act of sympathetic magic to induce a like action on the part of the rains, to fructify the earth and restore the life principle.[12]

It should be made very clear that in any of these cultures the meaning of the kingly god's death, and thus of the rites of the symbolic death of the king, was not the "killing of the father" as in the framework of the Oedipus complex. In Egypt and Mesopotamia the king god's son is his champion, his avenger or rescuer. The whole aim of the rite was the renewal and reinvigoration of the potency of the royal figure, who was the very embodiment of the powerful center of the cosmos. When king killing was performed, as apparently some legends say was done among some of the Indoeuropean peoples,[13] in eastern India and in Scandinavia and Ireland in the west, the purpose was the same, to preserve the power of the kingship by having only a fit figure of a man to carry the function.

Death in Psychic Form

The motif of death may take many forms. Often one hears of a dream immediately preceding the psychosis in which the patient is submerged in turbulent water and is drowning, perhaps in a panic. In the usual religious framework the death is sacrificial, perhaps a crucifixion or martyrdom, or some sort of ritual killing. The more paranoid variant is the acute fear of being the victim of murder, assassination, or poisoning. Often the impression of death is more concrete as a kind of entity that moves over the patient, with peculiar sensations and odors as its harbingers. In keeping with the fact that the patient is living all the while at the level of myth and ritual ideation, the image of death is characteristically coupled with rebirth as a single process in two phases.

An example can be found in the case of a young man of twenty-two (Case 5), who went through a preoccupation with death. As we were sitting together he began playing, in a good mood, with the crayons, humming a western song. His drawing took the form of a cowboy in gay colors. I almost passed this drawing off as doodling about the song, but did ask him rather casually whether cowboys meant something particular to him. He answered that he wanted to live on a ranch but that his wife opposed it, being a city girl. When I was curious about his wish, he elaborated, telling the story about his paternal grandfather, with whom he had always felt a special kind of affinity. The grandfather was a cowboy and an engaging, swashbuckling character of some charm, flighty, volatile, easily violent, and a footloose and lovable wanderer; he had come to an untimely end in a barroom brawl at the age of twenty-two, that is, about the current age of the grandson. His son, the patient's father, was born soon after and grew up under the shadow of this legendary character, and, as one might expect, developed all the opposite traits possible. He was restrained, law abiding, even rigid, and admirable for his qualities of responsibility. He became a policeman of good reputation. When I remarked on this tendency of the patient to take after his grandfather, the mild statement seemed to echo in his mind, for he scribbled statements later saying, "I am my own grandfather" and the like.

In this identification, then, we find a self-image derived from the father's father complex, that is, a father image that the father renounced and repressed, and that the son picked up. Its effect had motivated the son now on the ward to be obstreperous, aggressive, sometimes combative, and difficult to handle.

The next week the young man produced a drawing of a graveyard with a prominent tomb in the form of a cross; over the tomb the color black prevailed, conveying the depressive mood of the death theme. The associations with the drawing involved certain individuals on the ward toward whom he felt antipathy because they were aggressive and irresponsible; that is, they were receiving his projection of the grandfather complex.

Soon after, the young man produced a picture representing the death of the grandfather himself. He lies on the earth, and as his spirit leaves the body in rings of breath, flowers spring up around and through him, an image precisely resembling a representation of the dead Osiris. A sunflower above the feet is associated with the grandmother. I see this drawing as representing the death of the self-image that had given the young man a good deal of trouble, and that had grown to be less and less serviceable, in keeping with the usual fate of the self-image in the catatonic turmoil—dissolution and reconstitution in terms of death and renewal. The sunflower associated with the grandmother may connote something of the father's mother complex, constellating some of the patient's new potential for flowering into warmth and relatedness.

The myth and ritual form of death has two variants, as place and as process: the place is the realm of the ancestors, over which the deceased king reigns; the process is the descent and passage through death as a phase in the rejuvenation of the living king.[14] In the individual psychic experience, the imagery of a "death trip" thus signifies the entrance into a "space" of psychic depth, "spaced out" in a realm of the ancestral heritage, that is, in a space occupied by the archetypal affect images. Yet death also signifies the coming to the end of a phase in development, and the killing off of a self-image, that is, the sacrifice of the leading image of the central archetype, thus allowing its transformation into a new image.

3. THE RETURN TO THE BEGINNINGS

The notion of regression has become a byword among those accustomed to thinking in psychoanalytic terms both Freudian and Jungian, and it is generally understood that regression is an essential element in the nature of schizophrenic process. In fact, regression is so much part of the theory that the suspicion easily arises that the concept might be just an item of abstract doctrine. To be reassured of its validity, however, one need only listen to psychotic individuals expressing their feelings of being a little child or even an infant, to watch their behavior at certain moments, and to observe the kindergarten quality of their drawing.

Less familiar is the regular occurrence, along with these feelings of slipping back into one's own personal beginnings, of the accompanying fantasies of returning in time to the beginnings of the world in general. The backward movement is both to the image of the starting point of one's own existence and of the existence of all things. The myth and ritual expression of this affect image is the creation rite.

The Return in Israelite Myth and Ritual

Israel was no exception to the general custom in the Near East of celebrating the New Year with a creation rite and myth along with the other elements in the enthronement ceremonies.[1] It is likely that the story of the creation as it reached its final form in the Book of Genesis was the literary rendering of such a ritual text. The Royal Psalms, however, provide the more certain texts.[2] The outlines of the story are familiar, but less generally recognized is the fact that Yahweh does battle with chaos and performs the act of creation, overcoming the monster and taming the waters, in his role as the true king of Israel. One such psalm addresses Yahweh as the awesome king god who governs the assembly of the lesser deities and who has proved his might by the creation of the world:

For who in the sky can be compared with Yahweh.

. . .

A God who is awesome in the council of the holy ones.

. . .

It is Thou who dost rule over the swell of the sea;
When the waves thereof arise, it is Thou who dost still them.
It was Thou who didst crush Rahab like a corpse,
Scattering Thine enemies with Thy mighty Arm.
Thine are the heavens, Thine too is the earth;
It was Thou who didst found the world and all that filleth it.

It was Thou who didst create the north and the south;
Tabor and Hermon applaud Thy Name![3]

The following Royal Psalm is thought by some to be an actual ritual text of the creation rite. It is a very poetic ode addressed not only to the creator but to his creation as well; we note that Yahweh appears as storm god, "rider of the clouds," who secures the created world by containing the flood waters:

Bless the Lord, O my soul.
O Lord my God, thou art very great;
thou art clothed with honor and majesty:
Who coverest thyself with light as with a garment:
who stretchest out the heavens like a curtain:
Who layeth the beams of his chambers in the waters:
who maketh the clouds his chariot:
who walketh upon the wings of the wind:

. . .

Who maketh his angels spirits:
his ministers a flaming fire:
Who laid the foundations of the earth,
that it should not be removed for ever.
Thou coveredst it with the deep as with a garment:
the waters stood above the mountains.
Thou hast set a bound that they may not pass over;
that they turn not again to cover the earth.

. . .

He watereth the hills from his chambers:
the earth is satisfied with the fruit of thy works.
He causeth the grass to grow for the cattle,
and herb for the service of man:
that he may bring forth food out of the earth;

. . .

He appointed the moon for seasons:
the sun knoweth his going down.
Thou makest darkness, and it is night:
wherein all the beasts of the forest do creep forth.

. . .

O Lord, how manifold are thy works!
in wisdom hast thou made them all:
the earth is full of thy riches.

. . .

The glory of the Lord shall endure for ever:
the Lord shall rejoice in his works.
He looketh on the earth, and it trembleth:
he toucheth the hills, and they smoke.
I will sing unto the Lord as long as I live.[4]

The theme of the creation is carried further in the dramatic form of the enthronement festival by identifying the king with the first ancestor and first king, Adam, whose name means "The Man" as the prototype of mankind, and who reigned over the first paradise as Keeper of the Garden of God, "crowned with glory and honor," and in divine status comparable to the angels.[5] The meaning stands out clearly, if, in the ninth line, for "man" one substitutes "Adam":

O Lord our Lord,
how excellent is thy name in all the earth!
who hast set thy glory above the heavens.
Out of the mouth of babes and sucklings has thou ordained strength
because of thine enemies,
that thou mightest still the enemy and the avenger.

When I consider thy heavens, the work of thy fingers,
the moon and the stars, which thou hast ordained;
What is man, that thou art mindful of him?
and the son of man, that thou visitest him?
For thou hast made him a little lower than the angels,
and hast crowned him with glory and honor.
Thou madest him to have dominion over the works of thy hands;
thou hast put all things under his feet:
All sheep and oxen,
yea, and the beast of the field;
The fowl of the air, and the fish of the sea,
and whatsoever passeth through the paths of the sea.[6]

BACKGROUND OF THE IMAGE

In Egypt, the motif of the creation was woven into the ideology of the kingship as an essential and constant aspect of the royal role. The ascension of the king to his throne was equated in significance to the first rising of the sun in the east, and the throne to the first rising of solid land out of the surrounding flood of chaos at the dawn of creation. The same pictographic word is used to designate each of the three—throne, dawn and Primeval Hill.[7] The Primeval Hill, ceremonially designated by the double flight of steps to the raised platform of the throne, was one of the variants on the theme of the world mountain. It was represented as arising out of the midst of the Lake of Fire as an image of the primordial waters of chaos; over them passed the god Atum, personifying the wind or silent breath, to create the first locus of the ordered cosmos. In this image we recognize one of the roots of the Israelite image of creation by the "ruach Yahweh," the breath of God, the spirit passing over the waters.[8] The Lake of Fire added further to the comparison with the sunrise, in which the heavenly luminary stands for the very epitome of cosmic order, rising out of the night amid the flame of color.[9]

In Mesopotamia, the Akitu or New Year's Festival brought out most clearly the ritual that reenacted the beginnings of the world. The story of creation came into being as the dramatic text, and not as an explanation such as we might conceive with our modern outlook, rendering the account of the first origins of existence out of nothingness. The view of creation was rather that it was an ever-continuing component in the cycle of existence.[10] Just as the life of the vegetation waxed and waned, sprouting into vital growth and shriveling into death, so did the year itself and its principal manifestation, the sun. Time was seen as moving forward and backward in this cyclic fashion, the New Year marking the end of time and its renewal, a new beginning of existence. The creation myth and ritual was then no mere commemoration of a mighty act of the origin of things, but an actual, present, annual event of the renewed order arising out of chaos, and life out of death.[11] We find in the drama the same play of motifs of wind and flood as in the Israelite and Egyptian creation myths. The Sumerian antecedent of Marduk had been Enlil, Lord Storm, whose nature was the wind; accordingly, in the later version Marduk's powerful weapon was the wind as he did combat with the great mother monster, Tiamat, personifying the primordial waters of the abyss. The decisive stroke making order of chaos was his cleaving her body in two like an oyster shell, separating the upper and lower worlds.[12]

We are now left with the question, Why should there be a need for a creation myth, either in the ancient myth and ritual or in the modern renewal process? Mircea Eliade has written a searching study of man's need expressed through the ages to abolish time and to put himself and his world back to the beginning.[13] Eliade concludes that through the passage of time, through the course of a year in the ancient Near East, a sense of error and guilt builds up and accumulates because of the natural tendency of man to deviate from the prescribed ways as established at the beginning by the founding heroes and gods. Insofar as man's actions hold to those sacred ways he stays within the bounds of what is real and valuable; deviations from them are of no value and do not partake of the sense of reality with which the approved ways are endowed. The accumulation of error and guilt is wiped out if time is abolished and thrown back to the start once more. One cannot help thinking in this instance of the Aztecs and their custom of measuring their epochs in fifty-two-year cosmological cycles. At the end of these periods they literally started over again, even renewing their sacred and public buildings by erecting new outer layers that buried the old form in the massive walls, which thus grew ever thicker.[14]

The Return in Psychic Form

The return to the beginnings in psychotic fantasy most frequently draws on the myth of the Garden of Eden and of the first man and first woman, as the starting point of human history. Almost as often it slips into a more frankly modern idiom, envisioning the first formation of the world, the rise of the continents and origins of life, and the early migrations of races.

I will point out an instance of such a creation episode in a psychosis (Case 4) of a young woman whom I have discussed at greater length earlier.[15] She was twenty-three, and undergoing an acute episode with all the classical signs of disturbance.

She felt she had certain ordeals or trials to perform, exacted of her by her voices. She was told she must repeat the creation of the world from the beginning and participate in all the phases of its evolution. First she had to be under the sea for some time and there beheld all sorts of primordial monsters of the deep. Coming up on the land as the evolution of life progressed, she was witness to the age of the reptiles. As humanity began to come upon the scene, she lived among the primitives and joined them in their rituals and ceremonials; during this period she sang and danced rhythmic chants in her room, reciting little rhyming phrases and verses. Simultaneously, she was required to go back to her own beginnings, her birth and infancy, and to repeat her growth step by step up to her present age exactly and precisely: whenever she made an error she had to go back to the start again and repeat it all over. She said she could get as far as the age of sixteen, and no further. This limit was an accurate bit of psychology, for she had indeed only reached about that age level of maturity.

This case was an unusually clear example of the parallel of the personal and the cosmic beginnings. It shows how distinctly the personal and the archetypal processes go hand in hand. As I visualize it, the affect image of the cosmological process is the vehicle for the personal contents to come into play and find their resolution.

Sometimes one finds either the personal or the archetypal part of the process appearing without the other. In the young lady's imagery discussed in the section on the center (Case 1), the imagery of the center was used to recapitulate each phase of her personal development from her early years on, a series of six drawings to indicate the stages the self had gone through. In another example (Case 10), a young lady had an experience similar to the one just described, of seeing the creation of the world and the migrations of races over the landmasses. She had as her initial delusions the vision of herself as Eve in the Garden of Eden, thus located in time at the beginning of creation. However, her allusions to her infancy and childhood were not extensive. I sometimes wonder whether the imagery is, in such cases, present and functioning but not reported in the interviews, or whether the play of imagery is indeed somewhat irregular, varying from case to case in regard to which motifs occur and which do not.

The imagery has to do not only with a return to the starting point of things, but fully as much with a recapitulation of the steps of development of the world, and of history, and of one's own personal development. It thus becomes a redoing, phase by phase, of growth both on a personal and on an archetypal level. This recapitulation appears to me to be the meaning of the regression. Just as the imagery of death is chiefly instrumental in effecting a rebirth process, so the imagery of the return to the beginnings finds its significance principally as part and parcel of the process of recapitulating the steps of development.

I think there is little question that the established cultural canon appears immensely impressive, whether positively or negatively, to the kind of personality that is slated for a schizophrenic episode.[16] In my experience, this canon seems to be rendered to the growing child by the mother's conviction of its absoluteness. It therefore operates in much the same way as the canon of established ways described by Eliade, engendering a like guilt if not followed.[17] However, the problem in the modern psyche is not reestablishing the canon in its purified form, but letting it go, reshaping it, and reforming it.

The term *a cultural canon* may not sound as all-encompassing as the creation of a world, but one must remember that we are dealing with affect images. The individual's image of the world is a psychological and emotional kind of reality; it is the condensation of an entire "Weltanschauung," a world outlook or world view. It is a structured system of values and meanings that describes the totality of one's experience. This inner world is the interior reading of the outer one, the rendering in meaning of what otherwise is a mere mass of outer experience in the raw, random and unshaped by the work of the whole psyche. The image of the world in this sense is one of the forms that the image of the central archetype of the self assumes. This parallel is why the "world" of archaic times was the kingdom, centered in the figure of the king; it was a culture with an *ethos* and an *eidos,*[18] viewed as a totality to such an extent that other kingdoms were not considered to be part of the ordered cosmos.

The renewal process of the psychotic individual must revise this world outlook and this cultural canon from the ground up. This need entails the work of the affect images in their customary process of beginning the creation over again from the void and forming an entire new structure, this time hopefully in the image of what one is in one's own proper constitutional makeup, no longer of what one was given by the parental world.

4. THE CLASH OF OPPOSITES

An essential component of the creation process, as a regular accompaniment to it in traditional as well as psychotic forms, is the clash of opposite cosmic powers. This clash is known in the language of myth and ritual studies as the *ritual combat, sacred combat,* or *cosmic conflict.* Psychoanalytic studies have had much to say of the "world destruction fantasies" encountered in schizophrenia, of which interpretations have been made having to do with the loss of reality and object relations. However, a fresh look at the place of these images in their rightful context reveals further dimensions of meaning in this process.

The Cosmic Conflict in Israelite Myth and Ritual Form

As one examines the content of the Royal Psalms, one is impressed with how much they are occupied with the chastisement of the King's Enemies and with the suffering undergone at the hands of their foes. Yahweh appears distinctly in the role of heroic warrior and savior, with many of the attributes of his Canaanite predecessor, as Rider of the Clouds and Lord of the Storm. As Israel's King he performs exploits of might against the monster of the deep, Leviathan. The name of this creature is often given in forms derived directly from the Canaanite myth, namely Lotan or Tannin.

The ideology of this enemy is most significant for our present discussion in that it is steeped in an emotional flavor that we are tempted to call as paranoid as can be (considering that these are sacred texts). The Waters of the Abyss, the Flood, are equated not only to the monster and to Death, but significantly, to the "Kings of the Nations" who are threatening to besiege and persecute Israel and to undo it if they can. Thus Yahweh's mighty act of creation is identical both with his victory over the flood, and with his triumph as the god of order over the forces of chaos, and as king god over the king's enemies. The hostile foreign nations then represent the potential for disorder and the threat of the disintegration of the kingship, and of the kingdom, that is, the world.[1]

To complete the image, it must be understood that the kings of the foreign nations are representatives of their king gods, who are masters of their city states, and that these are the lesser deities in the divine assembly governed by Yahweh as their king of kings:

> *God* [or *Yahweh*] *taketh His stand in the divine assembly;*
> *Amidst the gods He pronounceth judgement.*
> *"How long will ye judge unjustly,*
> *And show partiality towards the wicked?*
>
> . . . .
>
> *Rescue the weak and the poor,*
> *Deliver them from the hand of the wicked,*
> *Who have neither knowledge nor understanding,*
> *But live persistently in darkness,*
> *So that all the foundations of the earth are shaken."*
>
> *"I admit that ye are gods,*
> *And all of you sons of the Most High.*
> *Nevertheless ye shall die like men,*
> *And fall like any ordinary prince."*
> *Arise O God (or Yahweh)! Judge the earth!*
> *For* Thou *shalt take possession of all the nations.*[2]

It is not only the foreign rebellious elements, but those within Israel that will be chastised by this law-giving god:

> *"If his children forsake My law,*
> *And walk not in My judgements,*
> *If they violate My statutes,*
> *And do not keep My commandments,*
> *I will attend to their rebellion with a rod*
> *And their iniquity with blows."*[3]

The people of Israel are called to this high task of the sacred combat against the forces of the enemy on behalf of the divine king:

Let the devout be thrilled at the thought of glory,
Let them applaud upon their beds,
With the acclamation of God in their throat,
And a two-edged sword in their hand!
To wreak vengeance upon the nations,
Chastisement upon the peoples,
To bind their kings with chains,
Their nobility with iron fetters,
To execute upon them the judgement prescribed,
Falleth to the honour of all His votaries.[4]

While the people of Israel are given protection and comfort by their divine king, the enemy is condemned to dwell in the arid wastelands; Yahweh brings rain and nurturance to his own, but the demonic enemy is deprived of these blessings and is rejected into outsideness:

God giveth the lonely a home wherein to dwell,
He skillfully setteth free those in bondage;
But the rebellious make their home in the arid waste!
O Yahweh, when Thou wentest forth before Thy people,
When Thou didst march through the desert,
The earth quaked, yea, the heavens poured
Before Yahweh, Him of Sinai,
Before Yahweh, the God of Israel.[5]

Yahweh is portrayed as a mighty warrior leading his hosts in the sacred combat, and saving them from the enemy, "Death":

The chariots of God are thousands upon thousands;
The Lord is amid them, the God of Sinai is in the sanctuary!
Thou hast ascended on high, leading Thy captives;
Thou hast taken tribute from amongst mankind,
Even those who rebelled at Yah's choice of a home!

. . .

God is for us a god who saveth,
And through Yahweh, the Lord, 'Death' is expelled.[6]

Meanwhile, the Davidic king is protagonist in the drama of the ritual combat against the enemy, undergoing the threat of submission to death as it overwhelms him, and crying in trust to his divine father to intervene to rescue him:[7]

Out of my distress I cried unto Yah;
Yah's answer was to set me at liberty.
With Yahweh on my side I do not fear
What man may do to me.
With Yahweh on my side to give me aid,
I gaze in triumph on them that hate me.

. . .

All nations surrounded me;
Through the Name of Yahweh I cut them off.[8]

A stirring and poetic account is then given of the epiphany of this triumphant storm god as he manifests himself in his full and terrible splendor. This poetry has the fantasmagoric quality that today might be called *psychedelic:*

In His Palace (or Temple) He heard my voice,
And my appeal came to His Ears.
The earth heaved and quaked,
While the foundations of the mountains quivered;
Yea, they rocked because He was wroth.
Smoke rose from His Nostril,
While fire leapt devouring from His Mouth;
Live coals came kindling therefrom.
He parted the heavens, and descended,
With a cloud beneath His Feet.
He rode upon a cherub and flew;
He sped on the wings of the wind.
Yahweh thundered in the heavens;
The Most High uttered His Voice.
He sent forth His arrows, scattering them abroad,

Even lightnings in abundance, making them resound.
Then the channels of the sea could be seen,
And the foundations of the world were laid bare,
At Thy rebuke, O Yahweh,
At the tempestuous breathing of Thy Nostril.
He reached from on high, He took me,
He drew me out of the many waters.
He delivered me from my powerful enemy,
From my foes, for they were too strong for me.
They confronted me on the day of my calamity;
But Yahweh became my support.
He set me at liberty;
He freed me, for He was pleased with me.
Yahweh doth recompense me according to my righteousness;
According to the purity of my hands He maketh me restoration.

. . .

Thou hath girded me with might for battle;
Thou dost subdue mine opponents beneath me.
Thou hast made mine enemies turn back before me,
And them that hate me I put to silence.[9]

BACKGROUND OF THE IMAGE

In the Egyptian form of the conflict, in the time of the gods when Seth had brought about the death of his brother Osiris in the attempt to wrest the kingship for himself, revenge had to be wrought upon him by Osiris' son and legitimate heir, Horus. This sky god, out of love for his father and for the sake of the stability of the order of the world, fought his destructive antagonist.[10] The king, as the living embodiment of Horus, did similar ceremonial battle with his enemies.[11] On the eve of the enthronement rites, or the rites of renewal at the New Year, or of the Sacred Marriage, among the proceedings was "the destruction of the king's enemies." Thus at the Raising of the Djed Pillar a mock fight between the men of two Delta cities (of Pe and of Dep) was dramatized with weapons of reeds and stalks.[12] At the Sacred Marriage of Edfu the king's enemies were represented as hippopotami, crocodiles, or fishes to be harpooned or trampled, as birds or animals to be snared and dispatched, or as animals to be sacrificed.[13] Designated by the boar in pictorial form, Seth represented also an opposition in many aspects: the earth against the sky, the darkness of the clouds against the light of the broad sky or the sun, the arid desert and its Asiatic or Nubian kingdoms against the fertile land of Egypt, or foreign hostile powers and domestic rebellious elements against the king's rule.[14]

In Mesopotamia the ritual myth[15] tells that before the world was created the gods of the old order under the leadership of the great Mother of All, Tiamat, felt enmity toward the new gods and challenged them. The king leading Tiamat's forces, Kingu, designated by a boar, was defeated by the magic spell of the wise water god, Enki. Now Tiamat was enraged and threatened the gods with extinction. The young Enlil (or Marduk later) was begotten of Enki for the very purpose of leading the gods against this formidable foe. We have already seen how this Lord Storm, or Wind, inflated Tiamat's belly with his seven winds and clove her in twain, creating the upper and lower worlds of her substance. With the admixture of the Tammuz role into the ritual drama, the king god succumbed to death for a short period, to be rescued by his son Ninurta (later Nabu), while in the festival itself the king underwent his humiliation.[16] Myth customarily has a multiplicity of images to express a motif, while the rational mentality finds this difficult to understand because of reason's bias toward clarity and consistency. Thus the Sacred Combat was dramatized by a foot race with a representative of the Storm Bird, Zu.[17] Also, as seen in cylinder seals that have been found, Marduk in his death was contained in the wings of a bird representing Tiamat, and such a bird was cloven in twain at the altar during the rites to signify her fate,[18] while at other times Marduk was shown overcoming her as dragon or hydra.

The Canaanite conflict was between Baal as the young Puissant Prince and god of the kingship, whose task was to master the life-giving waters, and Yamm as the Prince River, whose propensity was to overrun the land with his chaotic deluge.[19] Baal embarked on mortal combat with this dragon, Lord of the Flood, as a rival claimant to his throne who was even favored by the elderly god of the highest sky, El, of the old order. Baal's victory led then to his control of the flood. His other sacred combat was against Mot, Lord Death, King of the Underworld, as already mentioned.[20] Mot engulfed

Baal and contained him in death for a seven-year period, then to be overcome by Baal and himself undergo a seven-year demise. There was in this myth some of the vegetational ritual, since Mot's body was ground up and scattered like grain.

The Cosmic Conflict in Psychic Form

The psychotic persons in this syndrome give a picture of world destruction as the possible and fearful outcome of the cataclysmic warring of opposite forces in the world. During the 1950s, when most of the persons in this group of twelve were undergoing their psychotic episode, the regular expression of this clash was the vying for power between democracy and communism. The imagery described a world divided into balanced halves in opposition: there was this half of ours, our world with which we are familiar, and then that other half, the enemy side, unfamiliar, sinister, and threatening. All description of the conflict was couched in strictly mythological terms, as an Armageddon. Democracy was the side of the Good, often expressed as representing the forces of Christ, preserving the order and integration of the world and even the universe, while communism was the side of the Bad, usually of Evil and of the Devil, or perhaps the Antichrist, attempting to destroy the world or even all of creation, and to thrust it all into chaos and disintegration. Most often the person found himself or herself at the midpoint between the opposing sides, at the center, being made use of in some way by both of the factions; sometimes it was felt to be incumbent on the person to make a choice of allegiance to one or to the other.

For example, in the case of the young woman (Case 4)[21] whose creation fantasies we have just reviewed, these ideas occurred as part of that total picture. She found herself embroiled in a cosmic struggle between the Devil and Christ. The former was plotting to destroy the world by exploding it with the nuclear materials that he was devising, while the latter was pitting himself against the Devil in order to save the world. All the world was divided equally between the opposing forces, the communists belonging to the Devil and attempting a final disintegration of creation, and the democracies, under the banner of Christ, trying to preserve the world intact. She was hearing voices constantly, those of the Devil and of God. An alternative expression of the threat of disintegration was that the Pope himself was possessed by the Devil and was in hell, just as she was; his threefold tiara was torn into triangular fragments, and at the same time the Holy Trinity was similarly broken up. Thus the motif of dismemberment is all interwoven through that of the world destruction and of the intense collision of world powers. This person's arduous task of repeating the whole of creation then took on the connotation of her effort to side with the forces of order to preserve the integrity of the threatened world.

Another young woman (Case 12) exemplified very vividly the kind of implications one finds in this theme of the cosmic conflict. Shortly before admission she had been experiencing two different kinds of odors. There were the "odors of salvation," or "of life," which were sent by the Blessed Virgin Mary and which conveyed a feeling of great serenity; these were sensations of pure bliss. Opposed to these were "odors of death," sent by the Devil; these odors struck her with oppression and anguish, made vivid by giving her a heavy pain in the chest. She knew herself to be specially elected by the Blessed Virgin for a special mission, to initiate a movement to establish a new order in the world, and this election gave her confidence in her superior spirituality. One day she observed that the patients in the ward were lined up on opposite sides of the room and recognized these sides as the forces of democracy and of communism, mobilized against each other for a final war of Christ's forces against the Devil's. She had already perceived that some of the doctors were really communists, asking questions of her to test her faith. At another dramatic moment, she was looking out her window and beheld the world turning inside out. It was suddenly becoming the Devil's world now. After that, as she looked about the city she saw only a sinister sort of atmosphere and a degenerate look on peoples' faces. Evil, she knew, was contagious in just the same way as diseases, and was spreading, like an epidemic.

These delusional and hallucinatory impressions are not just ravings of the insane devoid of meaning, but are quite accurate accounts of the things that were happening at a level of depth in her makeup at that time. She was going to have to make her peace with the world of passion, carnality, instinct, and human sorrow and strife, all the "ugly" side of human nature that she had scrupulously shunned till now.

This imagery of the world factions in conflict is based on a symbolic and psychological geography that should be explained.[22] At this level of archaic representation, the society to which one belongs is not an amorphous aggregation of people like a modern city, but is given a form and meaning along well-defined lines. The society has a center and a periphery, and is oriented to the cardinal directions. The center is the focus of power that gives life and order, and is personified, as we have pointed out, in the figure of the sacral king. The kingdom is then an image of the world. Within its bounds is cosmic order, and its structure of values and meanings and its way of life are modeled on their prototype in the world of the gods.[23] Its kingship is a gift of the gods, and its ritual practices likewise are a reenactment of what the gods have done and instituted. The moral law is thus a reflection of the laws of the cosmos, and social order is merely an instance of the general cosmic order.[24] This emotional image is conferred on "our" world, "our" way of life, and "our" values and meanings—on all that is "inside" this favored world.

To be "outside" is a different matter altogether. What is beyond the periphery belongs to the opposite of all we have just said of the inside, and belongs not to the world of order but to chaos. It is at best barbarous, not yet illuminated with the knowledge of the gods and their boons to man's culture, and therefore of value as raw material for the creative process of extending the bounds of the ordered world, that is, for conquest.[25] At worst it is demon land, the terrain of the enemy principle of disorder, darkness, and all that is hostile to life. It thus has affinities with the underworld—what is outside and what is below are akin.[26]

The ritual of the sacred combat is thus the warring of the sacral king against the king's enemy, as the protagonists of light, life, and cosmic order on the one hand, and of darkness, death, and chaos on the other. It is the striving of the forces within the kingdom against the forces that typify the outer alien lands. Thus military conquest was regarded as having this mythological significance, as part of the king's cosmocratic function, that is, continuing the creation of cosmos out of chaos. This war-making is called the *historification* of the sacred combat—carrying out into political activity the pattern which had its origins in myth and ritual.[27]

This discussion sets the stage for the basic ground plan of the history of cultures, as a dialectical process between opposite tendencies: the rigid preservation of the traditional, ordered forms with the sanctity of the gods' gifts to men, and against this rigidity, the vigorous and restless upsetting of those forms to break their stasis and make way for new growth. The same pertains to the individual, if one but translates the process from the outer social form to the inner spiritual form of a culture. The individual's own personal structure of values and meanings, and way of life and outlook, is a culture in miniature, an interior one.[28] This culture is represented in the image of the kingdom world and of the enemy. Inside the kingdom are the psychological forces that would preserve it unchanged and intact, while outside it are the antagonistic enemy forces that would disrupt and dismantle it to make room for change and growth.

The development of the psyche at the level of these affect images may fail if it meets with a resistive consciousness. Jung has pointed out that the brittleness of the defensive ego in the schizoid personality causes this kind of person a mortal dread of any such compensatory movement from the autonomous psyche.[29] To a more fluid nature, the development would be a profound experience of transformation to behold the spectacle of one's world of illusions and biases collapsing in a soul-shaking upheaval; to one not resilient enough to allow such a turmoil, the threat of such a collapse is projected and seems to come from purely malicious agencies in the outer world.

With this imagery of the enemy we come to the heart of the paranoid process. When psychotic persons are filled with delusional fears of being poisoned, plotted against, done to death, and spied on by wired walls and magic devices to know their thoughts, it soon emerges that these are believed to be the fiendish connivings of an enemy, and that this enemy has a mythological cast. His intent is felt to be to bring about the person's undoing, and along with that the undoing of the nation, the world, or even the universe.

For instance, in the case of a psychotic student whose therapist I supervised, at the start of the acute episode weeks went by with the student's entire communication being confined to his paranoid conviction that his bedsprings were electronically wired to spy on him. His preoccupations were apparently frozen in this form in an unbelievably sterile image. When the therapist began to show an interest in what was behind this belief, in whom the student believed to be doing this spying, and why, suddenly a rich profusion of vivid imagery opened up, and the student's rigid and static quality of mind changed into animation. The reason for the spying, the student found, was that there was to be an imminent Second Coming of Christ with displays of divine glory and power from the heavens. The patient felt that he was involved in this apocalyptic event, perhaps in the leading role. Negatively, this discovery could be disapproved as a bit of triumphant "psychotic insight," but I would prefer to think of it as a long-overdue psychic activation that would produce movement, given the psyche's own strange mode of moving.

To the psychiatrist, usually preoccupied with his clinical views of what constitutes "reality," that is, object relations, and "normality," which implies good reality testing, the world destruction fantasies seem almost self-evident in their import: they represent the loss of object relations. He then assumes that the loss of the world in delusions is the pathological tendency of the schizophrenic to withdraw cathexes and to regress away from the demands of the outer world. The obliteration of the world looks dire enough to warrant the judgment that it must be pathological in its inception. Such a view would only overlook and bypass the well-known fact that these notions of the destructive work of the enemy have belonged to the most revered systems of myth, ritual, and metaphysical ideation throughout the millennia of the civilized era.

Such a view would also overlook the possibility that, just as the myth forms of this theme come into play in normal communal ceremonies, so also they might in the individual have a role to play in the maintaining of the normal balance of the psyche. We have noted already that the person who is slipping over the borderline into his inner experience identifies with the affect image of the center, especially in the form of the sacral king or messiah. This identification is the paranoid position, in the supreme powerfulness of the center. As soon as one steps into this exalted role, automatically its opposite is constellated as its antagonist. The sacral king who represents the highest rule of order has as his natural companion-piece the king's enemy, who carries the possibility of disorder and chaos issuing from the depths. In the same way that the heroic son seems to be an aspect of the image of the king god, so the king's enemy appears as one of the facets of the king god archetype. This negative pole of the affect image, when constellated, threatens to dislodge the carrier of its positive pole. That is, the ego has usurped a position that is too big for it, and has become inflated to the point of being psychotic. The move to destroy the supremacy of this power is corrective. It is a compensatory function, as with so many unconscious processes, that intends to initiate the process of death and renewal, and of world destruction and creation, as a healing measure.

5. THE REVERSAL OF OPPOSITES

An all-pervasive theme running through the psychotic process is a strongly loaded misgiving in regard to the opposite sex, whether within oneself or in the men or women of the outer world. There has been much comment in the literature on psychosis, beginning with Freud's commentary on the Schreber case,[1] about the role of homosexual strivings in the paranoid mechanism. Whether or not there happen to be actual homosexual wishes and impulses, certainly one does hear a great deal of apprehension on the part of psychotic persons that their sexual identities are threatened with reversal and also that the power of the opposite sex is overwhelming. I have come to see this theme of the threat of sexual reversal as part of a larger pattern of the reversal of opposites in general.

In the New Year Festivals a parallel to this motif of reversal as a form of the play of opposites is found in the chaotic phase of the proceedings, that wild overturn of the customary order that Gaster has given the apt epithet, "topsy-turvydom."[2] It is the period, in the festivals of certain of those cultures, in which the normal relationships are turned about.

The Reversal of Opposites in Israelite Myth and Ritual Form

How this overturn of order was expressed ceremonially in Israel is not clear, but certain Royal Psalms indicate at least that the normal social order, based on the covenant with their divine king, was temporarily nullified:

Thou hast repudiated the covenant with Thy Servant;
Thou hast brought his crown to pollution in the dust.
Thou hast broken down all his walls;
Thou hast laid his defenses in ruins.
All the passers by have despoiled him;
He has become a mockery to his neighbors.

. . .

Remember, O Lord, the mockery of Thy Servant,
How I bear the brunt of all the peoples.[3]

BACKGROUND OF THE IMAGE

In Mesopotamia, in the opening phase of the rites, when Tiamat was dominant and her chaos ruled, as Eliade phrases it, "all forms are supposed to be confounded in the marine abyss of the beginning, the *apsu*. Enthronement of a 'carnival' king, 'humiliation' of the real sovereign, overturning of the entire social order (according to Berossus, the slaves became the masters, and so on)—every feature suggests universal confusion, the abolition of order and hierarchy, 'orgy,' chaos."[4]

In reviewing some kindred rituals in the Near East, in the mysteries of Attis, essentially a variant on the motif of Osiris and Tammuz and Baal, Gaster finds that "The notion of topsy-turvydom or suspension of normal activities at the end of the life lease was symbolized by a general saturnalian license, characterized, as in other parts of the world, by masquerades and interchanges of garments."[5] This practice of transvestism has ancient roots and has often been associated with service to the Great Mother Goddess, in which the males dramatized their allegiance to her and identity with her by dressing in female attire.[6] Here, it should be emphasized, the sexual identity was only a special instance of the reversals of role and position. The imagery that seems to have to do with the reversal of opposites in general, such as power-subservience, dominance-submission, and male-female designates the overturn of the customary order.

The Reversal of Opposites in Psychic Form

In the schizophrenic process, perhaps the most common of these preoccupations and enraged suspicions is, among men, that they are being accused of being homosexuals, or among women, that they are being turned into men by some sort of underhanded devices such as medications or radiations. On the part of some of the men one hears of supreme dominance of some female figure, usually of mythological or religious stature, and on the part of some of the women, fantasies of gigantic power plays to eliminate men and thus preserve their own dominance. Then, too, the cosmic conflict or political clash is often recognized by the person to be an expression of the struggle between the male and female sides of his or her own nature.

This latter observation, concerning the clashes of factions as representing male and female components, gives a helpful indication of what we are to make of this class of imagery. What distinguishes it from the motif of the cosmic conflict, with which it seems to overlap? The phenomenology of this theme of male and female shows it to be all bound up with the idea of the play of opposites; we must regard it, then, as a special instance of the clash of powers. However, in this case the opposites turn into one another, or more exactly, one of the pair turns into the other or is overwhelmed by the other.

An example of the touchy apprehensiveness concerning sexual roles occurred in the case of a young man (Case 9), the major part of whose preoccupations revolved around the question of giving his allegiance to the communist world instead of the democratic. The trouble, he thought, with the democratic way is that it is too soft and weak, wishy-washy, religious and sentimental, and has no virility; the communist way, on the other hand, has guts, is strong and aggressive, and is the only way acceptable to any man who wants to be a man. This young man had been a Mormon minister, in keeping with the custom of Mormons, as an interim assignment when he was through school. He was currently renouncing this disciplined way of life, feeling that it discouraged the ways of manhood. In spite of remorse and regret over the disloyalty, he was considering transferring his allegiance to this enemy power and its superior concept of maleness. In his attitude toward his own country there was a certain uneasiness about his masculinity, as if he would lose it or at least weaken it if he remained within the American way of life. Naturally, it goes without saying that there was no question of any actual transfer of his citizenship or even his politics on the reality level; he was speaking altogether in terms of the mythological imagery representing world or cosmic opposites, cloaked in terms of political factions.

It is interesting that in this case, as with so many, the opposites are equated with the parental images and complexes. This equation signifies that some of the qualities assigned to the opposites are derived from the person's experience of the parents, and that they are therefore now encountered in projection on the parents. This case is therefore an instance of the principle that the person's preoccupation in the psychotic state is with the archetypal affect images, which have swung relatively free of the complexes ordinarily clustered around them and which only gradually find their way back into their emotional context. This person's mother was the parent who was tender and loving, and who pushed his religious interests so that he took them too seriously in adolescence; he was now turning right against their religion. His father, being cold and distant, "would have made a good communist," for he was unloving, detached, and preferred to live his life by logical thinking. The patient's swing toward the communist side, then, has the significance of his allying himself with the father at this point in his development, against the softening hold of the mother. As he put it, democracies are made of idealistic sissies, communism of practical he-men. He made his apprehensiveness about his sexual adequacy quite apparent.

An interesting light is thrown on the theme of reversal of sexual identity in a young woman of Latin-American background (Case 6). When she felt disliked, she presented herself as aggressive and hostile by being insulting and sarcastic. In her inflated state she announced that she knew too much and the world was afraid of her. She was Queen of the Aztecs, she proclaimed, specially elected by God to lead her people. However, this was her role not as a woman, but as a male doctor, for she had been living sixteen years as a boy and then became a man, and could "take on anyone." Her grandfather, that is, the mother's father, was Emperor of the Aztecs. Here enters the theme of the clash of opposites in political terms: the grandfather's four sons, her uncles, were undertaking a revolution against this tyrannous rule at the center of the Aztec World, and they would divide it up into four equal quadrants and reign as kings of governments marked by fairness and equality.

The issue is made a little more clear again by reference to the parental problem in which this group of ideas finds its setting. For the tyranny was an image representing the mother's dominating and controlling nature, and the grandfather emperor was therefore the image of her (the mother's) father complex, the component in the mother's makeup that gave her this power motivation. In Jungian terms, this component is called the mother's *animus,*[7] her masculine component, which moved her to aggressive or competitive ways and which had been bearing the impress of her father's ways. It was this maleness in the mother that was now under attack; it had been operating as the governing center of this young woman's psyche, but was now to be supplanted by a differentiated rule of four components belonging to the mother's sibling world as opposed to her parental world, promising to render the regime more equalitarian than authoritarian. Only by dispelling the power of the mother's father animus would it be possible for the patient to clarify her own sexual role, for up to now it has been confused. She described herself as ruling as queen, akin to the grandfather and therefore in a male role. A tendency to resolve this merging of masculine and feminine was indicated in her belief that she was about to give birth.

Our inquiry is therefore concerned with the meaning of the interplay of opposites. It appears that to schizophrenic persons, this interplay becomes an especially frightening possibility. Although the sexual identity is a major aspect of the phenomenon, it nonetheless is only one facet. Other facets involve possibilities that are equally opposite to the patient's identity, such as cultural, ethical, political, or religious values, attitudes, and beliefs. It is my impression that these persons are dismayed about this free interflow of the various opposites because of their need for a sort of absoluteness—the order of things must be dependable and right if one is to feel at all sure of anything. This attitude amounts to a rather brittle, if not rigid, and somewhat constricted range of permissiveness toward the possibilities of other ways. On the other hand, this free flowing into one another of various opposites may have as its purpose to mobilize and make familiar, and thus bring close to conscious awareness, those aspects of personality that have been left unconscious. The schizoid personality tends to be congealed in a sort of one-sidedness and defensiveness that resists modification and compensation from the unconscious. This is why the issue of opposites sounds much like the one just described in the motif of the cosmic conflict and clash of opposites.

6. *APOTHEOSIS*

Thus far the process under discussion has been on a negative bias: death, regression and return to the beginnings, cosmic conflict, world destruction, and the threat of reversal of the order of the opposites. All these images are the effects of slipping into the archetypal center and its powerful machinations. They are balanced, however, by a number of auspicious images that in the myth and ritual form constitute the later phases of the process. The apotheosis is a cluster of images around the theme of being raised to a highly exalted state either above all other humans or even above the human condition altogether. The most familiar of these delusional notions are those of being a world savior or messiah, and also of being king, emperor of the world, or indeed, of the universe.

The Apotheosis in Israelite Myth and Ritual

The Israelite New Year was a festival of enthronement, that is, of yearly reenthronement, and the Royal Psalms again are explicit as the spoken text of the rites. After his encounter with death in the sacred drama, the king calls to Yahweh for help, and at dawn the deity enters the scene in power in the role of savior, and is victor over the foe. The day of victory is proclaimed and the blessing of Yahweh is invoked for prosperity and increase, symbolized by the carrying of festal boughs indicating fertility:

This is the day on which Yahweh hath acted;
Let us rejoice and be glad therein.
O Yahweh, grant salvation!
O Yahweh, grant prosperity!

. . .

Blessed is he that cometh in the Name of Yahweh!
We greet you from the House of Yahweh;
Yahweh is God, and hath given us light!
Join in the dance with festal boughs
Up to the horns of the altar![1]

The triumphal procession is assembled at Israel's spring, Gihon, where very likely there is a baptismal lustration of the king and a ritual cup of the cosmic waters is given him:[2]

What a spectacle was Thy procession, O God,
The procession of my God, my King, into the sanctuary!
Singers went before, minstrels followed behind;
In the middle were maidens playing the timbrel.
In companies they greeted God,
Even Yahweh, from Israel's Spring.[3]

As Yahweh appears now at dawn as victor over the enemy, his mastery over the cosmic waters turns them to their rightful life-giving purpose. A basin in the temple designates the waters of the abyss, and also the temple is envisioned as standing directly over the abyss itself, issuing forth from a river to nourish the earth:[4]

As for 'The River,' its streams make glad the city of God,
The most holy abode of the Most High.
With God in her midst she cannot be shaken;
God doth help her as the morning appeareth.
The nations clamour, the kingdoms reel;
At the sound of His Voice the earth is in turmoil
Yahweh of Hosts is with us;
The God of Jacob is our stronghold.[5]

The procession joyfully circumambulates the holy mount and its walls, a ritual act that characteristically honors and pays homage to the center:

> *Let the daughters of Judah rejoice*
> *Because of Thine acts of judgement!*
> *March around Zion, Go round about her,*
> *Number her towers,*
> *Pay heed to her ramparts,*
> *Pass between her palaces,*
> *That ye may tell the coming generation*
> *That such is God!*
> *Our God, who abideth for ever,*
> *Is our leader against 'Death.'*[6]

From his position of mastery over the abyss ("The River"), his governance extends over all of the created world:

> *May he also rule from sea to sea,*
> *And from 'The River' to the ends of the earth.*
> *May the creatures of the wild bow down before him,*
> *And his enemies lick the dust.*[7]

Yahweh is master of the kingdoms of the world in his capacity as lord of the thunder and the storm, typical attributes of the warrior god of that part of the world:

> *Ye kingdoms of the earth, sing unto God,*
> *Sing the praises of the Lord,*
> *Of Him who rideth through the ancient and lofty heavens;*
> *Lo, He uttereth His voice, a mighty Voice!*
> *Ascribe might unto God,*
> *Whose majesty is over Israel,*
> *And His might in the clouds!*[8]

The awesomeness of this godhead is brought out in the following hymn of praise, in which the voice of his thunder is full of numinous dread and wonder. The hymn is borrowed from the earlier Canaanite cult of the thunder god.[9] His enthronement as king is at the same time his assumption of mastery and control over the flood, as he is seated at the center over the abyss:

The Voice of Yahweh soundeth over the waters;
The most glorious God hath thundered forth,
Even Yahweh, over the many waters.
The Voice of Yahweh is full of power;
The Voice of Yahweh is full of splendour.
The Voice of Yahweh shattereth the cedars,
Yahweh doth shatter the cedars of Lebanon.

. . .

He maketh Lebanon skip like a calf,
And Sirion like the young of the wild-ox.
The Voice of Yahweh cleaveth flames of fire;
The Voice of Yahweh convulseth the wilderness,
Yahweh doth convulse the wilderness of Kadesh.
The Voice of Yahweh doth make hinds to calve,
And causeth the birth of kids in haste,
While all His Temple echoeth the word 'Glory!'
Yahweh is enthroned over the flood:
Yahweh is enthroned as King for ever.
Yahweh will give strength to His people;
Yahweh will endow His people with welfare.[10]

Meanwhile the Davidic king is equally made victor over his enemies, by this intervention of the king god, and he thus assumes the exalted role of head of the nations and ruler of the world. The first Davidic kings were given the imposing title of King of Kings, matching the position of Yahweh as ruler of the assembly of the lesser king gods:[11]

Thou dost deliver me from my people's struggles;
Thou dost make me head of the nations;
People serve me that I have not known.

. . .

Yahweh liveth! *Blessed be my rock!*
The God who doth save me is supreme,

The God who hath granted me vengeance,
And subdued the peoples beneath me!

. . .

Therefore I will thank Thee amid the nations, O Yahweh,
I will sing praises to Thy Name,
To Him who doth give great victories to His king
And showeth devotion to His [*Anointed*],
To David and his seed for ever.[12]

The well-known Psalm of David gives the account of his exaltation into the kingship, his person sacrosanct as servant and son by adoption to his divine father. His anointment as the chosen one and the granting of the assurance of the covenant of mutual loyalty define his relation to the divine father. Meanwhile all are reminded that Yahweh is actually Israel's real king, just as he is also lord over the divine assembly of the king gods: the Davidic king is one of the Elohim like them:[13]

Of old Thou didst speak by a prophet
To Thy votaries, and saidst—
"I have bestowed aid upon a manly one,
I have exalted a youth from among the people.
"I have found David, My Servant;
With My holy oil I have anointed him,
"So that My Hand shall be His constant support,
Mine Arm also shall strengthen him."

. . .

"He shall cry unto Me, 'Thou art my Father,
My God and the Rock that is my salvation.'
"I on My part will make him My first-born,
The highest of earthly kings,
"Evermore will I keep My devotion for him
And my covenant in faithfulness to him.
"I will make his seed to endure for ever
And his throne as the days of heaven."

. . .

"I have made a covenant with My chosen one;
I have sworn to David My Servant.

"I will establish thy seed for ever;
Yea, I will maintain thy throne through all generations."
The heavens declare Thy wondrous work, O Yahweh,
Even Thy faithfulness in the assembly of the holy ones.
For who in the sky can be compared with Yahweh,
Is like Yahweh among the gods?
A God who is awesome in the council of the holy ones,
He is great and terrible above all who are about Him.
O Yahweh, God of Hosts, who is like unto Thee,
Strong, O Yah, and with Thy faithfulness all about thee?

. . .

For it is Yahweh who is really our shield;
It is the Holy One of Israel who is really our King.[14]

BACKGROUND OF THE IMAGE

Unlike Israel, Egypt had a true "divine kingship," in that the pharaoh was Horus made manifest, and Horus was embodied in the pharaoh.[15] The king's likeness to the sun became increasingly emphasized in time, with special reference to his role as upholder of justice, and thus the solar god, Re, was recognized as a major element in the nature of the kingship as well; in this case, the relation of the king to the god was one of sonship.[16] In the earliest form of the enthronement and reenthronement rite, the Sed Festival, the king dramatized the role of hero, avenging the death of his father Osiris and demonstrating his rightful claim to the throne by carrying a legal document to that effect in his hand as he danced the Dedication of the Field (the field representing the land).[17] A fourth divine nature lay in the identification of the king with the creator god, Atum, as he ascended the throne representing the Primeval Hill where Atum as First King stood over the Land.[18] A magnificent procession of the gods, designated by their standards and emblems, ushered in the ceremonies. Universal dominion was dramatized, as we have already noted, by the seating of the king on each of four thrones successively facing the four cardinal directions, and releasing arrows (in other ceremonies, geese) into these quarters of the world. The double crown was placed on his head, representing his rulership over the two halves of the world, South and North, or Upper and Lower Egypt.

In Mesopotamia, we have observed, the kings were not generally divine, but only in certain circumstances; that is, those individuals who were selected by the goddess Ishtar to be her bridegroom in the Sacred Marriage.[19] The honor thus conferred by her put the king in the role of Tammuz, son or brother and lover of the goddess, and giver of life to flocks and vegetation. In this respect the king took the part of Gardener of the Gods.[20] In other respects he was the earthly representative of Enlil, Lord Wind or Storm (Enlil of the Sumerians, later Marduk of the Akkadians, and again later Assur of the Assyrians). This role emphasized his warrior aspect, imposing order on the world by enforcement of law within the realm and of conquest without.[21] In either role, whatever the status of the royal personage, the kingship itself was distinctly of divine origin, for it had been a gift from Anu, supreme god of the high sky, "when king-ship was lowered from heaven" together with its emblems of the regalia.[22] From early Sumerian times in the fully expanded form of the kingship, the title claimed had the heady quality of universal overlordship, "Lord of the Four Quarters," "King of the Universe," or "King of the Four Directions," inasmuch as, again, the kingdom was equated with the world, its form a copy of the heavenly model of the cosmos, (which Gaster has given the term *topocosm,*[23] and Campbell has called *mesocosm*).[24]

The Canaanite kingship was in line with others of the Near East even though not much is known from the texts of the extent to which the king identified himself with the king god, or of the exact form of the enthronement drama. The inference seems clear, however, that the mythological model of the earthly king was in the complex figure of Baal, whose name means "Lord." He combined the features of the gods of the storm and of the vegetation; in his Enlil role he was storm god, warrior, and supreme ruler; in his Ninurta role, dragon slayer and vanquisher of Death (Mot); and in his Tammuz role, suffering death and descent into the underworld, to be rescued by his sister and lover, Anat.[25] After his victory over the dragon, Lord River, Baal was enthroned in his palace at the earth's center atop Mt. Zaphon directly over the abyss, from which he asserted control over the flood waters. The hymn praising his thunderous voice and might[26] was taken over intact by the Israelites as Psalm 29 (as just quoted above) to extol Yahweh in the same image.

The Apotheosis in Psychic Form

In examining the different forms of the theme of the apotheosis in persons undergoing the process of this syndrome, we may recognize several kinds of framework and idiom: religious, political, and heroic or cultural, which overlap so much that they are hardly distinct from one another.

In the religious vein, one may feel oneself to be a world reformer, prophet, or saint, in the milder forms. With a little more grandeur, one might be a founding father of a faith, or a messiah, sometimes identified with a historical personage of this calling. In the more extreme forms, one becomes a deity, most commonly among males as the Second Coming of Christ, and among females, as the Virgin Mary.

The political idiom, of course, takes the form of kingship and its derivatives. One may believe oneself to be a divine king or biblical king of some sort, and as just mentioned, king of the nation, the world, or even the universe. Often the idea is of being a new leader or founder of a nation, or perhaps president. Women patients commonly feel they are queen or wife to such leaders, and sometimes a biblical or historical queen in their own right.

The heroic motif is mostly heard among the male patients, in the form of being number one defender of the nation against perils, or overcoming enemies or monsters; they arrogate to themselves the qualities of a superman, and relate accounts of feats of daring, prowess, and great strength.

The cultural form of this heroism appears as a claim to extraordinary giftedness in wisdom or intellect or science; the person may believe him- or herself world-famous for creative genius or artistry in some field.

One person in my series rang all the changes in this theme of the apotheosis (Case 2). He has also been discussed in full in another book,[27] but his ideation also serves well to illustrate the imagery of the apotheosis.

His inflated self-image in his psychotic break makes itself explicit in each of the categories mentioned. In the political, he called himself "Ace High," an ace airman who led the defense of his country against its enemy, Communist Russia, which was plotting to capture not only this nation but also the world. As usual, communism was conceived as being on the side of the Devil, standing for darkness and slavery. However, at other moments this person expected to be made head of that enemy faction instead. He was also a second George Washington, founder of his country, also Prince Valiant, king of the nation, who sent 300 young men to the Korean War as a sacrifice for his kingdom; his own death also was such a sacrifice. In another vein, the Germans were plotting to capture the world and planning to make him their emperor of the world.

This person had fantasies of four kings, rulers of the four cardinal directions, but focusing on a conflict of major proportions between the King of the North and the King of the South.

In the religious idiom, Christ was understood to be leading the good half of the world against the Devil's. The young man saw himself as another Christ, come to lead that struggle, and to be crucified and to rise again from the dead. Paralleling the tale of the four kings was a mythlike account of the Garden of Eden and its being occupied first by the Trinity, Father, Son, and Holy Ghost, but then later "taken over" by the Devil. In a different context this person felt himself as Adam with his therapist as Eve, as First Man and First Woman, and their son as David and also Christ.

In the role of hero the patient performed many exploits of strength and daring. He was Richard the Lion-Hearted and had killed a tiger and strangled a serpent when only an infant. He was also a Japanese hero, who overcame monsters, and in the guise of a serpent developed a "vicious power to strike back," and slew a tarantula who was really a Japanese mother dressed as a warrior.

In the image of the supremely accomplished man he called himself the "man of steel," with the "strength of a hundred." The Germans wanted to make use of his gifts as chief of their superscientists who would master the world of the heavens and the universe through their skill in astronomy. They would shoot him to the moon by rocket ship because only he would be able to survive on it. He saw himself as the "most perfect man" and a "leading scientist."

The observation that Jung made in 1912,[28] that when the regression gets under way the image of the hero is constellated, and that the hero's basic nature is solar, is due for consideration at this point. Jung visualized the sun hero's "night sea journey," following his death in the west and toward his rebirth in the east, as the most fitting and universal expression of the descent into the underworld of the unconscious in the renewal process. It is curious that among psychotic individuals the only instance in my practice that I have encountered of this myth form was in this case, in the context of the many variations of the heroic motif. The image was very archaic, though clothed in modern dress. This person drew the round of the earth, as encompassed by a circular ocean around its periphery, and as divided by a vertical line into halves belonging to the democratic and the communistic factions. In maps of antiquity, notably the Greek with its Okeanus, and the Nordic, one sees evidence of a customary view of the world as thus bounded by the sea at its circumference. The young man then asked me to take him in my "underwater school," which went by submarine from this country to Russia under my captaincy. This indoctrination would then become an initiation experience for him, in which he could learn the hidden truths of "the other side."

While there are many types of hero cycles, from those of tribal societies up to the most developed urban ones, we seem to find this hero image in the modern psyche occurring as one among the several facets of the ideology of kingship. When Jung wrote of the solar hero, the history and the myth and ritual forms of the archaic kingship were not yet known as they are now. From the ideology of the sacral kingship are derived the several forms of hero, whether the "king's champion," the messianic reformer, or the sage, the enlightened one. In this mythological context, the sun god embodied the cosmic law and hence the social code. In variations where the sky god personified the cosmic order, the sun god captured the epitome of the regularity that that heavenly body so faithfully maintains from day to day and thus retained the essence of the sky principle of light and order.[29]

The hero as champion was portrayed as the slayer of dragons, giants, or monsters, and as the defender of the realm from the threat of its enemies. In the Egyptian Horus we discern the young royal champion of his father, avenging his death and becoming heir to his throne. In the Mesopotamian myth, young Ninurta similarly fought the dragon, acting as his father's champion rescuing him from the realm of death. It is interesting to find in the contemporary art forms this youthful hero depicted with club and lion pelt, revealing him as the original model of the later Heracles, hero of heroes.[30] It seems that this young royal hero figure is the youthful aspect of the king god, qualifying himself for the throne in the process of the renewal of the kingship.

The messianic hero has already been described in an earlier chapter as a more evolved and developed pattern of kingship ideology of which it is an internalized form. His role emphasizes the renewal and revivification of the spirit in the kingdom, with special reference to the people's spontaneous adherence to its structure of values and meanings, which derive from the cosmic law and which form the social code.

The motif of the supremely accomplished heroic man belongs equally to this ideology. The ideal of kingship had originated in the idea that the royal figure was the "unique man," supremely endowed with all the highest qualities of human nature.[31] In Egypt he alone possessed at first an immortal soul.[32] In China the Sage was the very embodiment of the fully accomplished human potential, the equal and equivalent of the Son of Heaven, the Emperor.[33]

These qualities of the Unique Man and of the fully accomplished human potential point the way toward our understanding of the meaning of this imagery, of this apotheosis in the idiom of the kingship. The king is the image of the center, personified. In the individual psychic form, the kingly ruler is the governing center of the inner world, supreme over the fourfold structure of the organization of this interior psychic cosmos. Just as the king once embodied the potency of the center in providing both the life-giving and the order-giving principles, so we must read this image today as signifying that the psychic center does the same, that it has a *Logos* function of promoting organization and an *Eros* function of promoting livingness. This central archetype or affect image contains within itself the full potential or range of possibilities of any psyche, just as the image suggests. The uniqueness of the individual is delineated and promised in this figure, and thus individuation and fulfillment are the particular work of this affect image. The principal means by which it accomplishes its ends are those of the renewal process.

The question that always remains to be worked out by any individual in whom this image is activated is how to relate in a healthy way to this powerful center. To identify with the central archetype obviously sets the paranoid process in motion: the inflation, the constellating of its opposite, and the threat of being undone. The more difficult task is to find a way to relate to this archetype while it does its work, without falling into such inflation by identifying with it.

7. THE UNION OF OPPOSITES

The mythological form of union with the opposite sex may be thought of as the converse of the fear of the reversal of opposites and of being overcome by the other sex. Here, in the ideology of the Sacred Marriage is the highest exaltation of the intercourse of masculine and feminine into its essence, its *eidos.* The Sacred Marriage refers not so much to the wedding or coitus of the mundane kind between two individuals, as to the sexual or marital union of mythological personages of quite nonindividual nature. As an affect image it represents an epitome of the meaning and emotion of love, not as in tender concern for a particular partner, but as in the absorption in the experience of the erotic passion. Not only is the motif intimately bound up with the interplay of opposites, but is equally with the new birth motif that follows.

The Sacred Marriage in Israelite Myth and Ritual

In Israel, needless to say, the strict ruling out of any trace of the Goddess from the scriptures left the records bereft of any reference to the Sacred Marriage. Indirectly we have evidence that until the reforms of the eighth century B.C., there remained survivals of Canaanite beliefs and practices in the temple, notably in the "Ashera," the conical stone emblems of the Goddess; she was partner to Yahweh as El Elyon, "The Highest," in the same manner as Ashtera had been to El in the Canaanite pantheon.[1] In the Royal Psalms, while there is no mention of a *hieros gamos* between Yahweh and a consort, it is said of the Davidic king that he was "born from the womb of Dawn," which is a direct reference to his being given ritual birth by this very goddess derived from Canaan.[2] Also, it is believed that the "booths of greenery," that were prominent in the New Year Feast of Tabernacles, had reference to the similar booth of greenery that housed the Mesopotamian sacred marriage.[3] While classical Judaism was bereft of a female principle, except for a metaphorical marriage of God to Israel,[4] this element is restored to its rightful place in the Christian reforms, with its myth form of the Annunciation and impregnation of the Virgin by the Holy Spirit.

However, there are Royal Psalms that are understood to be ritual texts of a sacred marriage performed at least by the Davidic king, the representative of Yahweh:[5]

My heart is inditing a good matter:
I speak of the things which I have made touching the king:
My tongue is the pen of a ready writer.
Thou art fairer than the children of men:
Grace is poured into thy lips:
Therefore God hath blessed thee forever

. . .

Thine arrows are sharp
in the heart of the king's enemies;
whereby the people fall under thee.
Thy throne, O God, is forever and ever:
The sceptre of thy kingdom is a right sceptre.
Thou lovest righteousness, and hatest wickedness:
Therefore God, thy God, hath anointed thee
With the oil of gladness above thy fellows.
All thy garments smell of myrrh, and aloes, and cassia,
Out of the ivory palaces, whereby they have made thee glad.

King's daughters were among thy honorable women:
Upon thy right hand did stand the queen in gold of Ophir.
Hearken, O daughter, and consider, and incline thine ear:
forget also thine own people, and thy father's house;
For he is thy Lord; and worship thou him.

. . .

The king's daughter is all glorious within.

. . .

She shall be brought unto the king in raiment of needlework.
The virgins her companions that follow her shall be brought unto thee.
In gladness and rejoicing shall they be brought:
They shall enter into the king's palace.
Instead of thy fathers shall be thy children,
Whom thou mayest make princes in all the earth.
I will make thy name to be remembered in all generations:
Therefore shall the people praise thee forever, and ever.[6]

BACKGROUND OF THE IMAGE

In archaic civilizations, as is well known, it was felt to be a vital necessity to ensure the productiveness of nature by ritual means. While in tribal societies these rituals might have taken the form of communal sexual activities, in the urban era they became part of the royal function. The king, as representative of the sky, united with a corresponding personification of the earth in a *hieros gamos,* usually in the New Year festival.

In Egypt, the most renowned instance of this divine union was that of the Sacred Marriage of Edfu, performed at the New Year of the summer harvest season.[7] In it the Falcon God, Horus, identical with the king, was brought in effigy by barge along the Nile to the Temple of Hathor, the Falcon Goddess: after a ritual combat, he resided with her fifteen days in nuptial union. According to this particular mythological constellation, the god appeared as Horus, the Elder, his aspect not as son of Isis and Osiris, but of Hathor, probably a more archaic derivation.[8] As often was the case in such royal ceremonial, the marriage was incestuous, incest being "the prerogative of the gods," and where kings were divine, of kings.

However, the more classical expression of the Sacred Marriage for our present purposes was that which served as the culmination of the Mesopotamian New Year festival. It was literally the high point of the festival, for the union was consummated atop the Ziggurat or stage tower, which had at its summit (where it touched the sky, so to speak) a *gigunu,* a shrine of greenery. In it the king as representative of the god embraced a hierodule, perhaps the queen or a priestess, personifying the Goddess. It was the wedding of sky and earth on the one hand, but along the lines of an earlier and more archaic ceremonial, of Tammuz and Ishtar, which was again an incestuous relation.[9] It will be recalled that the criterion of the divinity of Mesopotamian kings appears to have resided in the special grace conferred on the monarch by the Goddess, in her selection of him as her royal consort and in her entering into nuptial relations with him in this ceremony. The function of the king as Giver of Life predominates in this phase of the ritual, and its image is that of the Gardener of God, in which role the king tended the sacred tree on the Mountain of the Gods and ministered to its cyclic waxing and waning of life, which was personified in the figure of the dying god, Tammuz.[10] The significance of the Sacred Marriage in this ancient form was more the invigoration of the realm, its prosperity and its herds and its crops, than the conception of a divine child.

The Canaanite derivative of this ritual marriage has been poorly preserved in the tablets from Ras Shamra, but they at least make quite clear the fact of its inclusion in the myth of Baal. In a buffalo-filled canebrake the king god meets his sister Anath:

Puissant Baal lifts up his eyes,
Lifts up his eyes and beholds,
Beholds the Maiden Anath,
Fairest among Baal's sisters.
Before he rises, he stands,
At her feet he kneels and falls down.[11]

As a prelude to the union with her, mention is made of the sacred combat, as usual: "We'll thrust my foes into the earth, / To the ground them that rise 'gainst thy brother!"[12] There is an implication, which remains unclear (the dashes in the text indicate lost portions, not censorious editing) that the couple join as ox and cow:

He seizes and holds her womb;
She seizes and holds his stones.
Baal——to an ox.
——the Maiden Anath
——to conceive and bear.[13]

Once more, it goes without saying, the union is incestuous, between the Royal Brother-Sister Pair.

The Sacred Marriage in Psychic Form

A common expression of the image in the psychotic form is, among women, the belief that they have been selected as bride to Christ or to God, or perhaps have been visited by the Holy Spirit as the Virgin Mary had been; among men the corresponding form is election by the Goddess as spouse. The union may be consummated by partners who take the role of First Man and First Woman, Adam and Eve, or it may be likened to the cosmic marital union of Sun and Moon, or perhaps of King and Queen or Prince and Princess.

One patient of mine in her mid-thirties (Case 8), who had not worked out a satisfactory relation in her marriage, was inclined to be possessed by overwhelming infatuations in which were aroused not only strong sexual passions but religious ones, intermingled. In her psychosis she saw herself as Mary Magdalene in her dark, lower, and sexual self, and as Christine in her light, higher, and spiritual self. The latter name referred to her belief that she was Christ, for in her confusion of sexual identity she experienced herself as in some sense male, in some female. She would say, "I am the Lord Christ" or "God" or "the Son of God," but at other times, "I am the Daughter of Judah, the Prophetess," or "the Emissary of God." In this latter role she believed God had chosen her to give birth to his Divine Child, "because I am good," and "because I am already the mother of John the Baptist." This "will be a child of the Spirit," she asserted, and not of her husband; for she had been in love with a man and had seen in him the face of Christ, and she thought she had made love with him, and thus with Christ. Here the theme merges with the New Birth and New Society motifs, for she was convinced she was pregnant from this union, with a baby that "had been dirty but God made it clean again." He shall save the world, she declared, "for he shall be called David Emmanuel," a clear reference to the Messianic prophecies. Once she thought the child already born.

The sacred marriage as an affect image in this process is in all probability one of the most important of its elements. As already pointed out, it has still to do with opposites, but this time as their union and not as their strife. The imagery promises a new life-giving fertility and productiveness, and in some forms more specifically, the conceiving of a new life form in the person of a divine child.

What, then, is this fertility and new life in our psychological terms? We have a hint in the studies of ritual lamentations that preceded the marriage, the phase in which the earth has been bereft of the life-giver; the mourning is in the context of the desiccation and dormancy of the life in nature. The shedding of tears is more than the expression of grief, in this case, and has the function of sympathetic or mimetic magic, inducing the shedding of the rain waters on the ground like tears.[14] Psychologically, this image also implies that the flow of emotion has a life-producing significance. We can also make the statement, from the evidence of various expressions of the Wasteland motif, that the absence of water implies the cessation of life-giving affectivity. Then the erotic ceremonial of the sacred marriage induces the return of the warm and vital affective forces.[15]

What is so highly significant in this psychotic process is that the emotion roused with this affect image is specifically the loving one. Along with the sexuality comes an upwelling of loving passion, often accompanied by tenderness and concern—those very emotions that in the prepsychotic personality are customarily suppressed and stunted in their development, and that yet belong to the schizoid personality's sensitive makeup.

I therefore see in this symbolism the basic expression of the affect image for the capacity for lovingness, still existing only as an archetypal potential. This symbolism represents the *Eros* principle, which, as it differentiates and enters conscious experience, grows from the state of mere potential into actualization, and becomes the motivation for genuine personal concern and closeness in relationship. One should bear in mind that as an affect image the sacred marriage is purely "idealized," that is, a nonindividual and nonspecific representation, not at all of an actual loving relationship, but of the possibility of and readiness for such relationship.

8. NEW BIRTH

The motif of the New Birth represents in symbolic form the fruit of the entire renewal process, and thus takes on a considerable significance. It is closely related to the theme of dying that had initiated the episode, in that death and rebirth are the two poles of a single process. Also it is a companion piece to the image of the sacred marriage insofar as the latter represents the nuptial union with a deity or royal spouse that conceives the divine child or infant saviour. In this sense, the work of salvation is often clearly expressed as the restoring of peace and order between warring factions in the cosmic conflict, and thus what had been a clash of opposites becomes a uniting of them as a promise of world integration.

In the comparative myth and ritual forms, we have been observing that the New Year ceremonies were in essence a means of rejuvenating the sacral king and the kingship, and that renewal could take the form either of resurrection or resuscitation from death, or of conceiving a son and successor.

The New Birth in Israelite Myth and Ritual

Salvation and resuscitation from death are the principal expressions of renewal in the Israelite drama: by Yahweh's own intervention as savior a mighty act is performed that restores the king to life out of the grasp of death:

Hark to the cheers of victory
In the tents of the righteous!
Yahweh's Right Hand acteth mightily,
Yahweh's Right Hand is exalted,
Yahweh's Right Hand acteth mightily!
I am not to die but live,
And relate the deeds of Yah.
Yah hath chastened me sore,
But He hath not given me over to 'Death.'

Open for me the gates of righteousness,
That I may enter thereby and acknowledge Yah.

. . .

The stone which the builders rejected
Now doth crown the corner.
This is Yahweh's doing;
It is marvellous in our eyes.[1]

Among the Royal Psalms, the two that are most absolutely certain in their antiquity and in their function as texts of the rite are the "enthronement oracles," Psalms 2 and 110.[2] The first of these, after recapitulating the cosmic conflict with the foreign kings, specifically notes that the Davidic king is enthroned on Yahweh's own holy mount of Zion as his son by adoption, begotten and born on this day of the victory over Death; his dominion is to be universal over the whole of the created world:

Why did the nations become insurgent,
And the peoples fall to useless plotting?
The kings of the earth took up their stand,
The rulers conferred together,
Against Yahweh and against His Messiah.
"Let us snap their bonds asunder,
And let us fling their cords off from us."
He who is throned in heaven doth laugh;
The Lord maketh mock of them.
Then he doth speak to them in His anger,
And in His wrath He doth dismay them.
"But I, as you see, have set up My king
Upon Zion, My sacred mountain."
Let me tell of Yahweh's decree!
He hath said to me, "Thou art My son;
"This day have I begotten thee.
"Ask of me, and I will make
"The nations thine inheritance,
"The ends of the earth thy possession."[3]

The second royal oracle again enthrones the king on the holy mount of Yahweh at his right hand. The coronation day was at the same time the day of the king's ritual birth from the womb of the Dawn Goddess, according to the old Canaanite agrarian formula in which the sky god impregnates her with his dew.[4] He is to be a priest king, of the same order as the Canaanite kings of Jerusalem, Melchizedek ("king of righteousness") being the Canaanite royal host to Abraham on a historic occasion. The phrase "drinking of a stream by the way" refers to the ritual in which the king was given a cup of the cosmic waters at Israel's Spring, Gihon, at the start of the triumphal procession:

Oracle of Yahweh to my lord!
Sit thou at My Right Hand, while I make
Thine enemies a stool for thy feet.
Yahweh doth extend thy powerful sceptre;
Rule from Zion amidst thy foes!
Thou hast the homage of thy people on the day of thy birth
In sacred splendour from the womb of Dawn.
Thou hast the dew wherewith I have begotten thee;
Yahweh hath sworn beyond recall.
Thou art priest for ever
After the order of Melchizedek.
The Lord hath smitten away at thy right hand,
Judging kings in the day of His anger.
He hath filled with corpses amid the nations;
He hath smitten heads o'er all the wide earth,
Drinking of a stream by the way,
Thus holding His Head on high![5]

BACKGROUND OF THE IMAGE

In Egypt, both forms of new life occur in the myth and ritual. The deceased king, Osiris, was described in the myth as being sought and found and brought to life again by his sisters, Isis and Nephthys.[6] Also, Isis was impregnated by him and conceived Horus, who was destined to become King of the Living while his deceased father would become King of the Dead.[7] Before he could accede to the throne, Horus had to enter a contest with his wicked uncle Seth, who had tried to steal the throne from Osiris. One form of this encounter was a legal dispute before the company of the gods.[8] In this dispute, his mother Isis, to assure them of the validity of Horus' claim, took Horus to her breast and gave him suck. This moment is a favorite theme in Egyptian art, being an instance of the age-old theme of the madonna and child. The motif had existed in sculpture from much more ancient, neolithic times, when the dominant divinity was the Great Mother, represented often in her iconography as the mother suckling her divine child.[9] The Egyptian form was the earliest of this genre that had to do specifically with the divine kingship. The arrival of Horus on the scene was a turning point in the ritual narrative; up to then, the land was riven in conflict between Osiris of the Northern and Seth of the Southern Kingdom, while the victory of Horus now brought the "Union of the Two Lands" under the Double Crown,[10] an eloquent image of the resolution of opposites.

In Mesopotamia, the form of the death and resuscitation of the king god is roughly parallel, with certain significant differences. The myth and the ritual versions differ enough to give some difficulty in allocating the right parts to the right players. In his ritual "Tammuz role," the king god is temporarily overwhelmed by the powers of the Abyss. This role is modeled on the myth of the young vegetation god. Like Osiris, Tammuz is drowned and then sought and brought back to life by the Goddess.[11] In his Storm God role, as Enlil (later as Marduk), the king god is liberated from the hold of death by his son and hero champion Ninurta (or later Nabu). Though the Sacred Marriage follows the liberation from death, the motif of the conception of a divine child is not included in the ritual form. It is evident this divine son has already been born, thus to be the agent of rescue. The divine child motif occurs, however, in the creation myth accompanying the ritual.[12] Enki (Ea), the old wise one, was the first to do combat with the forces of Tiamat, overcoming her kingly delegate, Apsu, by putting a magic spell on him. As his reward he took possession of the watery Abyss, also called Apsu, for his own palace, and there with his consort conceived the divine child, the Storm God Enlil (or later Marduk). When the time came for the gods to face the monster Tiamat once more, Enki was able to bring forth a new hero champion to dispatch her. This sequence combines the motifs of combat, enthronement in control of the flood waters of the Abyss, and Sacred Marriage culminating in the birth of the Divine Child.

The Canaanite story of the new birth is unfortunately shrouded in obscurity because the tablets have been poorly preserved. After the sacred marriage of Baal and his sister consort, apparently in conjugal union as bovine partners, Baal ascended the throne on Zaphon and the maiden Anat came up to him:

In the pleasance, the Mount of Possession,
She cries aloud to Baal:
"Receive of Baal godly tidings,
Yea, receive, O Son of Dagon:
A wild-ox is born to Baal,
A buffalo to Rider of the Clouds."
Puissant Baal rejoices.[13]

One is reminded of the tale of Zeus pursuing and possessing Europa as bull and cow, a comparison not amiss in view of the direct historical descent that has been established from Canaan to Crete and from Crete to Greece.[14] Bull gods had existed from time immemorial through the Neolithic era, and vestiges of them remained in later times. In Egypt, for instance, one of Hathor's forms was a cow, (as well as vulture or falcon), and as the son of this mother the Horus king was sometimes called a Golden Calf or Strong Bull:[15] on Pepi's temple was inscribed:

Pepi comes to thee, O Re!
A calf of gold, born of heaven,
The soft one of gold, formed by the Hesat-cow.[16]

The New Birth in Psychic Form

The various instances of the new birth image in psychotic form are quite similar. One finds often that the very generalized characteristics of the newborn child or of the reborn state become more specific and individual only with the differentiation that both time and experience bring. Women most commonly express the idea of giving birth to some extraordinary child, savior, redeemer, messiah, or other form of world leader. They very frequently express their belief that they are pregnant, and this symbolic expression is the occasion for many a pregnancy test! Fortunately enough, this is one unconscious configuration that does not take on a psychosomatic form. Men, for obvious reasons, express the idea somewhat differently. The individual more commonly feels that he is going through a new birth or rebirth himself, and that he is being selected as the new savior or redeemer.

A male in his early thirties (Case 3), unmarried, and a Catholic, had the experience of being put through "the Three Ways of Initiation," which meant going to Hell, to Purgatory, and back again, which he compared to "Making the Way of the Cross." He saw the world as riven in a war between the Sodality of Our Lady of Fatima and Communism. In this he had been selected as the "special apostle and chief defender" of the Goddess, who was about to rule the world, and thus saw himself as possessing the characteristics and powers of Christ, as his Second Coming. Looking up at the ceiling one day, he had a vision of the Immaculate Conception (in this case, Mary). The idea of a marriage to the Virgin Mary was prevalent in many forms, although the forms Mary took all were in the image of redheads. There was Cora, who was the Sacred Heart; Rose, who was the Rose of Sharon; and Claire, who was Claire de Lune, and his sister. There was to be a birth, and this he visualized as twelve babies under the pillow. It was through Claire, his sister, that birth would come, and this offspring would be like an egg; he then drew the egg on paper. With this egg he drew his rebirth, which he was experiencing as the "Four Degrees of Initiation," which meant passing down and up through Purgatory, Hell, Heaven, and Earth. The result of rebirth he saw as the Victory of Heaven in the form of a new world order, that of the "World Mission of Our Lady of Fatima" in which there would prevail a new reign of tolerance for all creeds and colors without discrimination: this stage he drew as a circle in four quadrants of four colors, representing the four continents and four creeds and races.

Though this array of heady notions might seem quite uncon nected with real life, it did as a matter of fact have immediate bearing on the individual's conflict. He was fascinated by women, and admired and worshiped them at a distance but felt far too shy to approach them. He suffered fears of his sexual adequacy and consequent doubts about risking any closeness. In this context, the initiation he was undergoing involved, as he saw it, a difficult choice "between the Way of the Head and the Way of the Heart," with opposite callings to the priesthood or to marriage.

In this theme of new birth, then, regardless of the alternative forms it takes—new birth, rebirth, renewal, rejuvenation, or resurrection—the new life clearly is the image of a new governing figure that has the power to overcome his enemies and to establish a peaceful rule—that is, to transcend the clash of the opposites and bring a new unity. To find the psychological meaning of the image, we have only to transliterate these alternative forms into their equivalents on an experiential level.

The psyche in this process, as in its earlier phases, has become torn in a mortal conflict of cultural values, expressed in terms of "our side" against "the enemy." The images of death and of the clash of opposites appear to have as their goal the formation of a new image of the "center" that can redeem the psyche from its split state and give it a unity and wholeness. Such a symbolic resolution must begin as the representation of a generalized possibility or potential, and must differentiate with time and experience into ever more specific expressions describing just what attitudes, outlook, and values might serve such integrative interests. The renewal of the center thus becomes in time the reorganization of the self-image and thence of the entire self.

9. THE RENEWED SOCIETY

In the light of what has just been said concerning the conflict and resolution of cultural values, it is evident that the ideation of the new society interrelates closely with that of the new birth. In the play of images, this interrelationship reveals itself as a program for the new era under the coming leadership of the newly born divine being. Together, these images become a symbolic expression of a new order and new governing center, and often accompany a messianic advent of some sort.

The portrayal of the ideal state of society and its mores had its roots in the ancient New Year ceremonies. The ritual was designed to reestablish the right order and right relation to the divine patrons. These ways must return to the pristine condition at the beginning of time in the first rule of founding gods and heroes.

I have found confirmation of this derivation of messianic vision of a renewed society from the ritual forms we are describing. Mowinckel says of Deutero-Isaiah's prophecies, "He derived both the framework and the details from a feature of Israelite religion which was already central . . . namely those ideas and experiences which were associated with the most important festival of the temple cultus at Jerusalem . . . the festival of Yahweh's enthronement."[1] In those promises of a restoration, he says, "Point by point all the elements in the future hope and in eschatology can be traced back to corresponding conceptions in the enthronement festival."[2] This New Year rite reenacted the events of the *Urzeit*, the beginning time of the world, which then becomes transferred to the *Endzeit* (the end time). Mowinckel notes that "Eschatology is a reinterpretation of the mythology of the primordial time, as is clearly expressed in the *Epistle* of Barnabas: 'Lo, I make the last things like the first.'"[3]

The Determination of Destinies was an oracular procedure for searching the mind of the gods in order to know their favor or disfavor, and thus to ascertain whether things were in their right order or not. Each of the oracular readings took a somewhat primitive ceremonial form of what was later to emerge as fuller philosophical or spiritual expressions, in various cultures, of the harmonization of the realm's life with the "Will of Heaven." These expressions belonged to the more sophisticated era of the founding of the great religions and the great philosophies, mostly during the middle centuries of the first millennium B.C. There were prophets, seers, mystics, enlightened ones, sages, and philosophers at that juncture in the leading cultures of the time, who evolved a new concept of righteousness, not as mere obedience to the king and code, but as the realization that the atunement to the "will of heaven" was an individual accomplishment. The ideology of the kingship became thus democratized, individualized, and internalized. In each culture that produced such seers, there were visions of a golden age to come when perfect righteousness and virtue would prevail, and all men would become as the kings used to be, unique men and sons of heaven, carrying out the will of heaven on earth to order and sustain it.

This prophetic function, promising a new destiny for a new age, was, as I see it, the later and more differentiated and sophisticated version of the same intent that had been expressed in the more archaic "Determination of Destinies" of the New Year Rites.

The Renewed Society in Israelite Myth and Ritual

The prosperous order of both society and nature was believed by the Israelites to depend entirely on their earning the favor and approval of their divine king, Yahweh, and equally on the faithfulness of the Davidic king, who served as intermediary between the people and their god.[4] The order or disorder in the life of the sacral king at the heart of the realm determined the welfare of the natural and social world around him. "As it goes with the king, so goes it with the kingdom."[5]

At the New Year festival of Israel there was a Determination of Destinies not unlike the Mesopotamian procedure. Here divination was performed by the use of the Urim and Thummim, two tablets on the robe of the priest king that indicated positive and negative answers to questions.[6] The effort was to descry the "will of God" in respect to the pressing issues of the times, and accordingly to obey that will if things were to fare favorably under the rule of their king in heaven.

A Royal Psalm keynotes the basis of the Davidic king god's rule:

Thine is an Arm with might!
Thy Hand is strong, and Thy Right Hand on high.
Righteousness and justice are the foundation of Thy throne;
Devotion and fidelity are present before Thee.[7]

The foremost sign of divine favor is the manifestation of himself in his function of master over the flood waters, which he sends in their due season to fertilize the earth when the realm is in order, but which he withholds from the disobedient:

Thou wilt shed a generous rain, O God,
Over Thine inheritance, when it is exhausted,
That which Thou didst found, in which Thy family doth dwell,
Which in thy goodness Thou wilt keep in order for the humble,
O God.[8]

The king god's relation to the Davidic king is one of mutual loyalty to the covenant established from ancient times, and the kingly lineage is assured of perpetuity:[9]

I will not violate My covenant,
Nor alter that which hath passed My lips,
Once for all have I sworn by My Holiness,
To David I will not lie;
His seed shall endure for ever,
And his throne like the sun before Me,
Like the moon, which shall continue for ever,
A faithful witness in the sky.[10]

Again justice and righteousness are emphasized in the vision of a prosperous reign in this Royal Psalm of prayer for the blessing of the Davidic king. Welfare and peace and prosperity are indicated in the image of the rains sent by Yahweh, and divine favor is granted also in the form of perpetuity of David's lineage. The text makes clear the functions of the king as giver of order and giver of life, for righteousness resides in him and he acts like the rain itself:

O God, give Thy justice to the king,
And Thy righteousness to the king's son;
May he judge Thy people with righteousness
And Thy humble ones with justice.
Through righteousness let the mountains and hills
Bring welfare [*EVV.* '*peace*'*] *to the people.*
May he grant justice to the humble among the people;

. . .

(May he also continue) as long as the sun,
And, like the moon, through all generations.

**EVV* signifies standard English versions.

May he descend like rain upon the crop,
Like showers that water the earth.
May righteousness flourish in his days,
And welfare [EVV. 'peace'] abound till the moon
Be no more.[11]

An idyllic state of the realm is portrayed in these verses of blessing, in which the king's justice results in plenteous abundance and fruitfulness of the earth:

He will have pity upon the weak and needy;
Yea, the lives of the needy will he save.
He will protect their life from oppression and violence.
And their blood will be precious in his eyes.

. . .

So may one pray for him continually.
And bless him all the day long.
May there be a wealth of corn in the land
To the top of the mountains.
May the fruit thereof be as plenteous as Lebanon;
May they flower on the summit like the grass of the earth.
May his name endure for ever,
May his name continue as long as the sun;
Yea, may (all the families of the earth) bless themselves by him,
May all nations call him happy.[12]

An era of universal peace will result when Yahweh assumes the complete mastery over the nations:

Come, behold the deeds of Yahweh,
He maketh wars to cease throughout the earth.
He doth shatter the bow and snap the spear;
He doth burn the shields with fire.
"Be still and know that I, God,
Am high above the nations, high above the earth!"[13]

BACKGROUND OF THE IMAGE

The Egyptian pharaoh's functions were similarly, from the very beginning of the earliest dynasties, the giving of order and the giving of life.[14] Right order and justice were personified in Maat, daughter of the sun god, Re, and were divine attributes of the king's nature; he was son of the sun in his justice, and judged as a representative of Re.[15] The king's Ka, or "vital force," was the life-giving power given out to the realm through the person of the king from its source in the land of the ancestral dead, conveyed through him by the embrace of Horus by his father Osiris.[16] At his enthronement, the texts say the king prides himself in having achieved what had not been done since the time of Re at the beginning of time, namely restoring the pristine ideal conditions of the beginnings.[17] The world view of that culture saw the natural and social order as static; any innovations merely made manifest what had been potentially present in the original plan of creation. The order established at the beginning was normative for all time and was upheld by the king as its champion. Because the end of a year or of a reign, with the death phase of the ceremonies, represented the danger in disruption of the harmony between society and nature, the coronation equally represented a renewed order at the start of a new epoch, and hence partook of the quality of the original creation.[18]

In Mesopotamia the world view was different in that the order of nature and society was not an established static condition, but subject to the caprice of the gods. Humanity was created for the service of the gods. The great gods were the personifications of the powers in nature, and man's concern with the gods was to serve them out of desire to keep in harmony with nature and maintain a concord that otherwise tended to be unstable.[19] At each change of season and turning of the year, the gods could change the realm's fortune, because order was subject to the decrees of the gods in the divine assembly. The king could maintain the harmony with nature only by watching over the service to the gods; faithful service being rewarded with abundance and increase, the king's function was largely to act as husbandman to the land and not to disappoint the gods.[20] At the Second Determination of Destinies, there were expressions of fear that the fruits of the Sacred Marriage might be prevented by any guilt invoking the divine wrath. Failures, errors, or defilements might rob the rites of their beneficial consequences, and the gods in their divine assembly would judge whether or not to bestow their blessing for the ensuing period.[21] Man's happiness could reside only in living out the destiny for which he was created, to serve the gods well. Hence the period of atonement at the beginning of the festival was designed to restore right relations with the gods once more, and the Determination of Destinies was intended to assure the king of their favorable judgment.[22]

The Renewed Society in Psychic Form

In delusional fantasies the renewed society is usually pictured as a new golden age. This age is sometimes called a New Jerusalem, or Heavenly City, or Kingdom of God, when the expressions are conventionally Christian, and in such cases the new rule is on the part of a new Christ or New Mary. The image is of a reformed world and society, of perfect wisdom or virtue. It is frequently, however, more secular than Christian and may then be the outcome of political more than religious developments. The earmarks of the improved order are usually the same as of any vision of a golden age: a brotherhood of man, justice, equality, tolerance, love, kindness, and peace.

In order to show that the programs are, however, not always so identical in their import and feeling, I am going to quote the fantasies of two young women, which sketch out programs that are not only different but opposite in their import.

The first was a young woman (Case 10) who lived primarily in relationships and felt hampered by her professional identifications; I have discussed her in another work,[23] but the material bears repeating here in its comparison with the second young woman.

Her identifications were with Queen Elizabeth II, as a sweet and gentle young queen, and with the Earth Mother Goddess. In this role of Great Mother and Mother Eve she found herself creating a moon and stars and populating both them and the world. She had an especially tender feeling for the vegetation that grows from the earth—her earth—and felt a great concern for increasing its productivity to feed the excess population that she had caused. Also she felt an intense resentment of the activity of men in desecrating the earth by digging out from its depths the metals and minerals that belonged to it, that is, to her. She also had a fantasy of being the Virgin Mother and giving birth to the Redeemer.

Her image of the sacred city took the following form. She believed San Francisco to be the New Jerusalem, and the hospital to be the center, her palace made all of gold. In the stone grotto outside, on its altar, there took place a sacrifice of a certain man who was traitor to his country. Also in the grotto she witnessed the Nativity of the Savior, in which she felt herself to have a central role. The New Age was to involve a whole set of changes in the life of the city. All buildings, including public ones and industrial ones, were to be converted into homes, and the families were all to live together without having to leave to go to work. There were to be no industries and no use of metals, but rather all the families were to have their own plot of soil and were to grow from them the fruits of the earth. Part of the plan was also to reclaim land from the sea by filling in the coastal margins.

I would emphasize that the image of woman with which this individual identified is gentle, beneficent, creative, fertile, and nourishing; she did not identify with any male figure. There is a passing mention of elimination of men. The New Age and Holy City represents a revolt against the scientific and industrial way of life in favor of family life, relationship, nursing of the soil, and reverence for the earth.

The second young woman (Case 7) also has been given brief mention in a previous chapter. Her disposition was more cool and detached, and she lived primarily for her work, which tended to be administrative.

Her identifications were of two kinds. On the one hand she felt herself to be a witch with magic power and the Evil Eye, also to be Queen Elizabeth I as an evil queen, cold and ruthless, in both cases castrating to men. On the other hand, she believed herself to be several times reincarnated as a holy man, as Moses, Paul, Luther, and now herself, in each case a visionary leader.

Her image of the sacred city was depicted as follows. A new age was being ushered in, and the San Francisco Bay Area was the site for a New Bethlehem, which was to drop down from the sky. Spaceship balloons were to sail down from outer space, bringing new influences from heaven. All this activity was an achievement of science. There was to be no one new Savior or Christ, but the oldest son of each family was to be a "Son of Man," all Christs; they would be perfect men, knowing everything, and already knowing in childhood what we now only learn later. The result of this influx of these Sons of Man was to be an age in which people could live sensibly together, meaning a reconciliation between the opposing great political factions.

I wish to draw attention to the fact that the image of woman with which this individual identifies is evil and destructive, while the image of man is that of the holy seer and visionary. There is passing mention of elimination of women who are ineffective. The New Age and Holy City are explicitly descended from heaven and ruled by science and perfect knowledge. The rule of the Sons of Man also is masculine in character.

These two instances of the motif of the sacred and ideal society demonstrate the point that the same affect image can be woven into very different specific configurations, to give expression to a design of life and of societal participation that belongs uniquely to the individual's own general makeup. The affect image characteristically has this quality of generality and specificity, of collectivity and individuality.

This image of the new society is hard to see in its correct perspective because it appears so idyllic and idealistic as to have nothing to do with real life as it actually is. Is it mere wishful thinking and idle dreaming? The answer is that all such archetypal images are abstractions that represent only the essences of experience. In pure form they portray actual, effective, emotional potential, which with time and experience come closer to consciousness, and which then pass from their idealistic expression to their more differentiated forms. Similarly, the images of the hero, of the new birth, or of the marriage of prince and princess all are ideal epitomes of emotional experiences pictured in their most universal and schematic lineaments, awaiting differentiation.

In this case, the golden age or new society motif is the image of a culture seen as exteriorized, like all else either in psychosis or in ancient myth and ritual. Its actual meaning, however, can in time be recognized as describing the equivalent inner culture, that of the individual's own structure of values and meanings and outlook. The drive to reform society and to save the world belongs to the task of giving new shape to one's own inner world, which will then be expressed in terms of a design of life in actual social relations or societal participation.

10. THE QUADRATED WORLD

There has been a tendency of the human psyche for at least the last 5000 years to represent the world in the form of a quadrated circle. The motif belongs to the imagery of the center, differentiating it and making it explicit as the midpoint of a fully embodied geometrical structure.

I put this element of the process at the end of the discussion only because it is often apt to occur as the product of a considerable amount of work on the part of the unconscious process, as an expression of synthesis and resolution. However, the quadrated world image may occur at any point and in any phase along the way. Indeed, any of the elements of the process may be framed in the circle with a center—creation, cosmic conflict, sacred marriage, or any other—and one may therefore justifiably look on it as a sort of containing vessel of the process.

The comparative symbolism of the world image leaves something to be desired, inasmuch as it is not always easy to ascertain what the exact form was in each ancient culture. Unless surviving plastic art forms depict it, one must rely on verbal expressions, which are not always quite explicit. The key to understanding the imagery is that the ancient kingdom was conceived as a replica of the larger cosmos, and that it and the world were more or less interchangeable concepts. As already mentioned, Gaster has given this form of the world the term "topocosm"[1] and Campbell the term "mesocosm,"[2] to express this phenomenon of the cosmos in the large being reflected in the kingdom in the small.

The Quadrated World in Israelite Myth and Ritual

Neither Israel, nor its forebear, Canaan, reveal myth or ritual forms that indicate the shape of their universe. The only hint we have of the appearance of the motif is the identification of the king at his enthronement with the First Ancestral King, Adam, the Primodial Man, who was Keeper of the Garden of God in the Paradise of Eden, which seemed to have this form as a representation of the world image with four gates in the cardinal directions, and four rivers flowing from its center.[3]

BACKGROUND OF THE IMAGE

In Egypt the image is indicated in the hieroglyph for the word *city*, which is a circle sectioned by a cross on its side, that is, the so-called St. Andrew's cross.[4] In the ritual symbolism surrounding the figure of the king god, Horus, many allusions are made to the quadrating of the world. At the coronation, as we have seen, where the king reenacts the deeds of Horus, geese are dispatched into the four directions or arrows are shot in the same fashion. In iconography, Horus' four sons are represented in a lotus, and mention is made of four rivers emanating from his head.

In Mesopotamia, the titles of the kings of Sumer and Akkad indicate the quadrated structure of the world. They called themselves "King of the Universe," a claim validated by general social consensus and not by personal subjective inclination. One might say that sacral kings were the only individuals having fully legitimate right to the position of ruler of the universe without being tainted by paranoid thinking. These kings also called themselves "Lord of the Four Quarters," "Ruler of the Four Directions," governing "the four corners of the garden of the world." A stela of Hamurabi shows a rotating symbol of the sun or the sky suspended on a mechanism above and in front of the king god. This symbol has been called a sunwheel, but might better be considered an image of the sky with the sun at its center.[5] A late stela shows a map of the world with Babylon as ruling center and four pointed structures at the periphery pointing in the cardinal directions.[6]

Various parts of the Indoeuropean world have built cities, citadels, or military forts in the shape of quadrated circles and/or squares. Iranian cities of the fourth century B.C. were structured as circles with avenues and gates oriented to the cardinal directions,[7] and Indian cities took the same shape, in squares.[8] Nordic military orders were established in forts of quadrated circular plan.[9] In the case of Roman city-founding rituals, a furrow was ploughed by bulls circling around a center, the *mundus,* and within this circle a square was laid out for the walls and avenues dividing the city equally.[10]

In China, the design of the world was given perhaps most explicit form of any, in the Bronze Mirrors of Han times. These were little discs hung to establish a ritual center in temples, on whose reverse side were depicted in relief a plan of the cosmos and topocosm of the "Middle Kingdom": the square kingdom enclosing a burnished hemisphere at its center representing the sun, its gates oriented to the cardinal directions, outside which was a cross in a circle, signifying the "Four Seas" extending out within the circle of the dome of heaven.[11]

The Quadrated World in Psychic Form

The motif in the psychotic process is clearest in those individuals who drew the images on paper, but the verbal imagery was often enough to convey the picture.

A young man (Case 2) spoke of the four kings of the four directions at war "at the end," which was loosely associated with the idea of the Garden of Eden being in possession of the Trinity but then taken over by the Devil as the fourth.

Another young man (Case 3) at the beginning of his process, drew a space-time diagram that he called by the delightful term "back-o'clock," a dial with the numbers 9—6—3—12, reversing the normal order, with four lines indicating the cardinal directions and with the sun's luminous body at the center. The reversed time was a witty way of expressing his sense of regression to the beginnings of time. At the end of the process he depicted the new order of the world as the "World Mission Rosary," a circle in four segments of different colors representing the four continents, creeds, and colors or races. The mission started from a world center in a ceremony of carrying lighted candles out into these four areas. The most remarkable demonstration of the difference between a modern and an archaic view of the shape of the world was this individual's map of a journey. He had been an aviation navigator with a long wartime experience and with an education in engineering, so that all the intricate mathematics of plotting courses on maps was well known to him, on the ego level of the rational handling of these matters. But on the nonrational level his image of the world became astoundingly transformed into an oval with four continents as petals in the four directions, North and South America, Europe and Asia, and with a circle in the center as Central America.

Another young man (Case 5) similarly visualized the new order of the world as a new equality and mutual tolerance among four races, colors, and religions. His more personal, new order of relationships he symbolized in a world map consisting of four islands as continents in different colors, with a spiral line running around them and into the center.

A young woman (Case 6) also saw a new order of equality. In her case, she believed her grandfather to be the Emperor of the Aztecs, ruling autocratically at the center of the nation and about to be overthrown by his four sons; these would set up four independent kingdoms in the spirit of equality and justice as a new era for the Aztec world.

A quite unusually archaic glimpse of a world image occurred in a young woman, (Case 4) who had a vision of a world mountain being circled by a plane that stopped at each of four planets spaced symmetrically around it.

The most clear instance of this imagery as a vehicle for the process of resolution of the clash of opposites, and of a consequent synthesis, occurred in twelve drawings made by the young woman discussed in the section on the image of the center (Case 1).[12]

The last three drawings in the series she drew bring out with schematic clarity the paranoid problem and its means of resolution. Problem and resolution were both represented in a political framework, but she was able to recognize in this schema her own inner division and its healing by a renewal process.

In the tenth drawing, she described the fate of her former position of world rule. She sensed the scheming and plotting of a revolt by the lower classes: "I have had a hunch something has been going on around here." Up till this time the two rival parties had been the mother's and the father's, but now the husband's entered the scene, the communists. These revolutionaries came in from one side and wanted to level everything, destroying both parties and taking over the world. The husband had encouraged her development of her interests. She was fascinated and excited by this development, yet doubted her ability to solve it. She recognized in the third party her own new life, her new birth; she saw that these images are not to be taken concretely but symbolically. The two parties she now saw as the masculine and feminine parts of herself, creating a new baby (this idea did not come from me). So she made a companion drawing of the world, which showed these two parts in blue and red squares, with a black spot in the red or feminine one to designate the new birth as a pregnancy.

In the final, twelfth diagram, she stated her realization that there have to be four parties, the fourth being the socialists who believe in the loving principle, warmth, and brotherly love. She said, "I'm aware of great depths like the bottom of the sea." The four parties converged at the center, which at first was dark, in a great clash and war. These were not only four parties but also were the four quarters of the world or continents in the four cardinal directions, depicted in four colors. The socialists were in red because they brought a happy mood and brotherhood, and wanted to level off all the others to make only one class. Where these four converged and clashed there was a purple cross. During the crisis all was dark and black, but then when it quieted down it became warm again and the sun shone at the center, in bright yellow. The four were now structured around this circle as four limbs of a cross and also four concentric circles. She said that this image was like her insight at Easter, that Christ was at the center, not herself; he was in us all, common to all.

I must reemphasize that these new developments at each stage of her resolution were quite spontaneous on her part and came directly from her own psyche without prompting or suggestion on my part.

Concerning the psychology of this image of the world one can only say that this appears to be the habitual way in which the universe was visualized by men of archaic civilizations, and similarly by the archaic level of the psyche today. The image follows the same formula as other elements of the process that we have been discussing—what in archaic times and also what in the psychotic state appear as external phenomena belong properly to the inner life. Therefore, this image of the cosmos or of the world actually describes the form and qualities of the psyche. This inner kingdom has a center of governance and a periphery that defines its boundaries, separating what belongs to it from all the possibilities that do not. It is a structure that is ordered and integrated by its center and that is contained by its periphery. Its order represents a harmonious balance and resolution of opposites of all kinds. The psychic structure may be symbolized on all levels of size, from an image of the universe, to that of the world or the kingdom, down to a plan of the temple precincts or *temenos* in which a ritual occurs, or of the hospital in which the psychotic experience runs through its course. The image may even appear as the groundplan of the intimate relationships such as those of the parental family or the circle of friends.

Like all other affect images of this kind, any description of what they mean psychologically necessarily leaves them dangling in the mid-air of generalizations and abstractions. Only when a person gives some personal associative context to the elements of the image do we get the sense that there is a meaningful definition of what we are actually dealing with emotionally.

Chapter Six

From Monarch to Messiah

Archetypal forms tend to come into cultural expression when new departures and ventures in culture forming are under way, to render their meaning and to steer their dynamic energies into the unfamiliar avenues. Their first expressions soon lose their effective vitality and become stale and sterile outward forms of habit, in cases in which the culture continues to grow and modify its patterns. The original dynamism then moves into renewed forms and differentiations.

In the early years of the urban revolution of archaic times, so real was the faith of the people in the potent sacrality of the kingship in Egypt, in Mesopotamia, and in China that the burial of kings at their death was accompanied by the sacrifice of dozens of their retinue. This was only at the beginning, in the early years of this myth and ritual practice. This practice was not so much a sign of the kings' power to bully their subjects as a sign of their awesome spiritual potency, for the custom dwindled away even while the authority of the kings was growing in scope and absoluteness. This decline indicated the fate of the sacral kingship in general, for it lasted only a few centuries in any one culture. I have used the term *era of incarnated myth* to indicate this period of earnest and convinced belief in the sacredness of the kingship as real and its myth and ritual practices as necessary to the life and well-being of the realm. The genuine belief was characteristic only during the first flush of its newness.[1]

As the political aspect of the sacral kingship became increasingly secular, its claim to its divine implications became sterile and hardly more than an expression of grandiosity. The sacred component, however, did not just vanish, but underwent its own history. This aspect of the kingship became increasingly democratized. What had been so concretely externalized now underwent a process of internalization, of realization that the qualities and attributes of kingship now could belong to men in general. In the transition, the myth and ritual statements were carried over as applicable and appropriate to the ordinary man.

It is noteworthy that, in the most spiritually sophisticated civilizations of the ancient world, the middle of the first millennium B.C. became a cultural turning point. A new image began to take shape in the visions of the great seers, prophets and philosophers: in China, the philosophers of "The Hundred Schools"; in India, Gautama the Buddha; in Iran, Zarathustra; and in Israel, the prophets, most notably Isaiah. In all of these visions appeared a new dimension of the kingship, marked by the quality of righteousness. This dimension took two aspects: the seers visualized on the one hand the figure of an ideal ruler over a new golden age, and on the other, a condition of mankind in which the kingly qualities and functions were seen as belonging to the gifted man's spiritual life.

The Messiah in Israelite Myth

In Israel, the sacral kingship was in its full flower in the persons of David and Solomon. It was interrupted by the Exile four centuries later, and it grew into a future hope in the sixth century B.C., in the form of an image of a Messianic Hero who should act as Yahweh's agent in restoring Israel to her full glory. The development may be traced in epitome through the use of the term designating the consecration of kings by the application of a sacred oil. The Davidic kings were called "the anointed of the Lord"; when the advent of the new royal hero began to appear in the teachings of the prophets he was called "Messiah," a word meaning "anointed." Then when the Gospels were drawing parallels between Jesus and the Messianic Hero of the prophets they used the term "Christos," another word signifying "the anointed one," calling him thus "Jesus the Anointed" to imply his special messianic kingship.

Significantly for our present discussion, the earlier visions concerned at first the ideal of the traditional Davidic kingship before they began to reach beyond that into the more messianic image. This figure grew only at a later time when the actual monarchy no longer existed, after the Exile into Babylonia. The truly messianic hope was characterized primarily by the saving action of Yahweh through his chosen scion of the house of David, and by the eschatological vision of the end of time and the transformation of the world into a paradise, so that the last things should be like the first, the end of time like the beginning, *Endzeit* like *Urzeit.* An essential part of this development of great transformation visions was a growing evolution of the moral sense, in which personal piety took the place of the collective national moral well-being of the people as a nation.

The grand sweep of this development began in the eighth century B.C. when the danger of extermination at the hands of the Assyrians was making itself felt. The longing for wisdom and faithful obedience to the will of Yahweh on the part of the king was expressed as the only hope for the salvation of the nation. The fateful Exile followed, but by a miracle of tenacity to their faith and by the work of the prophets, Israel maintained its identity.[2] In the sixth century B.C., with the Return, hope was expressed for the restoration of the monarchy. This sacral kingship had been cut off like a tree, and now a green shoot or branch would grow again from this stump or root of Jesse, that is, the Davidic lineage. As this hope of a restored monarchy was dashed, the image of a more purely spiritual messianic leadership restoring the covenant faith of Israel began to take shape. This image was slowly transformed in the ensuing centuries into an image of the mythologically styled Son of Man, who should appear miraculously in the last centuries of the time of this world, save it from its enemies, and establish an interim kingdom before the whole cosmos would be consumed in flames and transfigured into a new creation. The Christian reform movement within this tradition proclaimed Jesus as the embodiment of this image of the Son of Man and incarnation of the Son of God, and as the fulfillment of the entire age-long messianic expectation. The evangelists rewove the prophetic utterances of earlier centuries into a new pattern of revelation and salvation.

I will therefore attempt to trace out this complex evolution of the messianic idea as clearly as possible. While it is full of exalted visionary poetry of the highest order, it is equally ensnared with tangles for the scholar. While it develops in richness and differentiation book by book, it does not do so evenly, for certain significant passages of the early books derive from the later prophetic circles and were interpolated into the traditional sayings of the early prophets.[3]

It will be seen that the early prophetic efforts to restore the ideal of the sacral kingship followed the lines of the chief elements of the New Year festivals of enthronement, and that gradually these elements evolved into more purely mythical form independent of their former ritual context. In this development the kingship imagery came less and less to concern government and increasingly to belong to the inner spiritual life of the people, as it became democratized.

For purposes of clarity I will divide the presentation of the material into phases: that of the hope for the restoration of the ideal of the Davidic kingship as expressed in the terms of the Enthronement rites; that of the democratized kingly ideology; that of the "Servant of the Lord"; that of the "Son of Man" theme in the apocalyptists; and that of the Christian reshaping of the prophetic visions.

RESTORATION OF THE IDEAL OF THE KINGSHIP

In the first phase, the eighth century B.C., Amos set the groundplan of the messianic idea in declaring the "day of the Lord" in which punishment and afflictions were the fruit of Israel's erring ways and sins. Specifically, this day would bring "exile, destruction, slaughter, humiliation, changes in the order of nature, and stoppage of the Torah":[4]

Lamentation shall be in the broad places,
And they shall say in all the streets, "Alas! Alas!"

. . .

Wherefore would ye have the day of the Lord?
It is darkness, and not light.[5]

Yet Israel's political downfall would lead to a realization of her errors, and repentance and salvation would follow. Amos thus established the basic pattern, which Klausner formulates thus: "Sin brings punishment, punishment brings repentance, which in turn brings the Days of the Messiah."[6]

Even more clearly, Hosea set down some of the fundamental elements of the messianic pattern. He declared that the tribulations were not pure vengeance from the Lord, but were designed to rouse Israel to repentance; they were thus the pains of childbirth leading to Israel's new life.[7] His phrase was: "The sorrows of a travailing woman shall come upon him."[8] This phrase gave rise to the concept of the "birth pangs of the Messiah," which became a recurrent motif throughout the scriptures.

Other elements were introduced at this time—the union of northern and southern kingdoms, separated after Solomon's reign; the motif of the ingathering of the scattered exiles; and the figure of an individual messiah, seen as a new kind of supreme man as political head of the nation.

And the children of Judah and the children of
Israel shall be gathered together, and they shall
appoint themselves one head, and shall go up out
of the land.[9]

This redemption from exile will be a new Exodus, and the messiah a new Moses:

Therefore, behold I will allure her,
And bring her into the wilderness,
And speak tenderly to her.

. . .

And she shall respond there as in the days
of her youth,
As in the day when she came up out of the land
of Egypt.[10]

Thus the prophets began to see in Moses the prototype of the new redeemer and savior of the people.[11] Also, they recognized in David the model and First Founding Ancestor[12] of the royal lineage out of which the Messiah should come, as a new David effecting a liberation of Israel from its enemies in the same manner as the first David, who rescued his people and their Ark of the Covenant at Shiloh.

Another highly significant theme introduced by Hosea is that of the image of a loving God wooing the nation, the "virgin daughter of Israel," as in the passage just quoted. She will forego the names of the Canaanite Baals, "Baali," and will instead refer to the Lord as her husband, "Ishi."[13] She will mend her ways and return to her Lord "as a wife of youthful innocence," Yahweh says to her.

> *And I will betroth thee unto me for ever;*
> *Yea, I will betroth thee unto me in righteousness,*
> *and in justice,*
> *And in loving kindness, and in compassion.*[14]

Along with this spiritual bliss will come perfect peace:

> *And I will break the bow and the sword and the*
> *battle out of the land,*
> *And I will make them to lie down safely.*[15]

According to Mowinckel,[16] all these early passages referring to the future hope were couched in terms of the restoration of the ideal of the Davidic kingship. The loftiest of these early poetic visions came from the hand of First Isaiah, author of the first thirty-nine chapters of the Book of Isaiah, contemporary with Amos and Hoseah. Isaiah saw in the scion of the house of David a form, even if still limited, of the Messiah. That is, he looked to the sacral king to uphold the nation in its times of peril and to continue acting as intermediary between the people and their true king, Yahweh, with whom he held the contract of homage and fealty, the Covenant.

Of especial interest to us is that the future hope for this ideal ruler, which was to evolve over the centuries in a way unique to

Israel, came into being here couched in language and imagery that sprang directly out of the myth and ritual of the Enthronement Rite of the New Year Festival.[17] Isaiah proclaims:

> *For a child has been born to us,*
> *a son has been given to us;*
> *the token of royalty shall be on his shoulder,*
> *and his name shall be called 'Wonderful Ruler,'*
> *'Divine Hero,' 'Father for ever,'*
> *and 'Prince of peace and well-being.'*
> *To increase the dominion,*
> *and [make] good fortune endless,*
> *upon the throne of David,*
> *and in his kingdom,*
> *to establish it with justice and righteousness*
> *from henceforth and for ever*
> *the zeal of Yahweh of Hosts*
> *will perform this.*[18]

Now, these enthusiastic tidings are ushered in with comments about the "trouble and darkness, dimness and anguish" that Israel was experiencing at the time of the threat of her oppression from the neighboring foreign powers. "Nevertheless," Isaiah announces,

> *The people who walked in darkness*
> *have seen a great light;*
> *those who dwell in a land of deep gloom*
> *upon them the light has shone.*[19]

The terms of Isaiah's description of this event are in every way appropriate to the myth and ritual of the divine kingship and, in it, the birth of the divine child. In the image of the coming from darkness into light Mowinckel sees references to the older Canaanite mythology of the rebirth of the king god from death. Elsewhere it is made clear that the Israelites understood him to be born from the womb of the Dawn Goddess, as the dew and the new light.[20] There is reference to this birth in the royal enthronement oracle of Psalm 110:

In the day of thy power,
In the beauties of holiness from the womb
of the morning:
Thou hast the dew of thy youth.[21]

The birth of the new prince of the House of David was now equated emotionally with the dawn of the new day of Yahweh's saving action, as it had been in the Enthronement Festival.

Isaiah thus draws on the ancient mythology of the birth of the divine child from the maiden goddess, even though he is proclaiming the actual birth of a prince from a mortal young woman, the queen:[22]

Behold the young woman has conceived,
and she will bear a son,
and she will call him Immanuel [*With-us-is-God*].
Curds and honey will he eat till [*he is old enough*]
to have discretion to refuse what is bad
and choose what is good.[23]

The milk and honey refers to the food of the gods in all probability, and thus the ritual food of the newly born divine child.

In these joyful visions was born the idea of the future hope and messianic expectation that was to evolve so dramatically over the following centuries of prophetic development. Isaiah's own writings were intended to greet the birth of the newly born prince of the House of David with all possible hope of restoring the traditional ideal of the Davidic kingship; in it the sacral king would bear within his person the virtues of righteousness, justice, and peace by which the nation would live.[24] Isaiah had not yet developed the notion of a future messiah who should save the people and restore Israel in an eschatological vision of the end of time. In the perspective of history, however, one may recognize in these passages a transition to the true messianic hope:

And there shall come forth a rod out of the stem of Jesse,
And a branch shall grow out of his roots.
And the Spirit of the Lord shall rest upon him,
the spirit of wisdom and understanding,

the spirit of counsel and might,
the spirit of knowledge and of the fear of the Lord;
And shall make him of quick understanding in the fear of the Lord:
and he shall not judge after the sight of his eyes,
neither reprove after the hearing of his ears;
But with righteousness shall he judge the poor,
and reprove with equity for the meek of the earth:
and he shall smite the earth with the rod of his mouth,
and with the breath of his lips shall he slay the wicked.
And righteousness shall be the girdle of his loins,
and faithfulness the girdle of his reins.[25]

These lines were composed for the birth of an actual scion of the House of David. According to an older view, the prophet had in mind Hezekiah, King of Judah, but more recent scholars have suggested that the lines might be derived from the later verses of Zechariah and interpolated into the older ones of Isaiah.[26] From this later date must come the metaphor of the green shoot out of the stem of the Davidic lineage, the new growth out of the tree of the monarchy so rudely cut down in the Exile. Zechariah was presumably the first to pronounce this renewal, in the sixth century B.C.:

Behold the man whose name is THE BRANCH;
and he shall grow up out of his place,
and he shall build the temple of the Lord:
Even he shall build the temple of the Lord;
and he shall bear the glory,
and shall sit and rule upon his throne;
and he shall be a priest upon his throne:
and the counsel of peace shall be between them both.[27]

The reference to the man called "the branch" is explained by the fact that the young prince of the House of David was at that time Zerubabel, a name which is translated as the "shoot from Babel," from Babylon. The circle of Isaiah's followers very likely then incorporated Zechariah's phrasing into the earlier book of Isaiah.

These several passages giving and explicating the significance of the name of the royal child bear all the connotations of a rejuvenation of the lineage of David and of its kingly powers. The naming at the birth of a sacral king and the amplifying of it, as in the verses, "He shall be called Wonderful, Counsellor, The Mighty God, The Everlasting Father, The Prince of Peace," all derive from the ancient custom of bestowing names of power and virtue on the young divine king of Egypt and on the sacral king of other cultures of the Near East.[28]

In one of the messianic passages from Micah, we note that this expected ruler is described as having been "from of old." Some scholars have sought in this reference an image of the Primordial First Man, existing from an eternal dimension.[29] However, the more recent consensus has been that the First Man motif only appeared later in the imagery of the "Son of Man" in the second and first centuries B.C., as in the Book of Enoch, after the prophetic era had closed. Micah's phrase "of old" seems to concern rather the lineage of David, that is, another embodiment of "David" and thus derived from his birthplace in Bethlehem and from olden days:[30]

But thou, Beth-lehem Ephratah,
though thou be little among the thousands of Judah
yet out of thee shall come forth unto me that is to be ruler of Israel;
those goings forth have been from of old, from everlasting.[31]

A hint of the "birthpangs" and of the royal birth recurs:

Therefore will he give them up,
until the time that she which travaileth
hath brought forth:
then the remnant of his brethren shall return
unto the children of Israel.[32]

Of particular interest for our present thesis of democratization is that the people of God, the "remnant" who are faithful to their covenant, are described in the same metaphorical terms as these Davidic kings, namely as dew and rainfall:

And the remnant of Jacob
Shall be in the midst of many people

As a dew from the Lord,
As showers upon the grass,
That tarrieth not for man,[33]
Nor waiteth for the sons of men.

That is, the royal imagery applies increasingly to the people themselves.

THE MESSIANIC FUTURE HOPE AND DEMOCRATIZATION

The Exile into Babylonia in the sixth century B.C. marked a profound change in the conceptualization of the ideal of the kingship, for with it the actuality of the monarchy came to an end, and the ideal and the real became differentiated from each other. Since in the sixth century there was no longer any actual king of the House of David, the ideal of the kingship was put off into the form of a future hope.

In place of the motif of adherence to the earlier "covenant faith" between the descendants of David and their liege lord, Yahweh,[34] there appears increasingly the theme of the destruction and ensuing restoration of Israel. The giving over of Israel to her enemies follows directly in the tradition of the ritual combat between the royal protagonist and his enemy in the Enthronement Festival, and the restoration has equal reference to the saving intervention of Yahweh in that ceremonial. Similarly, the growing image of a new order of the world and of the people derives from that same source, in which the return of the beginnings of time and the act of a fresh creation of the cosmos anew was an integral feature of the New Year rites. This was especially the case with Deutero-Isaiah, or Second Isaiah (Chapters 40 to 54 in the Book of Isaiah), as Mowinckel points out:

> Here Deutero-Isaiah was able to start from a developed system of ideas which was already in existence. He derived both the framework and the details from a feature of Israelite religion which was already central as early as the period of the monarchy, namely those ideas and experiences which were associated with the most important festival of the temple cultus at Jerusalem, the autumn and New Year festival . . . regarded as *the festival of Yahweh's enthronement.*[35]

Mowinckel goes on to elaborate the point:

> It is not difficult to see that the ideas of the enthronement festival must have been ready to hand for Deutero-Isaiah as the specific content of his promises and his faith in restoration. . . . The rituals and liturgies of the festival were full of promises about the glory brought by Yahweh, and thus assured for the future. This conviction was based on the covenant between Yahweh and Israel, which was the foundation of Israel's faith and of its very existence.[36]

In Deutero-Isaiah, according to Klausner, there is "almost no indication of an individual human Messiah, who will deliver his people and stand at their head, such as we found in the prophets preceding. The LORD Himself will be their redeemer."[37] Those that know righteousness are the servants of the Lord, and the term, "servant" is applied to the prophet himself, to his followers, and also to all who are faithful to God's covenant, thus the people Israel collectively, the "redeemed of the Lord." As in Jeremiah, they are described as having the law written in their hearts: "Hearken unto me, ye that know righteousness, / the people in whose heart is my law."[38] This matter of the Servant of the Lord will be discussed shortly.

Klausner also sees, in Isaiah chapters 24 to 27, and 34 to 35, the appearance of new apocalyptic themes springing out of the late years of Deutero-Isaiah's life, two decades from the close of the sixth century B.C.[39] Here he envisions an Age to Come in which there will be a cessation of death and a resurrection of the dead. The fearful day of the Lord is described in Isaiah in images of horrendous destruction and turmoil:

> *Behold, the Lord maketh the earth empty,*
> *and maketh it waste,*
> *and turneth it upside down,*
> *and scattereth abroad the inhabitants thereof.*
>
> . . .
>
> *The earth shall reel to and fro like a drunkard,*
> *and shall be removed like a cottage;*
>
> . . .
>
> *And it shall come to pass on that day,*
> *that the Lord shall punish the host of the high ones*
> *that are on high,*
> *and the kings of the earth upon the earth.*
>
> . . .

Then the moon shall be confounded,
and the sun ashamed,
when the Lord of hosts shall reign on Mount Zion,
and in Jerusalem,
and before his ancients gloriously.[40]

The theme of the cosmic conflict and ritual battle with the dragon monster of the deeps, that is, of chaos, is introduced in even clearer reference to the enthronement ritual:

In that day the Lord with his sore and great and strong sword
shall punish Leviathan the piercing serpent,
even Leviathan that crooked serpent;
and he shall slay the dragon that is in the sea.[41]

Yet this day of wrath is quickly followed by the Lord's saving action and comfort toward his people:

He will swallow up death in victory;
and the Lord will wipe away tears from off all faces;
and the rebuke of his people shall he take away
from off all the earth:
for the Lord hath spoken it.
And it shall be said in that day, Lo, this is our God;
we have waited for him, and he will save us.
this is the Lord; we have waited for him,
we will be glad and rejoice in his salvation.[42]

There are echoes of the enthronement festival and its songs extolling the seat of God's throne:

In that day shall this song be sung in the land of Judah;
We have a strong city;
salvation will God appoint for walls and bulwarks.
Open ye the gates,
that the righteous nation which keepeth the truth may enter in.[43]

Again we encounter the theme of the birthpangs of the Messiah:

Like as a woman with child,
that draweth near the time of her delivery,
is in pain, and crieth out in her pangs;
so have we been in thy sight, O Lord.[44]

Here occurs, among the saving actions of the Lord and the signs of new life, the earliest reference to the resurrection of the dead:

Thy dead men shall live,
together with my dead body shall they arise.
Awake and sing, ye that dwell in dust:
for thy dew is as the dew of herbs,
and the earth shall cast out the dead.[45]

The saving action of the Lord is bound together closely with the judgment, with the establishment of the law written in the heart and with the light of the people:

For a law shall proceed from me,
and I will make my judgment to rest
for light of the people.
My righteousness is near; my salvation is gone forth,
and mine arms shall judge the people.

. . .

Lift up your eyes to the heavens,
and look upon the earth beneath:
for the heavens shall vanish away like smoke,
and the earth shall wax old like a garment,
and they that dwell therein shall die in like manner:
but my salvation shall be forever,
and my righteousness shall not be abolished.
Hearken unto me, ye that know righteousness,
the people in whose heart is my law;
fear ye not.[46]

Third Isaiah (that is, Chapters 55 to 66) also draws on the enthronement festival for the expression of the stirring vision of a new heaven and a new earth, for it must be remembered that that was the feature of every New Year rite, in which time was put back to the beginning and a new creation of the cosmos was represented:

> *For, behold, I create a new heavens and a new earth:*
> *and the former shall not be remembered,*
> *nor come into mind.*
> *But be ye glad and rejoice for ever in that which I create:*
> *for, behold, I create Jerusalem a rejoicing,*
> *and her people a joy.*[47]

This New Jerusalem, and city of paradise, will then be glorified and set upon the center and highest point of the world where Yahweh will sit enthroned and all nations will come from the four quarters and pay homage to him.[48] This will be an era of the New Covenant (or New Testament) when the exiles will have returned from captivity and a scion of David will sit upon the throne:

> *I will make an everlasting covenant with you,*
> *the sure promises of favor to David.*
> *Behold, I have made him a witness to the peoples,*
> *a leader and commander over the peoples.*[49]

Jeremiah, another prophet of the sixth century B.C. describes that new day when the bad shepherds who have scattered the flock will be replaced by righteous rulers:

> *I will set shepherds over them*
> *who will shepherd them.*
>
> . . .
>
> *Behold, the days are coming, says Yahweh,*
> *when I shall raise up for David a righteous Shoot;*
> *and he will reign as king and wisely attain his aim;*
> *and he will execute justice and righteousness in the land.*
> *In his day Judah will be saved,*
> *and Israel will dwell in security.*[50]

He will be a priest king according to the ancient ideal, a true mediator between Yahweh and his people:

Their prince shall be one of themselves;
their ruler shall come from among them.
I will grant him access, and he shall approach me.

. . .

And you shall be my people [*as of old*],
and I will [*again*] *be your God.*[51]

This prince will be a king of the house of David:

But they shall serve the Lord their God,
And David their king,
Whom I will raise up unto them.[52]

Jeremiah's hope was that the current representative of the Davidic lineage would fulfill the role of such a priestly king, Zedekiah ("The Lord is our Righteousness"), but such expectations were soon dashed. In consequence, the immanent expectations were transformed from now on into a remote future hope.[53]

Jeremiah gave voice to a fundamental revolution in the spiritual life of Israel, in which there should be a "new covenant" between God and a people with a new heart and a new spirit:

But this is the covenant that I will make with the house of Israel after those days, saith the Lord: I will put My law in their inward parts, and in their heart will I write it; and I will be their God, and they shall be My people.[54]

This covenant is one of the more dramatic instances of the Revolution of Democratization. The moral sense that had been a concern of the nation as a whole with its collective rewards and punishments at the hands of their King, Yahweh, now was a matter for the individual to develop within himself and to take the consequences of his own piety or impiety. Formerly, the sacral king had taken on himself the burden of responsibility for upholding righteousness and justice, and thus for the moral well-being of the people.[55]

Even more definite is this ethical imperative in Ezekiel, the "Prophet of the Exile," who also began with hopes of the scion of David, Zedekiah, until the Destruction of the Temple and the nullification of the kingship. After that he mentioned a king in the house of David no more, but only the "Prince," who should be only a Good Shepherd and priest looking after the restored House of the Lord, as leader of a sort of religious republic and thus only as "first among equals" *(primus inter pares)*. By the same token, the New Jerusalem would be transfigured from a seat of government to a purely spiritual "heavenly city."[56]

In the early years of the fifth century B.C., Second Zechariah (from chapter 9 on) had exalted visions of the advent of a king who should restore Israel and bring peace and universal dominion:

Rejoice greatly, O daughter of Zion!

. . .

Behold thy king cometh unto thee,
He is triumphant and victorious,
Lowly and riding upon an ass,
Even upon a colt, the foal of an ass.

. . .

And he shall speak peace unto the nations;
And his dominion shall be from sea to sea,
And from the River to the ends of the earth.[57]

From Canaanite parallels it is recognized now that someone who rides upon an ass is a royal figure; in this case he is portrayed as both lowly and triumphant, both speaking peace and victorious.[58] The theme of universal rule over the peoples of the earth becomes increasingly strong in the later messianic prophecies:

And the LORD shall be King over all the earth;
In that day shall the LORD be One,
and His name one.[59]

Another theme that begins to appear and prevail, and that is first seen in Zechariah, is that of the suffering Messiah. It appears that the verses refer to an attack on Jerusalem and Judah by Gentiles:

And I will pour upon the house of David,
And upon the inhabitants of Jerusalem,
The spirit of grace and of supplication;

And they shall look unto the one
whom they have pierced;
And they shall mourn for him,
as one mourneth for his only son,
And shall be in bitterness for him,
as one that is in bitterness for his first-born.[60]

Although the vision was apparently referring to an episode of current history, the image was later applied to the messianic figure.

Finally, one of the great visions of democratization in a more general respect is found in Joel, indicating that prophecy, visions, and dreams are not to be any longer the prerogative of special functionaries, but of all the people:

And it shall come to pass afterward,
That I will pour out My spirit upon all flesh;
And your sons and your daughters shall prophesy,
Your old men shall dream dreams,
Your young men shall see visions;
And also upon the servants and upon the handmaids
In those days will I pour out My spirit.[61]

THE SERVANT OF THE LORD

Among the chapters of Deutero-Isaiah occur four distinct poetic entities, called the "Servant Songs," because they portray a man called "The Servant of the Lord." These verses represent not only some of the most exalted poetry in the Bible, but even rank supreme among the world's great religious poems. They also mark a new ideal of prophecy.

In themselves, these prophetic verses did not have a messianic meaning. Some centuries later, however, either Jesus or at least the evangelists in their rendering of Jesus' mission, turned these scriptures along with others to a new purpose, to demonstrate that Jesus' messianic mission was foretold from early times. It has been pointed out that, according to these evangelists, Jesus took the Fourth Servant Song as the program of his mission as suffering messiah and redeemer.[62] When they were written, however, these songs apparently were describing the spiritual significance of the life and role of a certain unknown prophet, who was lifted from contempt and exalted to the highest honor because he gave his life to redeem his people. The description of him contains no eschatological and no distinctly royal features; he was not a political figure and not of the house of David, therefore not viewed as the messiah at the time the songs were composed.[63]

There has been considerable disagreement among scholars as to whether this Suffering Servant was a representation of the people of Israel as a corporate body. Jewish tradition has understood the People as a social organism personified in this figure, as a "collective individual" who would suffer and be resurrected.[64] Others claim that this Servant of the Lord designated the sacral Davidic king who should suffer and die for his people as their representative and their personification.[65] A third view, which seems more substantial, has been that, while the word *servant* has been applied to the People Israel in various and sundry of the passages of Deutero-Isaiah, the Servant Songs are separate entities portraying a distinct figure of an individual human prophet. This man took on himself the role of representing Israel's suffering in a manner similar to a prophet, priest, or priest king, or sacral king, even though he was not a royal figure. He took the role on himself as a spiritual task for his people, but not in the actual function of kingship.[66] All contenders in this argument agreed, however, that the role of redeemer reached a new level of spiritual differentiation in this prophetic figure.

The First Servant Song is phrased in the manner of a "royal initiation oracle," calling a king to his task: "Behold, My Servant whom I uphold, / My chosen in whom I delight!" Among the further lines included in some renditions are ones that borrow from the language of the kingship: "[I will] give thee for a covenant of the people, / For a light to the Gentiles."[67]

The Second Song is modeled on the traditional psalm of thanksgiving; it uses the terms familiar in the sacral kingship referring to being elected from conception:

Yahweh has called me from the womb,
from my birth He has made mention of my name.

. . .

And He said to me, "You are My Servant,
by whom I will get myself glory."[68]

In the third of these lines the familiar King James version reads, "Thou art My Servant, O Israel," which was convenient to the traditional interpretation that the Servant was merely a personification of the realm. However, the mention of Israel has been found to be a later interpolation.[69]

The Third Song resembles a traditional psalm of lamentation except that it is addressed not to God, as that would require, but to men. The suffering was born willingly:

I was not rebellious . . .

. . .

I gave my back to the smiters,
and my cheeks to those that plucked out [*the beard*].[70]

The famous Fourth Servant Song has been valued as among the most exalted of the world's religious poetry. It explains the suffering taken by the Servant on himself as a vicarious guilt offering for the people:

He was despised and forsaken of men,
a man of pains and acquainted with sickness.

. . .

Yet ours were the sicknesses he carried,
ours the pains that he bore.

. . .

He was pierced for our rebellions,
he was crushed for our iniquities.

. . .

For he was cut off from the land of the living;
for our rebellions he was stricken to death.
His grave was made with the wicked,
with evil-doers his sepulchre.[71]

The first mention of resurrection from death in Judaism has been discerned in the following lines:

[He will deliver] his soul from distress;
he will see [light and live long],
and be satisfied with what he desires.[72]

Also he is granted a stature equal to that of kings. Because he bore these iniquities, the Lord says, "I will divide him a portion among the great, / and he will divide the spoil with the mighty."[73] This royal rank was often considered to be awarded to the righteous, a striking instance of the democratization of kingly forms.

THE SON OF MAN IN THE APOCALYPTISTS

One more major tradition was added to the accumulation of elements in the messianic image, besides those of the hope of the future king, the priestly prince, and the suffering servant of the Lord. This was the motif of the Son of Man, arising partly out of Iranian influences and partly out of the visionary experiences of the later apocalyptists.[74] Here I will present a small summary of the earliest of these, the group of "pseudepigraphs" assigned to Enoch, written from the first half of the second century to the first half of the first century B.C., and to Esdras and Baruch of the next.[75]

The name, Son of Man, has the meaning of "The Man," or "The Ideal of Man," just as Adam's name means "Man." In our language we might say this Son of Man represented the archetype of mankind, parallel to the image of the "Anthropos."[76] Like Adam, he belonged to a tradition concerning the Primordial Man, but in this case had close affinities with the Iranian Gayomart, the Primordial Man and King dwelling on the world mountain. He was therefore encompassing the *Urzeit* and *Endzeit,* the Golden Age of Paradise of the beginning and of the end of time.

The visions of Enoch revealed that this Son of Man was hidden under the wings of the Lord of Spirits from the time of the creation, and kept secret until his time should come. A whole new order of existence and of society was kept hidden in full preparation in paradise, to be revealed and effected at the end of time, in the fearful "Day of the Lord."[77] Eschatology, and the apocalyptic visions giving rise to it, were considered revelations of these secret future events; the visionary journeys took these apocalyptists to paradise itself, where they beheld these events and the secrets were disclosed to them.

In the Day of the Lord, the Son of Man would come riding on the clouds with thunders and lightnings; he would appear from the sea accompanied by the winds of the heavens, and causing great fear. He would quell the enemies of the Lord and hold a Great Judgment, separating the faithful from the rebellious.[78] Thereupon he would rule as king over an "Interim Kingdom" for a period of four hundred years, with a reign of perfect righteousness and justice, peace and abundance.[79] These years would be the fulfillment of the ideal of Israelite kingship.

Then would come the final "last things."[80] All of creation would be abolished, swallowed up in death and chaos once more. An immense hush would be cast over this void, an eerie seven-day silence representing the state of chaos before the creation. Then would unfold magnificently a "New Heaven and a New Earth." From their hiding in paradise the entire community of the souls of the righteous would appear again in a general resurrection of the dead, and angels and spirits and men would dwell together in this new world. The Son of Man would be enthroned at the right hand of the Lord of Spirits and rule in supreme righteousness and justice, peace and abundance in a kingdom without violence. This kingdom would be inhabited by the elect clothed in garments of light, and they would shine with their illumination. The New Jerusalem as a Heavenly City would be the center of this world to which the great and small of all the rest of the nations would come of their own accord to do homage to God as their supreme king.

BACKGROUND OF THE IMAGE

While in most of the ancient cultures the messianic ideology was an innovation springing up during the middle years of the first millennium B.C., with a strangely universal impetus, in Egypt something of the same pattern occurred in a more muted form more than a millennium and a half earlier.

We have noted already that as Horus was King of the Living, so was Osiris King of the Dead, and the life-giving principle was passed from the ancestors through him to Horus, and thus out to the realm. At first only the Pharaoh had an immortal soul and only he was the Unique Man, and by the same token, only he could become Osiris at this death. However, as Breasted so beautifully narrates in his book on Egyptian religion and thought,[81] through the force of history the power to achieve resurrection spread to the people. First the nobility who surrounded the king in an intimate entourage saw to it that they were buried near him and thus would be carried over into the next world and transfigured with him; then, in time, any commoner who had the financial means to pay for "the Egyptian way of death" could aspire to "become an Osiris" and have an immortal soul. The whole royal ritual, together with the texts that formerly had been meant solely for the king, became available eventually to the man in the street.

Hand in hand with this progress, the moral sense also underwent a similar metamorphosis.[82] The moral sense had first been embodied in the goddess Maat, the personification of "right order" and the daughter of Ra the sun god; the king, as representative of this sun principle, was the agency through whom Maat could hold sway in the life of the realm. With the growing usage of the concept of the Judgment of Souls at death by Osiris, before whose throne the deceased had to find himself justified, a moral sense gained headway. What had been the king's responsibility, to find himself without fault on this occasion (in his "negative confession"), became now the concern of every individual. In this fashion, the spread of the belief in the resurrection leads directly into the parallel belief in the moral responsibility of the individual.

Along with these changes, and with the crumbling of the sure order of the kingship at the demise of the Old Kingdom, there prevailed on the one hand a general disillusionment with the old order of things, but on the other, a new philosophic recognition of the value of moral worth.[83] A wise man arose who bore a close resemblance to the prophets of Israel of later times. Like them, the philosopher Ipuwer reprimanded the king, crying for a restoration of the pristine order of the realm and of the ideal rulership as at the time of the beginnings of creation. He had a vision of a new Reign of Righteousness to be comparable with that first Golden Age, and a new ruler without evil, a good shepherd of the people gathering them when their numbers are few and their hearts are fevered:

> It shall come that he brings coolness upon the heart. Men shall say: "He is the herdsman of all men. Evil is not in his heart. Though herds may be small, still he has spent the day caring for them." . . . Would that he might perceive their character from the [very] first generation! Then he would smite down evil; he would stretch forth the arm against it; he would destroy the seed thereof and their inheritance. . . . [But] there is no pilot in their hour. Where is he today? Is he then sleeping? Behold, the glory thereof cannot be seen."[84]

The Gathas, or writings of Zarathustra in Iran,[85] envisioned a new kingdom with a reign of order of such power as to effect a renovation of the world and a transformation of the universe. As at the occasion of the first creation, there will again take place a cosmic conflict of the forces of Light against those of Darkness, of Truth against the Lie, and out of this will emerge the New Creation. A Prince will arise, who as a redeemer will realize a new Dominion of Righteousness. This will be a new Golden Age, a future version of the one that had been established in the past by the First Ancestral King, Yima, as an Abode of the Blessed (Vara). This Yima, like his Indian counterpart, Yama, was originally Lord of the Realm of Death, and thus had a function somewhat similar to that of Osiris.[86] Zarathustra made the interesting statement that any among the people could become a savior, if he sought the Righteousness of the Lord. The new Redeemer would be the Saoshyant, a kind of Messianic Hero, a constellation of new mythology that profoundly affected the Messianic expectations of Israel.[87]

The Christian Renderings of the Messianic Image

The New Covenant in the writings of the evangelists was considered by the Christian community as the culmination of the development of the messianic expectation. In my tracing of the evolution of the messianic image, I am going to commit some violence to it in not discussing the later Jewish development of the theme after the appearance of Christianity, but my intention has been only to sketch out the Judeo-Christian history of our present tradition.

The gospels claimed a final incarnation of the major elements of the messianic hope discussed above. These writings are replete with quotations from the prophets and the apocalyptists to demonstrate the point that Jesus and his life and his mighty works were the full fruition of all that the ancient scriptures had anticipated.

Jesus' miraculous conception and birth were seen as that of the divine child described in Isaiah. At his baptism he was named the adopted son of God in the same words as in the royal enthronement oracle, Psalm 2. Coming out of Bethlehem, as Micah had written, he was seen as the new ruler of the House of David. As the Anointed of the Lord, the Christ, he was the King reigning over a new Kingdom of God, now an inner spiritual entity presided over by him as a priestly Prince and Good Shepherd, whose kingdom was not of this world, in a manner of Jeremiah's and Ezekiel's visions.

The Servant Songs, especially the fourth, were the evangelists' model for the basic program of the mission of Jesus.[88] As this Suffering Servant of the Lord, he was understood to take on himself the sins of the people, to give himself as a ransom for the many, pierced and chastized, and to pour out his soul unto death as redeemer of mankind, and to be restored to life in the resurrection.

Elaborating his role as the "Son of Man," many eschatological allusions were made to his appearing in glory on clouds, his overcoming of Satan, his Last Judgment, his bringing of the new order of the world for a millennium, and his being enthroned seated at the right hand of the Father.

In Paul's visions he was revealed as the New Adam, to replace the Old Adam (the Primordial Man, as the former image of the ideal of man) with this new spiritual dimension introduced by him into man's history. He was experienced now by Paul as the "Christ within," a living being within the hearts of men who could accordingly now themselves become "Sons of God." As in the visions of the prophets, the messiah would become the embodiment of the corporate life of the People Israel, so now the corporate life of the company of the faithful in the church was perceived by Paul as the very "Body of Christ" with its many members.

What could be a more explicit statement of the final internalization and democratization of the myth and ritual forms of the sacral kingship, crowning an 800-year effort on the part of great prophets and visionaries!

The Messiah in Psychic Form

Having reviewed the variations on the theme of the messianic figure, our main object of interest at this point is the transition from the grandiose ideas of world rule to the more ethical concerns with the destiny of the messianic image as an inner psychic experience.

The young woman already discussed (Case 1) in the section on the center, in Chapter Five, made such a shift away from her initial inflation, in which she was divine and in a ruling position, the whole world waiting for her to make her decision between opposing political parties in an election. At Easter time she voiced concerns that revealed a more healthy relation to the center, by recognizing the figure of Christ as an inner spiritual factor in all persons.

On Easter, the twenty-seventh day of her hospitalization, she heard a sermon in the chapel on the subject of resurrection. This sermon struck home, and she became deeply engrossed in ruminations on the meaning of death and resurrection in general, particularly Christ's. Concurrently came a marked improvement in her insight, as indicated by the following excerpt:

> She believes there is death only of the body, not the mind. She wants someone to explain religion. Christ could be any one of us, being like the power within us. She rehearses her former ideas of god-like power, and thinks she had these because she was always the center of attraction at home. She needs more interests and self-expression to put her imagination to use. She observes that in the drawings she is getting outside her circle. She agrees with the therapist that Christ is a symbolic being in our minds. Only the mind is real, not the body, and Christ is in all of us; he was in the tomb and has risen, and that happens to all of us. We can all be Christs.
>
> She draws the pews and altar in the chapel where she was meditating over this. At the right she depicts her fantasies about the death and resurrection of Christ, beginning with a tomb. "I thought it could be any one of us; it needn't be Christ's life—I think we could all be killed and planted in a tomb." We celebrate Christ's life because it is an ideal one which we imitate. There is no heaven, but we come back and "face it" here again, always enclosed in this life. She draws Christ come back, as a double triangle in red and black halves. Since he went through suffering, he is like us and is one of us; he is both cheerful and bad.
>
> She realizes now that she is not at the center and laughs at the idea. No one person can see the whole world; that is why there are so many people.

> She begins a second drawing in red, to represent Christ at the center and all the many people in the world. The ones who "give more" are bigger and redder, the nearer they are to Christ. He is the example, the symbol in us all, and his life is the model. He is at the center, "not me."[89]

By the gradations of the color red the patient intended to express the degree of participation in this experience of Christ and Christian love by the various individuals in the world. She intended at first to differentiate the light and dark aspects of people, but the final drawing gave the impression only of a bald straightforward statement, with no subtleties or complications, or even any oppositions of principles or colors.[90] When the patient later gave her associations to the color of red she named fire and emotion, and the redness in her drawing conveyed this feeling of warmth, even heat. Fire is a symbolic image traditionally used to express the experience of that central archetype that Christ represented[91] and with which the patient was now coming to terms.

The ability to realize that what had been at first naively externalized and taken concretely should be recognized as internal and taken figuratively—that, in my experience, is the crucial factor determining whether a psychotic experience is proceeding unfavorably toward disintegration or creatively toward reorganization with new gains for the personality's further development.

Chapter Seven

The Renewal of the Center

In the search for the parallels to the symbolic process that occurs in the acute schizophrenic episode, we have reviewed the myth and ritual of renewal of the center in ceremonial forms that arose with the first urban civilizations. In so doing, we have encountered some psychological principles that govern the evolution of such collective cultural forms, and that in turn add further to our understanding of the psychotic experience.

When we are considering the cultures of the ancient Near East at the time of the urban revolution, we must recognize the profound difference in their psychology from ours of today. A new kind of consciousness was emerging at that great turning point in history. Three major features of that vitally burgeoning form of culture stand out. Chief among them is the restructuring of society according to function in the general community, rather than according to family and clan; this mode of organization occasioned the gradual development of a new ethic and moral sense. With this elaboration of various kinds of productivity in the Bronze Age economy, the accumulation of wealth led to a theretofore unheard of acquisition of centralized power, of dominance, and of aggressive expansion of territory in the new-style kingdoms and empires. The invention of writing occurred in the midst of these conditions, as an expression of the higher level of organization and complexity of the cultures and of the consciousness required to manage them.

In this crucial period of cultural innovation and the consequent need for adaptations to new ways, we witness one of the regular features of rapid culture change. That feature is the creation of myth and ritual forms that would render the meaning of these innovations for the society's spiritual life and would guide the psychic motivations into these channels.

The phenomenology of these forms, which I have set forth both in this book and in *Lord of the Four Quarters,* shows that the processes pertaining to the transformation and directing of these psychic energies were concentrated in a ceremonial center. Considering this concentration from a retrospective vantage point, we can say that the image of the psychic center was projected out on a sacral king and his ceremonials. In a prospective view, the image of the center came into being in the collective and concrete outward forms and ceremonies and in time became internalized as properties of the individual psyche.

To put this tranformation in another perspective, the recently emerging consciousness of that time was a property only of kings and their nobles. Individuality, spiritual cultivation, and psychic renewal or regeneration were the concern of a small ruling class alone. In the prevailing idiom of that time, the sacral king was the Great Individual, the Unique Man, possessed of divine potencies (in the case of early Egypt he was the only man endowed with an immortal soul). In most of those cultures the lesser aristocracy gradually came to share these spiritual qualities with royalty; specially endowed souls were considered the equivalent of kings. Only in time did these privileges slowly filter down to become the properties of the spiritual life of the man in the street, as we are accustomed to think of them now. The motivations for the ordering of society, for regeneration of the spiritual life, and for the fostering of the ethical sense, were thus handled at first by the ceremonials at the governing center of the society, in the form of the ritual dramas of renewal.

From this extensive history, then, we can suggest that the evolution of consciousness moves from the external to the internal form of experiencing, and from the center outwards, and from the top of the social hierarchy downwards to the people. The new psychic potentials taking shape at great turning points are first made known in myth and ritual expression, which are evidently the creation of the gifted, charismatic leaders who evolve them out of visionary states and other altered states of consciousness. In this book I have tried to demonstrate that this evolution can be traced, in specific detail, in history. In it I have taken a sampling of the myth and ritual form at each of three levels: the ritual drama belonging to the externalized, central, and apical phase, when the sacral king personified the entire potential of mankind's future development; the later internalizing, decentralizing, democratizing work of messianic visions; and, together with these, the appearance of the same myth and ritual forms in the inner experience of visionary states in individuals of today.

We learn from history that these myth and ritual forms not only come into being to give expression to the potential of future developments of consciousness, but also pass away out of collective experience when they have done their work. That is, to the degree that the sacral kingship has become internalized as a psychic reality within the individual, the outward ceremonial of monarchy has correspondingly lost its compelling vitality as necessary to the welfare of society. Kingly myth and ritual played their part in evolution and were phased out, but have not left the scene; they merely reappear on a different level of experience.

It is my thesis that the visionary states we call psychosis recapitulate this entire history, as another instance of ontogeny repeating phylogeny. The renewal process attempts to evolve a new level of consciousness in the individual, and to accomplish this, induces an identification first with the mythology of sacral kingship, then with that of messianic democratization, and finally reaches a vision of the potential spiritual consciousness for life in the world society of today.

These explorations into the historical myth and ritual forms of the renewal process have made abundantly clear the basic premise with which I first began them. It is that only with a full grasp of the nature of humankind and the human psyche in all its many aspects can we hope to understand the significance of these profoundly "altered states of consciousness" called psychotic, which involve the entire organism in a state of distress. More specifically, only when we have become familiar with the components of the processes by which the psyche reorganizes itself can we learn how best to take advantage of what nature is doing in each individual case. Our ancient forebears in the healing arts had a very clear appreciation of the *vis mediatrix naturae,* the healing power of nature, however rough may have been their perceptions and formulations of its actual mechanisms. In the still young science of psychology, our knowledge is still scarcely adequate to the task of understanding nature's work. Yet, if we are to master this field, we need to recapture the spirit of this respect for the *vis mediatrix naturae* and learn how to cooperate with it in the form of the psyche's own efforts at self-healing. Studies of this kind are, then, comparable to the basic science of the physiological chemistry of organic processes, in contrast to the applied science or art of clinical medicine.

This book is a study of the phenomenology of the human psyche's own habits of renewing itself. Such an exploration leads, of course, to the natural next question: How are these processes made effective in therapy? Do people get better when these processes are given due attention? To what practical application can we put our knowledge of them?

As I see it, these are legitimate next questions, but they follow after those with which this book is concerned. First it must be established that there is such a phenomenon as a renewal process. I hope to have demonstrated that such an entity exists by the examination of motifs in individual case material and the parallels to them in the collective myth and ritual forms of our cultural heritage. By these illustrative devices, I hope to have indicated how these motifs are relevant to the urgent emotional issues with which psychotic individuals are grappling in their own reorganizational processes. That relevance, as I see it, is the major concern of therapy. In psychotherapy, we do not "make" people "get over" their condition. What we do is cooperate with what the psyche is attempting in each case, and by relating to it, to make it conscious and understandable. The phenomenon that can be observed with most clarity is a sequence of emotional issues coming into play one after another, and their resolution, which is accomplished both by insight and by working them through in the life setting.

Overall improvement in a person's general integration and personality development is a much more complex matter. To evaluate such improvement requires a battery of clinical assessment tests using more or less objective scales. Our difficulty with such assessments is that, while they might indicate such overall gains by the personality, the tests do not show how such gains are to be correlated with the content of the specific psychic processes. The question may always be raised, How does one know that clinical improvement has anything to do with the specific contents of the psychotic renewal process? This question has been a stumbling block in the relation between medical psychiatry and psychotherapy. Psychotherapy is content to focus on specific emotional issues and to work with them at close range, hoping that general improvement will become evident in time. Medical psychiatry maintains as a fixed aim the handling of psychiatric crises and their symptomatology; its goal is to get the "patient" back into reasonably effective adaptation and to clear up the symptoms. Dealing with content is in such clinical circles regarded as irrelevant and unfruitful.

In an effort to cope with the secondary question of how inner psychic process relates to improvement, the Diabasis project in San Francisco is launching a three-year investigation of schizophrenic episodes in young adults. In that time, we hope to have observed some hundred cases in this drug-free, nonhospital residence setting, and to have compared them with an equal number treated in the more customary psychiatric setting of a hospital facility. In this study we have a unique opportunity for overcoming the difficulty, because we will be keeping daily records of the inner processes revealed in the "mental content" and of the therapeutic sessions in which these processes are brought into play. We will also have periodic evaluations of the clinical progress for a prolonged follow-up period. The general intent is to demonstrate the effectiveness of this type of therapeutic milieu in a nonhospital, drug-free facility. The aims and objectives stated in our evaluation design are listed in the following section.

The goals of the project are:

1. To prevent the necessity of rehospitalization, and thus to establish that the method we advocate avoids the costly revolving door phenomenon to a significant extent.
2. To prevent chronicity, and thus to establish that this method avoids the customary low level of psychological functioning following psychotic episodes, and that, on the contrary, fosters development.
3. To make possible effective living after the psychotic episode, and to help further:
   a. More rewarding relationships.
   b. More autonomy from old family ties.
   c. More capacity for pursuing vocational goals and self-support.
4. To determine which kinds of psychotic individuals are best able to make fruitful use of this kind of residential program, and the criteria by which these individuals are to be recognized.

The objectives of the project are:

1. Of clients admitted in the third year, that is, after two years of the staff's learning experience, 75 percent will need no further rehospitalization, providing they stay in residence over ten days.
2. On follow-up evaluations, indications of worsening after discharge will occur in not more than 25 percent of all clients (the usual average being 45 percent).
3. Growth and development will register on a continuous upward curve in the evaluation scales on follow-up in the major number of cases.
4. In order to determine which kinds of individuals do best in this residential program, the items of mental content (that is, ideational and delusional) will be categorized, and quantified positive and negative correlations made with the degree of progress in each case.

These appear to be bold claims for the success of our methods, but they are based on the actual experience of our first trial run, between 1974 and 1975, of a little less than a year as a community mental health facility.

Now as concerns the specifics of the inner psychic process, my intention is to attempt correlations between the nature of certain components of the renewal process and the outcome of the episode in respect to certain items of personality development. Although these correlations have not been planned in detail at the time of this writing, what I will be looking for can be briefly and roughly indicated here:

1. *The Center.* Will the cases that bring the image of the center into play most prominently be the cases that show evidence of most intensive integrative work of the personality?
2. *Death.* Will cases that experience the most stressful sense of dying be the ones that most thoroughly let go their previous, prepsychotic modes of handling their emotional life?
3. *Return to the Beginnings.* Will cases that elaborate a distinct creation myth show evidence of a revitalized sense of meaningfulness in their world, as an expression of a new world view?
4. *The Cosmic Conflict.* Will cases with a vivid motif of clashing world powers show evidence of a reexamination of their moral and value system?
5. *The Reversal of Opposites.* Will cases who reveal fear of the opposite sex, or of change into the opposite sex, show evidence of developing a consciousness of their contrasexual component (anima or animus)?
6. *Apotheosis.* If, in the ideas of grandeur, the tenor of the motif begins with all-powerfulness and shifts toward all-lovingness, will the personality inventories show an increased capacity for relatedness?
7. *The Sacred Marriage.* Will the emotional vividness of the sacred marriage motif vary together with indications of an influx of vital creative energy?

8. *The New Birth.* Can it be demonstrated that the motif of the new birth correlates with the reorganization of the self-image and symbolizes its new form?
9. *The New Society.* Will the details of the messianic vision of a renewed society reappear in the individual's preferences for a compatible form of cultural context for him or her to live in?
10. *The Quadrated World.* Will the form of the individual's world image in a balanced set of opposites reveal his or her capacity to integrate opposites and sustain paradoxes?

I will also be asking, in respect to the entire array of these ten components:

1. Do these image sequences of the renewal process appear in most cases in the acute episode, or in only a few?
2. Does the occurrence of the complete set of all ten components indicate a more favorable outcome in terms of reorganizing the self?

It becomes all too evident in enumerating these possible correlations how enormously difficult it may be to formulate them with any precision or accuracy. An obvious obstacle, to begin with, is the absence of any personality assessment before the onset of the psychosis, with which to make any comparisons in the later development of the personality. Beyond that, it may be found to be a challenging task to trace the evolution of certain traits all the way from their expression in symbolic form to their appearance in quantifiable personality profiles.

However, it appears to me that unless we make this effort, we will go on making blind assumptions about the "psychopathology" of the psychotic episode and missing all the while the value of the work that the psyche is doing to redress its imbalances through its renewal process.

Appendix: Case Protocols

The following sections are summaries of the mental content of the renewal process, for twelve cases in the series of psychotic persons with whom I worked in psychotherapy. The imagery was "delusional," in the sense that the individuals believed them to be truly happening in outer reality. I have condensed and rearranged the content from my notes taken down immediately following my interviews, and also from the nurses' progress notes. The letters and numbers in each sequence, of course, represent the elements in the renewal process described in this volume:

A. The split self-image, positive and negative.
B. Ideas of a drama or ritual performance.

1. The center.
2. Death.
3. The return to the beginnings, cosmic and personal.
4. The clash of opposites; the cosmic conflict.
5. The reversal of opposites; fear of the opposite sex.

6. The apotheosis.
7. The union of opposites; the sacred marriage.
8. The new birth.
9. The renewed society.
10. The quadrated world image.

I have drawn from this material in Chapter Five to provide illustrations of the various elements of the renewal process as they occur in therapy. In these instances I was attempting to demonstrate how these motifs connect with the urgent emotional issues in these persons' lives and thus have a bearing on their growth process. In this appendix I am showing how the entire image sequence tends to make its appearance in each case, merely in the flow of verbal and visual statements, apart from their life context.

The twelve patients exhibited imagery related to the ten basic elements of the renewal process.

Cases	1	2	3	4	5	6	7	8	9	10	11	12
A. Self-Images	+	+	+	+	+	+	+	+	+	+	+	+
B. Drama or Ritual	—	—	+	+	+	+	—	—	+	+	+	+
1. World Center	+	+	+	+	+	+	+	—	—	+	—	+
2. Death and Afterlife	+	+	+	+	+	+	+	+	+	+	+	+
3. Return to Beginnings	+	+	+	+	+	+	+	+	—	+	+	+
4. Cosmic Conflict	+	+	+	+	+	+	+	+	+	+	+	+
5. Threat of Other Sex	+	+	+	+	+	+	+	+	+	+	+	+
6. Apotheosis	+	+	+	+	+	+	+	+	+	+	+	+
7. Sacred Marriage	+	+	+	+	+	+	+	+	—	+	+	+
8. New Birth	+	+	+	+	+	+	+	+	+	+	+	+
9. New Society	+	+	+	+	+	+	+	+	+	+	—	+
10. Quadrated World	+	+	+	+	+	+	+	—	—	+	—	+

Case 1 (1949)

A. She had looked on herself as "gabby and superficial," and her feelings as not grownup. In her psychosis she saw herself as having two sides: one side gay, the other quiet, or one cheerful and one bad, or one pushed aside and one the center of attraction.

B. Ideas of ritual or drama were missing.

1. The location of events in a world center was prominent throughout the process; first she was on the fence at the center between the two opposing sides of the world, between which there was to be a vote; then, as the opposing sides came into conflict, war was at the center. At one point, Christ was at the center of the world and she was "just a little bit" off to one side.

2. She felt threatened at the start with "punishment for a bad life," she believed she was being "framed for murder," and she heard eight shots. She feared being framed and poisoned, and feared odors. A little later she developed a new view of death—that it was the "Christ in all of us" who is "killed and planted in a tomb"—but that "Christ's death is only of the body," and he is risen again. She believed she had died and was resurrected, and that "this is the afterlife here"; "death is a planting," and "you come back the same." At her most regressed level, she saw herself at the center of attention in a circle ringed by the mother, father, and husband, in which she said, "I guess I love me," and called herself "such a self-centered child." At this point she thought herself to be Churchill's daughter.

3. There was the barest intimation of a creation idea, that she was "responsible for everything," and that she was "at the center, being watched"; she was "the cause of everything," especially bad and hurtful things.

4. She saw the world as divided into opposite camps. There was to be a vote between the sides, which were at first the mother's and father's sides, connected with the sun and moon. Later, there was a war at the center between the two; then a third party entered in to take it all over; and, finally, a fourth party, the communists, entered the war.

5. She felt herself being changed into a man by pills.

6. When at the center, she had extraordinary powers, controlling the sun, the moon, and the rain: "I tie up the whole world because I am ruling them," and "all the world has come to see me."

7. There was a marriage between the "masculine and feminine parts of me, creating a new baby."

8. This baby was the "third party," which was a "new life, a new birth"; she saw the clash of the four parties at the center and knew

that "the new birth will come of this." These parties clashed to bring a new order.

9. The Republicans were the mother's upper-class party, the Democrats the father's; the revolutionaries, both socialist and communist, were the husband's lower-class revolutionaries, and the socialists were "on one level, a happy medium. They believe in the brotherhood of man, and they're sociable, all one class"; the socialists were "after the upper class, to destroy the upper and level it off."

10. An early picture of the world showed a circle in a square, because "some think the world is square, others think it's round." The corners of the square were the future life. The picture contained sun and moon. The final drawing of the clash of the four parties showed a quadrated circle, with a war at the center, then darkness, and finally the sun coming out at the center, giving warmth and peace.

Case 2 (1951–1952)

A. This individual had extremely debased feelings about himself: "For twenty years I've been the little guy behind the eight-ball"; "I'm called a ghost, just a white garment walking through the halls." He felt like a "sad-sack," "Like castor oil, that passes right through and nobody likes," and "Like the cigarette you don't want to smoke." His "spirit's been killed, like an old horse that can't go any more" . . . like an orphan stolen from the garbage collection . . . out in the shadow, alone, a black curtain between him and others. On the other hand, he called himself "Ace High," the most perfect man and the nation's hero, with a body of steel, who can crush anything, and the world's leading scientist.

B. Ideas of a ritual or drama were not expressed.

1. The theme of a world center was not greatly stressed but was implied in the form of allusions to the Garden of Eden, where the Father, the Mother, and the Son (himself, and also Christ) were, and where they bet the Devil against God. When they left, the Devil took over Eden. Those three figures and the Devil made up the "Four Aces," drawn as a cross in a circle.

2. He believed he was a sacrifice in the war against Hell, along with his 300 companions. People thought he was Christ, who was

sacrificed but rose again in the spirit; the dead claw their way out of the grave, and those risen dead are the crazy people (in the hospital). He was being framed, and the communists' goal was to assassinate him and burn and bury him alive. He was taken to a room below, in his sleep, and "jumped on, pommeled and pounded up, balls and all."

3. The regression was expressed mainly in the form of the rebirth process: he said to his resident psychotherapist, a woman, "We are reborn every nineteen years. We go back to our mother's womb and are reborn again. . . . It takes my mother to get my strength. I knew you were my mother. The Garden of Eden will live forever." There was a period when, for a few interviews, he spoke of his birth and events of his infancy in delusional form: "I'm Richard the Lion-Hearted; they've been assassinating me all my life . . . that means I killed a tiger when I was born. . . . I was born a lion before I was a boy. . . . I killed the serpent, the black python when just a new baby. . . . that was the first trial, the first assassination attempt. . . . I was born in Japan, and the Chinese Communists stole me away. . . . "I was born in Russia, and taken by the Japs."

3. Ideas of the beginning of time occurred in a few interviews in which the Garden of Eden theme predominated. He said to the resident, "You were the first woman, I was the first man; we were Adam and Eve, and our first son was David, and Christ was our son . . . the woman and the man of iron. . . . You sent Christ from the moon and he was crucified. . . . You saved my life; the Garden of Eden will live forever; you went to the north and I went to the south; we always looked for our tree. . . . we started the Christmas tree."

4. He believed himself the hero leading the country's struggle against communism: "I sacrificed my life for my country. . . . Hell has the Ace against the three (Adam, Eve, and Christ). . . . The war of the kings will be the end, but I could save the world from Hell; these are the four kings of the North, East, South, and West. . . . If you release me the Communists will die out, else there'll be the A-bomb." The Russians were trying to get the whole world, but he was being transported to Moscow by submarine—then the United States would own Russia; Russians were trying to assassinate him.

5. He had many complaints about the strength of woman: women wear the pants, are the tougher fighters, carry the gun, and want the men to go to war and cut off the boys' tails, and are murderers of their sons and husbands; they are stronger ten to one. He had been a woman all his life, and his father had broken his penis; but now he was restored to manhood again.

6. He saw himself as king of the United States; he was Richard the Lion-Hearted; also George Washington. As Prince Valiant he had a seven-pointed star and jewel crown, and shield in the form of a heart. He was leader of the German race, their emperor, and invincible, and would rule the world as a knight; they would attack tomorrow to take over the world and to capture their favorite son; he was the first of ten in power over the universe.

7. The sacred marriage was included in his story of the Garden of Eden, in which the resident psychotherapist and he, as first man and first woman, united to produce their son David, and later Christ. He also saw the resident as Mary, himself as Joseph. With their child they were nailed to the Cross, but rose again in the spirit.

8. The new birth occurred in the idea of being reborn every nineteen years, and of giving birth to David and Christ.

9. The idea of a new society came in the form of superscientists of Germany coming to take over the world, with a new power over the universe.

10. The quadrated world was depicted in several ways—notably in the four kings of the four directions, the "four aces," who were at war. He drew a picture of this world, but the drawing showed no resolution of the tension in a peaceable settlement. The design combined the Garden of Eden motif with that of the four kings.

Case 3 (1954)

A. This individual spoke of himself as beneath everyone, and as lonely, and called himself "Skunk." On the other hand, when he was admitted, he felt he was "brought here by God," and was especially chosen to serve Our Lady.

B. He had ideas that play-acting was going on, and said that the people helping him were Hollywood actors.

1. In my first interview, he drew a diagram on the wall tile that described a square, a circle, and a cross, all concentric. At the center he stressed a point and identified it with himself; from then on he spoke of himself or the Holy Ghost being at the center.

2. At this center there was a "going up and down," for he was to go to Hell and Purgatory and back, these being the "Three Ways of Initiation." A little earlier he felt that he was "making the way of the cross" and imagined he felt the nails in him. At other times he thought he was being poisoned and sometimes shouted, "Go ahead, kill me, kill me!"

3. He thought of time as going backward, and he drew a diagram of the sun at the center of the cosmos and the four directions as time in reverse, and called the diagram "back-o'clock."

4. He saw the world as divided in a mortal struggle between Catholicism and the forces of the Devil, in the form of the Sodality of Our Lady leading the war against communism; it was Bishop Sheen against the Movie Set (that is, the Reds). Sometimes he heard the Devil talking to him.

5. He saw the world as being dominated by the divine woman, since it was about to be ruled by Our Lady of Fatima, of whom he was a special apostle and chief defender. He felt an urgent need to marry, and gave indications of great aggravation when there was any hint of a homosexual advance toward him on the ward, and was put into a tremendous rage on these occasions.

6. He saw himself as having the characteristics and powers of Christ, and as being the Second Coming. He drew diagrams of himself as the Holy Ghost in a quarternity of Father, Mary, Jesus, and himself as Holy Ghost (whom he once called Dope). He was also the successor to the fifteenth President.

7. One day he gazed upward and said he was seeing the Immaculate Conception. All redheads were recognized as Mary, whom he was to marry: one was Cora, which meant the Sacred Heart; one Rose, or the Rose of Sharon; and one Claire, the moon, or "claire de lune."

8. Along with these ideas of marrying Mary were many comments about birth, and a wish for twelve babies. Claire was the same as his sister, and he associated her with conception, with birth; this

birth was like an egg, which he drew. He also thought of the fourth degree of initiation as a rebirth.

9. He envisioned a new splendid order to be brought into the world by the World Mission of Our Lady of Fatima. There was a ceremony in which lighted candles were carried from a center, to all parts of the world. This ceremony would be Victory in Heaven, and in this order there would be tolerance for all colors and creeds without discrimination.

10. He drew this new order as a world in four continents; he also drew a rosary in four colors as the World Mission Rosary.

Case 4 (1954–1955)

A. This person thought of herself as too scatterbrained and silly to be liked; yet she had secret hopes of becoming a great mystic in the manner of a famous historical example.

B. Early in the process, she felt herself to be taking part in primitive rituals and dances and chants, which she carried out with energy in her hyperactive phase; she felt she had to carry out certain assignments as ordeals or trials, as follows.

1. She was in the middle between two warring world factions.

2. She was dead, in an afterlife state and in hell; the Devil was in her bones, which were turned backwards. Here she had to crawl through a skeleton and out of the mouth, while around her, her friends were in animal masks. The Pope was also in hell, and his tiara torn into triangular bits, while at the same time and by the same token, the Holy Trinity was similarly dismembered.

3. She was also having to go back to the beginnings of creation, to repeat it from the start and to go through the whole process of evolution step by step. She was in the primordial sea with its monsters, then on the land in the age of reptiles, and then among primitives and their rituals. At the same time she had to return to her own birth and repeat the stages of her growth up to the present without error; she could only reach the age of sixteen.

4. The world was divided in a cosmic conflict between two battling camps, and she was at the center between them. The Devil, using radioactive substances, was trying to destroy the world, and

Christ was opposing him to try to save it; the former was in the forces of communism, the latter, in the forces of democracy.

5. At the same time these forces were her own male and female sides in opposition. The Devil and God were speaking with conflicting voices in her ear.

7. (The order of elements has been transposed to keep the sequence of her fantasy.) She was having nightly intercourse with God in the semblance of her father and/or her boyfriend.

6. This intercourse made of her a kind of Virgin Mother, a chosen mystic with a world role in the cosmic conflict. She had a vision of herself and her lover as King and Queen of the Universe, being twin brother and sister, and prince and princess; she and he stood on globes, and another couple did also, on another pair of globes, which were planets.

8. This vision was followed by the birth of a Divine Child, a savior in a new form that was to release the world from the cosmic conflict; the communists made an effort to steal this baby, but a woman called the Queen of the Sea used magic to protect it.

9. She had a vision of the Blessed Virgin and Christ at the window, in which Our Lady gave her a special message to the world that the women should keep their marriage vows; this message was to bring a reform in the morals of society, under her own leadership in this special mission.

10. She had another vision of the world as a mountain, being circled by a plane that stopped at each of four planets around it: God, Mercury, Mars, and Venus (Mars was where colored people belonged, and work horses with black tails).

Case 5 (1955)

A. This individual saw himself as one not to be taken seriously as apologetic and foolish, so he "played the clown to carry it off"—he took the role of Peck's bad boy, the little joker. He also felt like a ghost, an idea associated with his identifying with his paternal grandfather who had been to him, and even to his father, a legend only; this grandfather had been a bon vivant, a lanky, colorful roisterer who died in a barroom brawl. This individual's tall stature was like this forebear, and so he called himself Giant—as Giant he could beat up anyone and gain respect.

B. There was only a vague allusion to his ward-mates playing roles.

1. When introducing the grandfather as his own prototype, especially longing to live on a ranch as he had, the young man drew a picture of him as a cowboy hero, and a moment later drew a quadrated world.

2. Some days later he represented the death of the grandfather with flowers growing out from his body, and a complex sunflower plant rising at his feet, which had to do with the grandmother and new life. He wrote as he talked: "I'm my own grandpa," and "not time to die yet," and "Who wants to die?" There was great anxiety and depression over this feeling, drawn as a graveyard with a black cross in the middle.

3. He sought life on a ranch, getting back to primitive fundamentals and to his ancestral heritage; he represented it cosmically, as the creation of a new world. He also reviewed his early years, drawing events of school years and home in the shapes of circles and squares.

4. He believed the world to be drawn up in a conflict between the north and the south sides; he was at the south, the Devil's side, controlled by lions; it was "Mac and me," and Mac was king. He was thus leagued with the Devil when he was feeling overcome by death; at other times he was the hero leading the struggle for God.

5. He feared the feminine: he was enraged at anything suggesting homosexual passes, and once shouted, "No one can make a goddamn woman of me." He envisioned the Trinity as female, made up of the Blue Moon, the Virgin Mary, and his wife.

6. He believed himself to be the Hero who would discover the Emperor Norton's treasure and thus would gain power to lead the world to salvation. He drew himself as one member of the Holy Trinity, made up of Father, Son, and Holy Ghost, the latter being himself in his clown and ghost image.

7. He represented his marriage as the union of Sun and Moon, which "stick together." These two, together with the Holy Ghost, made up the Trinity; a blue star was added, being the Blessed Virgin Mary and/or his wife.

8. From that union of the Trinity and the Virgin, and also that of the Sun and Moon, came a child that was divine and that was also his baby girl.

9. He saw his special mission as restoring a firm law and order in society; as the hero, he would join the forces of law enforcement toward this end.

10. He visualized the world divided into four races and colors, and four religions, which would have to be granted their equality. He drew a map of the world in four islands or continents.

Case 6 (1955–1956)

A. This individual was quick to set up antagonistic relationships by presenting herself as insulting, sarcastic, and hostile, which is a mood she seemed to enter when feeling disliked; yet she also took over the management of any situation needing her help as a nurse. On entering therapy she said the reason she had to come in was that she knew too much and the world was afraid of her.

B. She called all the movie stars her personal friends and felt herself to be reliving the story of the movie "Not as a Stranger."

1. Her delusions wove around a theme of her Aztec ancestry. Her grandfather was at present the Emperor of the Aztec nation and was visualized as reigning at its center.

2. She herself was communing with the Aztec ancestors and meeting their famous personages among the dead, and was living amongst them in their spirit world.

3. The ancestors were telling her of "their secret past," the story returning to the earliest origins of their people and the formation of their nation. During this time she was tearing up her clothes and reshaping the pieces into Aztec costumes—quite like a child, as she herself remarked.

4. She held secret communications at the window by drawing the curtain across the light, which had to do with radioactivity. For there was a revolution going on, a war by her uncles in a federation against the tyrannical government of the emperor, their father.

6. She herself was Queen of the Aztecs, especially elected by God to lead her people.

5. She was queen, not as a woman, but as a doctor, for she had been "living sixteen years as a boy and then became a man," and could "take on anyone."

7. There were indications of her being the mate to the King of the Aztecs.

8. She expressed concern over a pregnancy. Her "father was the Holy Ghost," and thus her own birth was a spiritual one.

9. The new order among the Aztecs as set up by the uncles was to be an era of fair government and equality to supercede the former tyranny.

10. The grandfather's four sons were to make an arrangement among themselves to overthrow his central government and to divide up the kingdom into four equal areas, over each of which one would reign as king.

Case 7 (1956)

A. She had customarily found herself cold and teasing toward men and disliked herself for it, and at the onset of her illness her first delusion was that she was a witch who had the Evil Eye and magic power. She also identified with Queen Elizabeth the First as a cold and ruthless figure of power.

B. Ideas of ritual and drama were not expressed.

1. She felt that the San Francisco Bay Area was a world center being engulfed either by fire or water and dropping down to become a new hell while a new heavenly city would replace it. She was at the center of conflicting world powers.

2. She thought she was being punished for her evil and wanted to be baptized, and that she had died and was in an afterlife state, along with the hospital personnel.

3. She had visions of the time of creation and early evolution, and of the first primitive peoples migrating across the continents and over the English Channel to the British Isles. She found herself preoccupied with sinister visions of holes in the earth that she had known in early childhood, and she thought herself back there again and felt very young.

4. She was frightened at being caught up in a struggle for power between Communism and Democracy, between which two

camps the whole world was divided. She was at the center of plots and counterplots, both sides wanting to make use of her knowledge, and she feared being poisoned.

5. She believed the feminine women were to be sent away to South America to be given work.

6. One day she was watching a lightning storm and had visions of a series of great holy men—Moses, Paul, and Luther—and in great exultation received the revelation that she was to be the fourth, and thus to be the leader of a fourth major new religious era. Each leader was a reincarnation of the same great divine spirit.

7. There were vague allusions to her being a new Virgin Mother (Elizabeth as the Virgin Queen), but this role was kept secret. This idea was overshadowed by a greater picture of things to come.

9. When the Bay Area became the New Hell, a New Bethlehem was to drop from the sky in spaceships, and a whole new order was to be brought to the world as an achievement of science.

10. This city was to be understood as a new version of the Heavenly City, the New Jerusalem, and its place as the center of the world.

8. There was to be no one new Savior, but every oldest son was to be a Son of Man.

9. All oldest sons were to be perfect men, knowing everything of importance for human welfare, even as children. The result was to be that people were to have the wisdom to enable them to live sensibly together in peace.

Case 8 (1957)

A. She looked down on her own womanly self, and disliked anything feminine, adopting the same attitude toward herself that the mother and brother had held toward her. She felt she was not good enough for her husband, yet also too good for him. She had two names, the first of which held the connotation of this insufficient person; the second—Christine—she favored as representing her Christlike better self.

B. The idea of playing dramatic or ritual roles was not explicit.

1. The setting of a world center was not mentioned.

2. She had fears of death, and also had concerns about the Crucifixion, inasmuch as she was identified with Christ. On one occasion she said, "But the Devil won't let me die." She had a panicky feeling of being suffocated by a pillow in her bed.

3. This feeling reenacted an episode of her infancy in which her brother tried to do just that. She mentioned once her being obedient "like a child to his mother." There were beliefs about the immanent destruction of the world.

4. There were apparently no clearcut ideas of frank world conflict but the equivalent ones concerned the opposition of good and evil, or the Devil and God. She "fled from G—" (the doctor, in seeing whom she once hallucinated the image of the Devil) "to God and back again." Also she said often, "My right hand doesn't know my left hand," or "I can't tell what my left hand is doing." There was a conflict between her two natures, one Mary Magdalene as the dark, lower, sexual woman, the other as Christine, the bright, higher, spiritual self that was Christlike. The opposition of these seemed to become an issue of world importance. On some occasions she had war in mind, pointing to Asian women and saying, "You're Japanese; we fought you," or "You're Korean and you're a Communist."

5. There was considerable confusion of sexual roles. She not only thought she was Christ, but said often, "I'm a man." Once, she looked at a nurse at her room window and shouted, "I see a woman, yet you say it's a male—let him be male if it be Thy will."

6. Her divine identifications were several. She said "I am the Lord Jesus Christ," or "I am God—the Son of God." She also thought of herself as the Daughter of Judah, a prophetess, the chosen instrument and emissary of God.

8. God chose her to give birth to a child because she was good and already the mother of John the Baptist. This was a child of the spirit and her husband was not the father.

7. She saw the face of Christ in a man she was in love with, and thought she had made love with him.

8. She was convinced she was pregnant and thought, "the baby had been dirty, but God made it clean again," and "He shall save the world, for he shall be called David Emmanuel." On one occasion she thought the child had been already born.

9. At the onset of her disturbance, she proclaimed, "Christ is about to appear at 10 o'clock"; she had ideas of a new salvation of the world.

Case 9 (1958)

A. This individual thought of himself as "no good"; he had "bad thoughts." His father used to tell him, "You're bad; you're bad," and so he thought he was bad, and therefore could never look people in the eye; he could not because he was weak. Yet he had set about "winning people's respect through admiration and fear," by establishing himself as a "tough reformer."

B. He thought there was some connection between himself and television performances.

1. No location of a world center was mentioned.

2. He had fears of being killed and had latent suicidal and homicidal tendencies.

3. He expressed no ideas of return to the beginnings, but he spent much time "trying to figure out my childhood actions."

4. He was particularly preoccupied with the relative merits of democracy and communism, the former being too soft, wishy-washy, and weak, the latter being tough, aggressive, and strong. He vacillated as to which he would prefer, and he presented the conflict between these two world powers as a struggle within himself. When he did not believe in communism, it was "because it is cold"; he hated his father, because his father was cold, "like a machine." His wish was to "get my father into a situation where I can tear down his defenses, so I can prove to him that he has emotions, then he and mother can be together." Democracy, on the other hand, he saw as too soft, and religious and sentimental, like his mother. Communism was practical, made up of practical he-men, while democracies were made up of idealistic sissies.

5. What made him feel guilty and unable to look people in the eye was the woman psychiatrist he had had previously. He displayed a fair amount of concern over his sexual adequacy.

6. He saw himself as a hero for the reform of the world through communism: "The whole world is wrong and I'm right—I'm going to change the world." He said he had an extraordinary power over

other people's values and power to convert people to his way of thinking.

7. Ideas of a sacred marriage did not make their appearance clearly.

8. He made occasional mention of the rebirth he was undergoing.

9. He thought of himself as a heroic reformer who would change the order of society: he would work for the Communist Party and save the world, for he was "in conflict with society" and would "give society one last chance to do something" for him and then would turn Communist.

10. There were no clear indications of a quadrated world image.

Case 10 (1958–1959)

A. This individual had always entertained a painful misgiving about herself, that she was an "oddball," essentially alone, unlike the others, and eccentric. She expressed this feeling in a tendency to play the trouble-maker and the slightly "zany" part. Yet she had notions of having a special calling in connection with the medical profession, which then slipped over into the delusional system.

B. She did not, overall, feel herself to be playing a dramatic role, but on two occasions she did so, each with a ritual significance. Once, she looked out at the stone grotto outside and had a vision of a dramatic performance of the story of the Nativity. On another occasion, she saw herself, when sitting with others at the table, as Christ with the Twelve in the Last Supper, which was being broadcast on television to the entire world.

1. The motif of a world center came in the form of the Garden of Eden, the New Jerusalem, and the middle between two opposing sides in the world conflict.

3. The Garden of Eden was her opening delusional experience, in which she felt herself to be Mother Eve.

2. At that time she thought everyone in the world had died except three women and one man here.

3. Soon she saw this experience as the beginnings of creation, and expected everyone to be "going around as primitives, all naked."

She saw her watch as made of solid gold, so that time stood still. At the same time, she was aware of returning to the state of a very young girl, needing warmth and touch, and writing a letter to Santa Claus asking for a "Tweedy Teddy Bear with his chuckle-buckle belt," expressing her delight with her therapist.

2. On admission, she thought she had died and was living in an afterlife state, the people around her here were "the Bread of Heaven," all having died. The theme of crucifixion was prevalent in her drawings, notably in one that showed a crowned serpent on the cross. Her vision of Nativity in the Grotto was preceded by a vision of a sacrifice of one "Lopex," a traitor to his country, shown on an altar being beheaded.

4. She expected an invasion from the communists and sensed their plots as a threat to her person.

5. Meanwhile, men were to be abolished and their sperm kept in jars against the time of the need of men when the communists invaded. All the masculine aspect of the culture was to be abolished as well, so that science and industry were to be given up, and all metals returned to Mother Earth from whom men had stolen them. People were to revert to the life of household and soil. She depicted her soul as a woman with a cup running over, as in the Twenty-Third Psalm. On the other hand, she once saw Man, in the person of the therapist, as a rapist, brutalizing women and using them sexually.

6. One day she saw herself glorified as a divine creatrix and she "created three stars and the moon itself, and peopled them"; she had a feeling "of being the whole universe," making worlds and peoples. She was Old Mother Earth herself. On another day, she had a vision of people climbing up a stairway toward her to adore her "as a holy person," Christlike, dressed in blue (male), white (Christlike) and black (the Devil), and a blanket over her (Mother Eve).

7. As Elizabeth of England, the sweet and gentle Queen of Peace, she was married to Perry, Prince of Peace (the title of King James of the Bible); there was much talk of marriage of Queen and King, also of her being both male and female as Christ and Eve.

8. Birth was a repeated theme inasmuch as she conceived herself as a Virgin Mother giving birth to a New Redeemer, and thought

she was pregnant at the time. She not only saw the Nativity in the Grotto as her own birth-giving role, but she also recognized the Christ Child in her pillow, and found twelve babies under her blanket. In fact, she saw all the women on the ward as pregnant.

9. The work to be done was to rewrite the Bible to bring a new gospel of love and kindness to heal the world of its illnesses. The new order of society was to be the return to the household and soil, so that family life would replace industry and science. She envisioned this as the New Jerusalem, a New Heaven and a New Earth as in the Apocalypse; this was to be San Francisco, the City of Peace.

10. This new world was drawn in the shape of a cross, a four-square city. Its center was her palace—the hospital—all of gold, and by it the Tree for the healing of the nations.

Case 11 (1959–1960)

A. This individual tended to assume that people would dislike her and find her stupid, also disagreeable and witchlike. Yet she also felt herself to be greatly superior to other people in intelligence, and blamed herself for being vain, proud, and haughty. This superiority developed into the feeling of special election in her psychosis.

B. She believed herself to be implicated in dramas taking place on television.

2. On admission, and for several weeks, she was the picture of fear, cringing and hiding her face in her hands. Later she said, of this time, "I was frightened of my own shadow." In this period she believed she was going to be put to death.

1. She voiced no ideas of a world center.

3. She expressed feelings of being a little girl and made many demands for extra food and attention, especially getting her mother to bring in all kinds of special goodies of her own making. She lamented for weeks over longing to go home again, and repeated the request to do so many times a day. She would say, "I want to be sent back to my mother and father—I'm their little baby in blue."

4. She believed she heard, at the outbreak of her disorder, the Last Trumpet sounding the call for the final mammoth conflict between the forces of Good and of Evil.

3. This conflict was to be an Armaggedon that would mark the

End of the World. She believed herself embroiled in this struggle in some way that was not defined, but that seemed to add to her extreme fears.

5. She expressed misgivings about her womanhood—that she did not look like a woman and had been a tomboy all her life. Her aggressiveness was marked and sharp, and she tended to seek a refuge of superiority over others in her intellectual capabilities.

6. She hinted that, when she heard the trumpet announcing the end, she knew that she was elected to an important world mission; its nature she left undefined, except to say that it was "pretty tremendous."

7. She evaded, and yet hinted at, the mission having to do with being a spouse of God.

8. She did express many concerns with rebirth and the idea of giving birth.

On the whole, these delusional ideas were powerful but were kept as her secret revelations and knowledge, and at no point did she openly volunteer to tell them to me.

Case 12 (1961)

A. This individual early learned to believe that she was unlovable and alone in the world, however much she might gain favor and liking. Yet she resolved to be strong and strive for perfection, and that way to get the love of God, even if she could not have the usual kind. Recently, she found herself purer than the priests she consulted for spiritual counseling, and was warned by them of her haughtiness and arrogance: this pose of superiority developed into her feeling of special election. In her exaltation, she found herself, "not quite of this world," (dating from a time about half a year before admission); she felt specially called by the Blessed Mother, and felt her "heart lifted up as if floating on a cloud."

B. She felt that to enter into the frivolous emotions and concerns of ordinary people seemed "just a game," "a huge joke," and that "we all have parts to play in this act," which was "the folly of the cross," a submission to the humiliation of the world.

2. In a few hours of sustained prayer (a few weeks before admission) she sensed the "odors of death" and of evil, and felt pain

across her breasts, and knew that she was about to die; this demise she took to mean the death of the ego, to be reborn. A little later, the "sweet odors" came, those that signified the presence of the Blessed Mother.

1. She was told by the Virgin Mary to circle around the City of San Francisco, signifying God's intention to help that city through her (this delusional action led to her admission). The city was to be the center and starting point of the new order.

3. Yet the powers of death and evil were stirring and she believed herself to be Eve the Temptress, returned now to the primitive emotions and ways of the Garden of Eden at the beginning. She saw "the world turning inside out," all the things that had been hidden now being on the outside, and her previous way of seeing things being destroyed.

4. On the ward she thought she was being given "truth serum" as a brain-washing technique, which signified to her that these plotters were communists and that she must keep silent "as a test of the strength of her religious faith." When the patients gathered in two groups at opposite sides of the ward, she understood this event to be a war with "two opposing battle lines drawn up," of communism against Christianity, and Evil against Good. Within her own self she felt the opposition as sweet odors and evil ones, representing those of life and those of death—the former from the Blessed Mother and the latter from the Devil. Sin she felt to be a contagion of cold germs passed from one to another.

5. She felt some anxiety over people's misunderstanding her sexuality, that they might be thinking she was Lesbian as two other patients were. She showed some fear of men's sexuality, believing the doctors to be rapists and to be using the patients for a white slavery racket. She made many differentiations between men's and women's roles, one living by the head, the other by the heart, or one's sin being purity, the other's pride.

6. The Virgin Mary made herself known to her by the beautiful odors like incense, and gave her to know that she was specially elected to help the work of changing the world. She signed herself into the hospital on the understanding that she was here to help others, as the first step in helping humanity. She found a significant resemblance between herself and Jacqueline Kennedy, the First

Lady, and thought therefore that she had some important role in national affairs.

7. She knew herself to be married to God, as a Virgin Mother.

8. She knew herself to be pregnant with a divine child by the Spirit, which was to be a holy birth. She also felt herself going through a rebirth, and as is frequently the case with women psychotics, to be "reborn in the heart of the Virgin."

9. She had ideas of a new order under the Blessed Mother, which would be the redemption of the world, in which she would play a leading part.

10. She expressed her problem, later in the process, as the suffering represented in the cross; it shows the tension of living in both the spirit and the flesh, a vertical arm designating the aspiration of the spirit, a horizontal arm the reaching out and relating to the world. This symbolism represented the folly of the cross, the willingness to live in the world, even though one belongs to the spirit.

Notes

Introduction

1. G. Santayana, *Poems* (New York: Scribner's, 1923).

2. J. W. Perry, "Reconstitutive Process in the Psychopathology of the Self," *Annals of the New York Academy of Sciences*, 1962, *96*, 853–876.

3. J. W. Perry, *Lord of the Four Quarters: Myths of the Royal Father* (New York: Braziller, 1966).

4. J. W. Perry, "Image, Complex, and Transference in Schizophrenia," in A. Burton (Ed.) *Psychotherapy of the Psychoses* (New York: Basic Books, 1961).

5. J. W. Perry, *The Far Side of Madness* (Englewood Cliffs, N.J.: Prentice-Hall, 1974).

6. C. G. Jung, *Collected Works*, Vol. 5: *Symbols of Transformation* (R F. C. Hull, Trans.), Bollingen Series 20 (New York: Pantheon, 1956).

7. A. T. Boisen, *The Exploration of the Inner World* (Chicago: Willet, Clark, 1936).

8. H. G. Baynes, *Mythology of the Soul* (London: Methuen, 1949).

9. P. Federn, *Ego Psychology and the Psychoses* (New York: Basic Books, 1952).

10. E. von Domarus, "The Specific Laws of Logic in Schizophrenia," in J. S. Kasanin (Ed.), *Language and Thought in Schizophrenia* (Berkeley: University of California Press, 1944); A. Storch, "The Primitive Archaic Forms of Inner Experience and Thought in Schizophrenia." *Association*

for Research in Nervous and Mental Disease (New York: Funk & Wagnalls, 1924).

11. S. Freud, "Psychoanalytic Notes Upon an Autobiographical Account of a Case of Paranoia," in *Collected Papers,* Vol. 3 (London: Hogarth, 1950).

12. I. M. Kogan, "Weltuntergangserlebnis and Wiedergeburtsphantasie bei einem Schizophrenen," *Internationale Zeitschrift für Psychoanalyse,* 1932, *18,* 86–104; W. A. Spring, "Observations on World Destruction Fantasies," *Psychoanalytic Quarterly,* 1939, *8,* 363–376.

13. M. R. Kaufmann, "Religious Delusions in Schizophrenia," *International Journal of Psychoanalysis,*" 1939, *20.*

14. H. S. Sullivan, *Schizophrenia as a Human Process* (New York: Norton, 1962).

15. F. Fromm-Reichmann, "Notes on the Development and Treatment of Schizophrenics by Psychoanalytic Therapy," *Psychiatry,* 1948, *11,* 263–272.

16. S. Arieti, *Interpretation of Schizophrenia* (New York: Brunner, 1955).

17. M. Horowitz, *Image Formation and Cognition* (New York: Appleton-Century-Crofts, 1970).

18. M. Sechehaye, *Symbolic Realization* (New York: International Universities Press, 1957).

19. M. Barnes and J. Burke, *Mary Barnes: Two Accounts of a Journey Through Madness* (New York: Harcourt Brace Jovanovich, 1971).

20. S. Grof, *Realms of the Human Unconscious* (New York: Viking Press, 1975).

Chapter 1. Healing Factors in the Psychotic Episode

1. C. G. Jung, "On the Importance of the Unconscious in Psychopathology," in *Collected Works,* Vol. 3: *Psychogenesis of Mental Disease,* Bollingen Series 20 (New York: Pantheon, 1960).

2. C. G. Jung.

3. H. S. Sullivan, "Schizophrenia: Its Conservative and Malignant Features," in *Schizophrenia as a Human Process* (New York: Norton, 1962).

4. A. T. Boisen, *The Exploration of the Inner World* (New York: Willet, Clark, 1936).

5. M. Sechehaye, *Symbolic Realization* (New York: International Universities Press, 1957).

6. R. D. Laing, *The Politics of Experience* (New York: Pantheon, 1967).

7. T. J. Scheff, *Being Mentally Ill* (Chicago: Aldine Press, 1966).

8. M. Foucault, *Madness and Civilization* (R. Howard, Trans.) (New York: Pantheon, 1965).

Chapter 2. Emotional Development and the Self-Image

1. J. W. Perry, "Emotions and Object Relations," *Journal of Analytical Psychology,* 1970, *15,* 1–12.

2. C. G. Jung, "The Relations Between the Ego and the Unconscious," in *Collected Works,* Vol. 7: *Two Essays on Analytical Psychology,* Bollingen Series 20 (New York: Pantheon, 1953), Pt. 2, Chap. 2.

3. H. G. Baynes, *Mythology of the Soul* (London: Methuen, 1949), p. 163.

4. J. W. Perry, "Emotions and Object Relations."

5. C. G. Jung, *Collected Works,* Vol. 2: *Experimental Researches.* Bollingen Series 20 (Princeton: Princeton University Press, 1973).

6. C. G. Jung, "The Psychology of Dementia Praecox," *Collected Works,* Vol. 3: *The Psychogenesis of Mental Disease,* Bollingen Series 20 (New York: Pantheon, 1960), Chap. 2 and pp. 67–69; "A Review of the Complex Theory," in *Collected Works,* Vol. 18: *The Structure and Dynamics of the Psyche.* Bollingen Series 20 (New York: Pantheon, 1960), *Analytical Psychology,* The Tavistock Lectures (New York: Pantheon, 1968), Lecture Two.

7. C. G. Jung, "The Relations Between the Ego and the Unconscious."

8. C. G. Jung, "The Structure of the Psyche," in *Collected Works,* Vol. 18: *The Structure and Dynamics of the Psyche.*

9. C. G. Jung, "Instinct and the Unconscious," in *Collected Works,* Vol. 18: *The Structure and Dynamics of the Psyche.*

10. C. G. Jung, "Mind and Earth," in *Collected Works,* Vol. 10: *Civilization in Transition,* Bollingen Series 20 (New York: Pantheon, 1964), pp. 31–33; "Recent Thoughts on Schizophrenia" and "Schizophrenia," in *Collected Works,* Vol. 3: *The Psychogenesis of Mental Disease. See also* "Foreword," in J. Jacobi, *Complex/Archetype/Symbol* (New York: Pantheon, 1959).

11. C. G. Jung, "On Psychic Energy," in *Collected Works,* Vol. 18: *Structure and Dynamics of the Psyche,* p. 11; and M. Fordham, "The Origins of the Ego in Childhood," in M. Fordham (Ed.), *New Developments in Analytical Psychology* (London: Routledge & Kegan Paul, 1955).

12. J. W. Perry, "Emotions and Object Relations."

13. C. G. Jung, "Spirit and Life," in *Collected Works,* Vol. 18: *The Structure and Dynamics of the Psyche,* pp. 330–332; "The Psychology of Dementia Praecox," in *Collected Works,* Vol. 3: *The Psychogenesis of Mental Disease,* pp. 40–46, 67.

14. C. G. Jung, "A Review of the Complex Theory," in *Collected Works,* Vol. 18: *The Structure and Dynamics of the Psyche.*

15. C. G. Jung, "The Relations Between the Ego and the Unconscious," p. 195.

16. C. G. Jung, "The Association Method," in *Collected Works,* Vol. 2: *Experimental Researches,* pp. 439–463.

17. C. G. Jung, "The Psychology of Dementia Praecox," in *Collected Works,* Vol. 2: *The Psychogenesis of Mental Disease,* Chap. 2; "On Psychic Energy," in *Collected Works,* Vol. 18: *Structure and Dynamics of the Psyche.*

18. C. G. Jung, "The Relations Between the Ego and the Unconscious," Pt. 2, p. 175 ff.; "General Aspects of Dream Psychology," in *Collected Works,* Vol. 18; *The Structure and Dynamics of the Psyche,* pp. 252–257.

19. C. G. Jung, "The Structure of the Psyche"; "Psychological Aspects of the Mother Archetype," in *Collected Works,* Vol. 9: *The Archetypes and the Collective Unconscious,* Bollingen Series 20 (New York: Pantheon, 1959), Pt. 1.

20. J. W. Perry, "Emotions and Object Relations."

21. C. G. Jung, "General Aspects of Dream Psychology," pp. 264–275.

22. J. W. Perry, "Emotions and Object Relations."

23. C. G. Jung, "Conscious, Unconscious, and Individuation," in *Collected Works,* Vol. 9: *The Archetypes and the Collective Unconscious,* p. 279.

24. C. G. Jung, "The Phenomenology of the Spirit in Fairytales," in *Collected Works,* Vol. 9: *The Archetypes and the Collective Unconscious,* pp. 246–251.

25. J. W. Perry, "Emotions and Object Relations."

26. M. Fordham, "The Origins of the Ego in Childhood," in M. Fordham (Ed.), *New Developments in Analytical Psychology* (London: Routledge & Kegan Paul, 1955); *The Life of Childhood* (London: Routledge & Kegan Paul, 1944), Chap. 5.

27. M. Fordham, *The Life of Childhood.* Pt. 1, Chap. 1; C. G. Jung, "Analytical Psychology and Education," in *Collected Works,* Vol. 17: *The Development of Personality,* Bollingen Series 20 (New York: Pantheon, 1954), pp. 123–132.

28. F. Wickes, *The Inner World of Childhood* (New York: Farrar, Straus & Giroux, 1927) Chaps. 2 and 3; and C. G. Jung, "The Association Method," Lecture 2, pp. 439–463.

29. C. G. Jung, "The Psychology of the Unconscious," in *Collected Works,* Vol. 7: *Two Essays on Analytical Psychology,* pp. 12–17.

30. E. Neumann, *The Origins and History of Consciousness* (New York: Pantheon, 1954).

31. J. W. Perry, "Emotions and Object Relations; and C. G. Jung, "The Association Method," Lecture 2.

32. J. W. Perry, "Image, Complex, and Transference in Schizophrenia," in A. Burton (Ed.), *Psychotherapy of the Psychoses,* (New York: Basic Books, 1961); "Love and Power in Madness," *The Far Side of Madness,* Ch. 10.

33. C. G. Jung, "Analytical Psychology and Education," in *Collected Works,* Vol. 17: *The Development of Personality,* Lecture 3; and F. Wickes, *The Inner World of Childhood,* Chaps. 2 and 3.

34. G. Bateson and others, "Towards a Theory of Schizophrenia," *Behavioral Sciences,* 1956, *1,* 251–264.

35. R. D. Laing, and A. Esterson, *Sanity, Madness, and the Family* (Baltimore: Pelican Books, 1970); D. Jackson and others, "Psychiatrist's Conception of the Schizophrenogenic Parent," *AMA Archives of Neurology and Psychiatry*, 1958, *79*; L. Wynne and others, "Pseudomutuality in the Family Relations of Schizophrenics," *Psychiatry*, 1958, *21*, 205; C. P. Rosenbaum, *The Meaning of Madness* (New York: Science House, 1970), Chap. 7, for an excellent review of the recent literature on the family relations in schizophrenia.

36. C. G. Jung, "Analytical Psychology and Education," in *Collected Works*, Vol. 17: *The Development of Personality*, pp. 78, 127–128; F. Wickes, *The Inner World of Childhood*.

37. J. W. Perry, *The Self in Psychotic Process* (Berkeley: University of California Press, 1953).

38. C. G. Jung, "Conscious, Unconscious, and Individuation," and "Concerning Mandala Symbolism," in *Collected Works*, Vol. 9: *The Archetypes and the Collective Unconscious*, Pt. 1.

39. C. G. Jung, "Concerning Mandala Symbolism," in *Collected Works*, Vol. 9: *The Archetypes and the Collective Unconscious*, Pt. 1. J. W. Perry, *The Self in Psychotic Process*.

40. C. G. Jung, "Rex and Regina," in *Collected Works*, Vol. 14: *Mysterium Coniunctionis*, Bollingen Series 20 (New York: Pantheon, 1963), Pt. 4.

41. J. W. Perry, "Reconstitutive Process in the Psychopathology of the Self," in *Annals of the New York Academy of Sciences*, 1962, *96*, 853–876. Compare with the term *stadial development*, as used by Neumann, *The Origins and History of Consciousness*.

42. A. Van Gennep, *The Rites of Passage* (Chicago: University of Chicago Press, 1960); J. L. Henderson, *Thresholds of Initiation* (Middletown, Conn.: Wesleyan University Press, 1967).

43. J. W. Perry, "Acute Catatonic Schizophrenia," *Journal of Analytical Psychology*, 1957, *2*, 137–152.

Chapter 3. The Chronically Regressive Personality

1. C. G. Jung, *Collected Works*, Vol. 5: *Symbols of Transformation*, Bollingen Series 20 (New York: Pantheon, 1956), Chap. 7; E. Neumann, *The Origins and History of Consciousness* (New York: Pantheon, 1954), Pt. 1, Sec. A, Chaps. 1 and 2; E. Neumann, *The Great Mother*, Bollingen Series 47 (New York: Pantheon, 1955) Pt. 2, Chap. 11.

2. J. W. Perry, "Acute Catatonic Schizophrenia," *Journal of Analytical Psychology*, 1957, *2*, 137–152; S. Arieti, *Interpretation of Schizophrenia* (New York: Brunner, 1955), Pt. 2, Chap. 3, Sec. 1.

3. P. Metman, "The Ego in Schizophrenia," *Journal of Analytical Psychology*, 1956, *1*, 161–176; also, 1957, *2*, 51–70.

4. C. G. Jung, *Psychological Types* (New York: Harcourt, Brace, 1926), pp. 543–546. The term *feeling* here designates one of the functions of

consciousness, which discriminates judgments of value; it is not the same as emotion and affect, which operate through the autonomous complexes.

5. C. G. Jung, "On Psychic Energy," in *Collected Works,* Vol. 18: *The Structure and Dynamics of the Psyche,* Bollingen Series 20 (New York: Pantheon, 1960). The term *libido* here designates a general psychic energy, whose values are indicated on the unconscious level by the affective charge of a content, on the conscious level by the feeling conferred on a content.

6. C. G. Jung, "On the Psychogenesis of Schizophrenia," "Recent Thoughts on Schizophrenia," and "Schizophrenia," in *Collected Works,* Vol. 3: *The Psychogenesis of Mental Disease,* Bollingen Series 20 (New York: Pantheon, 1960).

7. C. G. Jung, "Relations Between the Ego and the Unconscious," in *Collected Works,* Vol. 7: *Two Essays on Analytical Psychology,* Bollingen Series 20 (New York: Pantheon, 1953), Chap. 2.

8. C. G. Jung, "On Psychic Energy," in *Collected Works,* Vol. 8: *The Structure and Dynamics of the Psyche.*

9. C. G. Jung, *Collected Works,* Vol. 5: *Symbols of Transformation; Collected Works,* Vol. 12: *Psychology and Alchemy,* Bollingen Series 20 (New York: Pantheon, 1953) Pt. 3, Chap. 4, Secs. 5 and 6; E. Neumann, *The Origins and History of Consciousness,* Pt. 1, Sec. B.

10. C. G. Jung, "The Psychology of the Unconscious," in *Collected Works,* Vol. 7: *Two Essays on Analytical Psychology,* Chaps. 3 and 4.

11. C. G. Jung, "The Psychology of the Unconscious," in *Collected Works,* Vol. 7: *Two Essays on Analytical Psychology,* Chaps. 3 and 4.

12. C. G. Jung, "The Psychology of the Unconscious," in *Collected Works,* Vol. 7: *Two Essays on Analytical Psychology,* Chaps. 3 and 4; "Commentary on the Secret of the Golden Flower," in *Collected Works,* Vol. 13: *Alchemical Studies,* Bollingen Series 20 (New York: Pantheon, 1971), Para. 60.

13. C. G. Jung, "Definitions," in *Psychological Types.*

14. C. G. Jung, "A Psychological View of Conscience," in *Collected Works,* Vol. 10: *Civilization in Transition,* Bollingen Series 20 (New York: Pantheon, 1964).

15. E. C. Whitmont, *The Symbolic Quest* (New York: Putnam, 1969), Chap. 13.

16. M. Eliade, *The Myth of the Eternal Return* (New York: Pantheon, 1954), pp. 21–48.

17. C. G. Jung, "A Psychological View of Conscience," in *Collected Works,* Vol. 10: *Civilization in Transition.*

18. M. Eliade, pp. 34–37; S. H. Hooke, *Myth and Ritual* (London: Oxford, 1933), pp. 215, 221.

19. C. G. Jung, *Collected Works,* Vol. 5: *Symbols of Transformation,* pp. 258–260; M.-L. von Franz, *The Problem of the Puer Aeternus* (New York: Spring Publications, 1970).

20. E. Neumann, *The Origins and History of Consciousness.*

21. C. G. Jung, "Schizophrenia," in *Collected Works,* Vol. 3: *The Psychogenesis of Mental Disease.*

Chapter 4. The Acute Psychotic Regression

1. H. Frankfort, *Kingship and the Gods* (Chicago: University of Chicago Press, 1948); F. E. Burrows, "Some Cosmological Patterns in Babylonian Religion," in S. H. Hooke (Ed.), *The Labyrinth* (New York: Macmillan, 1935).
2. S. H. Hooke (Ed.), "Myth and Ritual Patterns of the Ancient Near East," in *Myth and Ritual* (London: Oxford University Press, 1933), p. 9.
3. M. Eliade, *The Myth of the Eternal Return,* Bollingen Series 46 (New York: Pantheon, 1954), pp. 53, 66–72.
4. G. d'Alviella, "Initiation," in J. Hastings (Ed.), *Encyclopedia of Religion and Ethics,* Vol. 8. (New York: Scribner's, 1911), p. 316.
5. T. H. Gaster, *Thespis: Ritual, Myth, and Drama in the Near East* (Garden City: Doubleday, 1961), pp. 26–34.
6. J. G. Frazer, "Balder the Beautiful," in *The Golden Bough,* Pt. 7, Vol. 2 (London: Macmillan, 1919), Sec. 5.
7. C. G. Jung, "Rex and Regina," in *Collected Works,* Vol. 14: *Mysterium Coniunctionis,* Bollingen Series 20 (New York: Pantheon, 1963).
8. F. E. Burrows, "Some Cosmological Patterns in Babylonian Religion," p. 54.
9. G. Murray, "Excursus on the Ritual Forms Preserved in Greek Tragedy," in J. Harrison, *Themis* (Cambridge, England: Cambridge University Press, 1927).
10. E. O. James, *Christian Myth and Ritual* (London: J. Murray, 1937), Chap. 3.
11. A. R. Johnson, "The Role of the King in the Jerusalem Cultus," in S. H. Hooke (Ed.), *The Labyrinth.*
12. J. W. Perry, *The Self in Psychotic Process* (Berkeley: University of California Press, 1953), Chap. 9.
13. F. E. Burrows, "Some Cosmological Patterns in Babylonian Religion"; M. Eliade, *The Myth of the Eternal Return;* J. W. Perry, *Lord of the Four Quarters: Myths of the Royal Father* (New York: Braziller, 1966), Intro.
14. A. M. Hocart, *Kingship* (London: Oxford Press, 1927), Chap. 3.
15. S. Arieti, *Interpretation of Schizophrenia* (New York: Basic Books, 1955).
16. A. M. Blackman, "Myth and Ritual in Ancient Egypt," in S. H. Hooke (Ed.), *Myth and Ritual* (London: Oxford Press, 1933), Chap. 2; M. Eliade, *The Myth of the Eternal Return,* Chap. 2.
17. G. Murray, "Excursus on the Ritual Forms Preserved in Greek Tragedy"; T. H. Gaster, *Thespis.*

18. C. G. Jung, *Collected Works,* Vol. 12: *Psychology and Alchemy.* Bollingen Series 20 (New York: Pantheon, 1953), pp. 315–326.

19. G. R. Levy, *The Gate of Horn* (London: Faber & Faber, 1948), pp. 98–100, Plate 11-b.

20. C. G. Jung, *Collected Works,* Vol. 12: *Psychology and Alchemy,* p. 201; *Collected Works,* Vol. 14: *Mysterium Coniunctionis,* p. 70.

21. J. W. Perry, *The Self in Psychotic Process,* pp. 30, 70.

Chapter 5. The Ritual Drama of Renewal

1. W. R. Smith, *The Religion of the Semites* (New York: Meridian Books, 1956), pp. 18–21. (Originally published 1901.)

2. J. Harrison, *Themis* (Cambridge, England: Cambridge University Press, 1927), Chap. 2.

3. T. H. Gaster, *Thespis: Ritual, Myth, and Drama in the Ancient Near East* (Garden City, N.Y.: Doubleday), 1961.

4. J. W. Perry, *Lord of the Four Quarters: Myths of the Royal Father* (New York: Braziller, 1966).

5. A. M. Hocart, *Kingship* (London: Oxford University Press, 1927); E. O. James, *Christian Myth and Ritual* (New York: World Publishing Co., 1965). (Originally published 1937.)

6. H. W. Fairman, "The Kingship Rituals of Egypt," in S. H. Hooke (Ed.), *Myth, Ritual, and Kingship* (Oxford: Clarendon, 1958); H. Frankfort, *Kingship and the Gods,* (Chicago: University of Chicago Press, 1948); A. M. Blackman, "Myth and Ritual in Ancient Egypt," in S. H. Hooke (Ed.), *Myth and Ritual,* (London: Oxford University Press, 1933); T. H. Gaster; E. O. James, *Myth and Ritual in the Ancient Near East* (New York: Praeger, 1958).

7. H. Frankfort, *Kingship and the Gods,* p. 25.

8. H. Frankfort, *Kingship and the Gods,* pp. 151–152.

9. H. Frankfort, *Kingship and the Gods,* Chap. 8.

10. A. M. Blackman.

11. H. Frankfort, *Kingship and the Gods,* pp. 133–135.

12. H. Frankfort, *Kingship and the Gods,* pp. 151–154.

13. H. Frankfort, *Kingship and the Gods,* p. 154.

14. H. Frankfort, *Kingship and the Gods,* p. 179.

15. H. Frankfort, *Kingship and the Gods,* Chap. 13.

16. H. W. Fairman, pp. 86–91.

17. H. Frankfort, *Kingship and the Gods,* pp. 169–176.

18. H. Frankfort, *Kingship and the Gods,* pp. 178–179.

19. H. Frankfort, *Kingship and the Gods,* pp. 149–157.

20. H. Frankfort, *Kingship and the Gods,* p. 88; H. W. Fairman, pp. 84–87.

21. A. Sachs, "Akkadian Rituals," in J. B. Pritchard (Ed.), *Ancient Near Eastern Texts Relating to the Old Testament* (Princeton: Princeton University

Press, 1955). See also "Temple Program for the New Year Festival at Babylon," in H. Frankfort, *Kingship and the Gods,* pp. 317–318; also pp. 319–333 for a detailed description of Ola rites.

22. E. A. Speiser, "Akkadian Myths and Epics," in J. B. Pritchard (Ed.), *Ancient Near Eastern Texts Relating to the Old Testament* (Princeton: Princeton University Press, 1955). See "The Creation Epic," pp. 60–72.

23. E. Burrows, "Some Cosmological Patterns in Babylonian Religion," in S. H. Hooke (Ed.), *The Labyrinth* (New York: Macmillan, 1935).

24. M. Eliade, *The Myth of the Eternal Return,* Bollingen Series 46 (New York: Pantheon, 1954) p. 15; E. A. Speiser, Tablet VI; See pp. 62–63, p. 69, and fn. 100.

25. H. Frankfort, *Kingship and the Gods,* pp. 313–316.

26. S. N. Kramer, "Sumerian Myths and Epic Tales," in J. B. Pritchard (Ed.), *Ancient Near Eastern Texts Relating to the Old Testament* (Princeton: Princeton University Press, 1955) v. "Innana's Descent to the Nether World," p. 52; H. Frankfort.

27. S. N. Kramer, *Sumerian Mythology* (New York: Harper & Row, 1961), pp. 10–25.

28. H. Frankfort, *Kingship and the Gods,* p. 329.

29. H. Frankfort, *Kingship and the Gods,* pp. 293, 324–325.

30. M. Eliade, p. 57.

31. H. Frankfort, *Kingship and the Gods,* Chap. 17.

32. H. Frankfort, *Kingship and the Gods,* Chap. 16.

33. T. Jacobsen, "Mesopotamia," in H. Frankfort (Ed.), *Before Philosophy* (London: Penguin, 1949), pp. 151–153.

34. H. Frankfort, *Kingship and the Gods,* pp. 295–301.

35. H. Frankfort, *Kingship and the Gods,* pp. 297–298.

36. H. Frankfort, *Kingship and the Gods,* pp. 285–286.

37. H. Frankfort, *Kingship and the Gods,* p. 301.

38. H. Frankfort, *Kingship and the Gods,* pp. 325–326, and pp. 331–333.

39. G. Widengren, "The King and the Tree of Life in Ancient Near Eastern Religion," In *Uppsala Universitets Ărsskrift,* Vol. 4 (Uppsala, Sweden: Lundequisttika Bokhendeln, 1951), p. 18.

40. R. De Langhe, "Myth, Ritual and Kingship in the Ras Shamra Tablets," in S. H. Hooke (Ed.), *Myth, Ritual and Kingship* pp. 130–134, 139–140; T. H. Gaster, Chaps. 2 and 3; C. H. Gordon, "Canaanite Mythology," in S. N. Kramer (Ed.), *Mythologies of the Ancient World* (Garden City, N.Y.: Doubleday, 1961).

41. W. F. Albright, *The Archeology of Palestine* (Baltimore: Penguin, 1960), p. 183.

42. A. Bentzen, *King and Messiah* (London: Lutterworth, 1955), pp. 19–21; E. O. James, *Seasonal Feasts and Festivals* (New York: Barnes & Noble, 1961); E. O. James, *Myth and Ritual in the Ancient Near East;* A. R. Johnson, "The Role of the King in the Jerusalem Cultus," in S. H. Hooke (Ed.), *The Labyrinth.*

43. S. Mowinckel, *He That Cometh,* G. W. Anderson, Trans. (New York: Abingdon, 1954); A. Bentzen.

44. W. F. Albright.

45. A. Bentzen, pp. 58, 65.

46. G. Widengren, "Early Hebrew Myths and Their Interpretation," in S. H. Hooke (Ed.), *Myth, Ritual, and Kingship.*

47. A. Bentzen, p. 19; E. O. James, *Myth and Ritual in the Ancient Near East,* p. 99–120.

48. A. R. Johnson, *Sacral Kingship in Ancient Israel* (Cardiff: University of Wales Press, 1955), Chap. 1.

49. See G. Widengren, "Early Hebrew Myths and Their Interpretation," pp. 149–159, for a review of the literature establishing this formulation of the New Year Festival; see A. R. Johnson for the detailed rendering of the ritual.

50. Psalm 48:9, trans. by A. R. Johnson in *Sacral Kingship in Ancient Israel,* pp. 77–81.

51. T. H. Gaster, p. 183; E. Burrows.

52. A. R. Johnson, *Sacral Kingship in Ancient Israel,* p. 81–93; H. Birkeland, *The Evildoers in the Book of Psalms* (Oslo: Det Norske Videnskaps–Akademi i Oslo, 1955).

53. G. Widengren, "Early Hebrew Myths and Their Interpretation," p. 175.

54. G. Widengren, "Early Hebrew Myths and Their Interpretation," pp. 164–174.

55. A. R. Johnson, *Sacral Kingship in Ancient Israel,* pp. 92–93.

56. A. R. Johnson, *Sacral Kingship in Ancient Israel,* pp. 102–103, quoting Psalm 89.

57. T. H. Gaster, pp. 62, 68.

58. G. Widengren, "Early Hebrew Myths and Their Interpretation," p. 191, quoting Psalm 47; A. Bentzen, p. 26.

59. A. R. Johnson, *Sacral Kingship in Ancient Israel,* pp. 74–76, alluding to Psalm 24.

60. G. Widengren, "Early Hebrew Myths and Their Interpretation," pp. 177–191.

61. S. Mowinckel, pp. 75, 103.

62. G. Widengren, "Early Hebrew Myths and Their Interpretation," p. 167.

63. G. Widengren, "Early Hebrew Myths and Their Interpretation," pp. 165–169; A. Bentzen, pp. 44–46.

64. T. H. Gaster, pp. 42–43; M. Eliade, pp. 53, 66–72.

65. G. d'Alviella, "Initiation," in J. Hastings (Ed.), *Encyclopedia of Religion and Ethics,* Vol. 8 (New York: Scribner's, 1911), p. 316b.

66. H. Gunkel, *Schöpfung und Chaos* (Göttingen, West Germany: Vandenhoeck & Ruprecht, 1895).

67. A. R. Johnson, "The Role of the King in the Jerusalem Cultus."
68. J. W. Perry, *Lord of the Four Quarters.*

Section 1. The Center

1. Psalm 48:1–3, trans. by A. R. Johnson in *Sacral Kingship in Ancient Israel.*
2. Psalm 48:4–8, trans. by A. R. Johnson in *Sacral Kingship in Ancient Israel,* pp. 78–79.
3. A. R. Johnson, *Sacral Kingship in Ancient Israel,* p. 79.
4. Psalm 102:19, trans. by A. R. Johnson in *Sacral Kingship in Ancient Israel.*
5. Psalm 46:4, trans. by A. R. Johnson in *Sacral Kingship in Ancient Israel.*
6. H. Frankfort, *Kingship and the Gods,* pp. 151–152, 25.
7. E. A. Speiser, "The Creation Epic," Tablet VI, v. 62–63, p. 69, and fn. 100; M. Eliade, p. 15.
8. T. H. Gaster, p. 183; E. Burrows.
9. J. W. Perry, *The Self in Psychotic Process* (Berkeley: University of California Press, 1953).

Section 2. Death

1. Psalm 89:38–42, 44–45, trans. by A. R. Johnson in *Sacral Kingship in Ancient Israel.*
2. Psalm 18:3–6, trans. by A. R. Johnson in *Sacral Kingship in Ancient Israel,* p. 107–108.
3. A. Bentzen, pp. 25, 42, quoting Psalm 42:4.
4. Psalm 42:1–5, in R. B. Chamberlin and others (Eds.), *The Dartmouth Bible* (Boston: Houghton Mifflin, 1961).
5. Psalm 42:7–10, in R. B. Chamberlin and others (Eds.).
6. A. M. Blackman.
7. R. Anthes, "Mythology in Ancient Egypt," in S. N. Kramer (Ed.), *Mythologies of the Ancient World* (Garden City, N.Y.: Doubleday, 1961) pp. 69–72.
8. J. H. Breasted, *Development of Religion and Thought in Ancient Egypt* (New York: Harper & Row, 1959). Lecture 8. (Originally published 1912.)
9. H. Frankfort, *Cylinder Seals: A Documentary on the Art and Religion of the Ancient Near East* (London: Macmillan, 1939), Plate XXI, a.

10. H. Frankfort, *Kingship and the Gods,* Plates 50–52.

11. H. L. Ginsberg, "Ugaritic Myths, Epics, and Legends," in J. B. Pritchard (Ed.), *Ancient Near Eastern Texts Relating to the Old Testament* (Princeton: Princeton University Press, 1955), pp. 135–139.

12. T. H. Gaster, p. 33.

13. J. W. Perry, *Lord of the Four Quarters,* pp. 21–22.

14. H. Frankfort, *Kingship and the Gods,* Chaps. 7 and 10.

Section 3. Return to the Beginnings

1. H. Gunkel, *Schöpfung und Chaos;* E. O. James, *Myth and Ritual in the Ancient Near East,* Chap. 5.

2. A. R. Johnson, *Sacral Kingship in Ancient Israel.*

3. Psalm 89:6,7,9–12 trans. by A. R. Johnson in *Sacral Kingship in Ancient Israel,* p. 99.

4. Psalm 104:1–9, 13–14, 19–20, 24, 30–33 in R. B. Chamberlin and others (Eds.) *The Dartmouth Bible.*

5. G. Widengren, "Early Hebrew Myths and Their Interpretation," pp. 165–169.

6. Psalm 8:1–9, in R. B. Chamberlin and others, *The Dartmouth Bible.*

7. H. Frankfort, *Kingship and the Gods,* pp. 150–157.

8. H. Frankfort, *Kingship and the Gods,* p. 161.

9. H. Frankfort, *Kingship and the Gods,* pp. 154–155.

10. H. Frankfort, *Kingship and the Gods,* p. 319.

11. M. Eliade, Chaps. 1 and 2. This thesis is best presented by V. Grønbech, *The Culture of the Teutons,* Vol. 2 (London: Oxford University Press, 1931), pp. 288–292, 216–223.

12. H. Frankfort, *Kingship and the Gods,* pp. 234–235.

13. M. Eliade, especially Chaps. 2 and 3.

14. G. C. Vaillant, *The Aztecs of Mexico* (Baltimore: Penguin Books, 1953), pp. 194–196. (Originally published 1941.)

15. See Chapter 4.

16. P. Metman, "The Ego in Schizophrenia," *Journal of Analytical Psychology,* 1956, *1,* 161–176; and, 1957, *2,* 51–70.

17. M. Eliade, especially pp. 34–37.

18. See G. Bateson, *Naven* (Stanford, Calif.: Stanford University Press, 1958), for definitions of these terms.

Section 4. The Clash of Opposites

1. H. Birkeland; A. R. Johnson, *Sacral Kingship in Ancient Israel,* Chap. 4.

2. Psalm 82:1–2, 4–8 trans. by A. R. Johnson in *Sacral Kingship in Ancient Israel,* pp. 89–90.

3. Psalm 89:30–32 trans. by A. R. Johnson in *Sacral Kingship in Ancient Israel,* p. 25.

4. Psalm 149:5–9, trans. by A. R. Johnson in *Sacral Kingship in Ancient Israel,* p. 82.

5. Psalm 68:6–8, trans. by A. R. Johnson in *Sacral Kingship in Ancient Israel,* pp. 70–71.

6. Psalms 68:17–18, 20, trans. by A. R. Johnson in *Sacral Kingship in Ancient Israel,* pp. 72–73.

7. S. Mowinckel, pp. 80–89; E. O. James, *Myth and Ritual in the Ancient Near East,* p. 99.

8. Psalm 118:5–7, 10, trans. by A. R. Johnson in *Sacral Kingship in Ancient Israel,* p. 115.

9. Psalm 18:6–20, 39–40, trans. by A. R. Johnson in *Sacral Kingship in Ancient Israel,* pp. 109–113.

10. R. Anthes, "Mythology in Ancient Egypt," in S. N. Kramer, (Ed.), *Mythologies of the Ancient World,* pp. 69–72.

11. H. W. Fairman, p. 87ff.

12. H. Frankfort, *Kingship and the Gods,* p. 179.

13. H. W. Fairman, pp. 92–93.

14. H. Frankfort, *Kingship and the Gods,* p. 183ff.

15. E. A. Speiser, p. 60ff; H. Frankfort, *Kingship and the Gods,* p. 284ff.

16. H. Frankfort, *Kingship and the Gods,* pp. 321–324 and 284–293.

17. S. H. Hooke, "The Myth and Ritual Patterns of the Ancient East," in S. H. Hooke (Ed.), *Myth and Ritual* (Oxford: Clarendon, 1958).

18. H. Frankfort, *Kingship and the Gods,* p. 328–329.

19. T. H. Gaster, pp. 114–126; H. L. Ginsberg, pp. 130–131.

20. T. H. Gaster; H. L. Ginsberg, p. 135.

21. J. W. Perry, "Acute Catatonic Schizophrenia," *Journal of Analytical Psychology,* 1957, *2,* 137–152.

22. J. W. Perry, *Lord of the Four Quarters,* Intro.

23. M. Eliade, Chap. 1.

24. T. Jacobsen.

25. J. W. Perry, *Lord of the Four Quarters,* pp. 20–21.

26. S. N. Kramer, *Sumerian Mythology,* p. 76.

27. T. H. Gaster, pp. 38–41; A. Bentzen, pp. 16, 32.

28. J. W. Perry, "Societal Implications of the Renewal Process," *Spring*, 1971, 153–167.

29. C. G. Jung, "On the Importance of the Unconscious in Psychopathology," in *Collected Works*, Vol. 3: *The Psychogenesis of Mental Disease*, Bollingen Series 20 (New York: Pantheon, 1960).

Section 5. The Reversal of Opposites

1. S. Freud, "Psychoanalytic Notes Upon an Autobiographical Account of a Case of Paranoia," *Collected Papers*, Vol. 3 (London: Hogarth, 1950).

2. T. H. Gaster, pp. 68, 62.

3. Psalm 89:39–41, 50 trans. by A. R. Johnson, in *Sacral Kingship in Ancient Israel*, pp. 102–104.

4. M. Eliade, p. 57, citing Berossus' *Babyloniaca.*

5. T. H. Gaster, p. 68.

6. W. R. Halliday, "A Note on Herodotus VI. 83 and the Hybristika," *Annual of the British School of Athens*, 1909–1910, *16*, 212. M. E. Harding, *Woman's Mysteries* (New York: Pantheon, 1955), Chap. 10; E. Neumann, *The Origins and History of Consciousness*, Bollingen Series 42 (New York: Pantheon, 1954), pp. 58–61, 78–79; J. G. Frazer, "Adonis, Attis, Osiris," in *The Golden Bough*, Vol. 2 (London: Macmillan, 1919), Pt. 4, pp. 263–264.

7. C. G. Jung, "The Relations Between the Ego and the Unconscious," in *Collected Works*, Vol. 7: *Two Essays on Analytical Psychology*, Bolligen Series 20 (New York: Pantheon, 1953), Pt. 2, Chap. 2.

Section 6. Apotheosis

1. Psalm 118:24–27, trans. by A. R. Johnson in *Sacral Kingship in Ancient Israel*, p. 118.

2. A. R. Johnson, *Sacral Kingship in Ancient Israel*, p. 110.

3. Psalm 68:24–26, trans. by A. R. Johnson in *Sacral Kingship in Ancient Israel*, p. 74.

4. E. Burrows, p. 49; A. R. Johnson, *Sacral Kingship in Ancient Israel*, pp. 52–53.

5. Psalm 46:4–7, trans. by A. R. Johnson in *Sacral Kingship in Ancient Israel,* p. 85.

6. Psalm 48:11–14, trans. by A. R. Johnson in *Sacral Kingship in Ancient Israel,* pp. 80–81.

7. Psalm 72:8–9, trans. by A. R. Johnson in *Sacral Kingship in Ancient Israel,* p. 8.

8. Psalm 68:32–4, trans. by A. R. Johnson in *Sacral Kingship in Ancient Israel,* p. 76.

9. T. H. Gaster, pp. 443–446.

10. Psalms 29:3–11, trans. by A. R. Johnson in *Sacral Kingship in Ancient Israel,* p. 56.

11. A. R. Johnson, *Sacral Kingship in Ancient Israel,* pp. 25, 92–3.

12. Psalm 18:43, 46–47, 49–50, trans. by A. R. Johnson in *Sacral Kingship in Ancient Israel,* pp. 113–114.

13. A. Bentzen, pp. 19–20; S. Mowinckel, pp. 62, 76–80.

14. Psalm 89:19–21, 26–29, 3–8, 18, trans. by A. R. Johnson in *Sacral Kingship in Ancient Israel,* pp. 101, 98–99, 100.

15. A. M. Blackman; H. Frankfort, *Kingship and the Gods,* pp. 32–34, 39–44.

16. H. Frankfort, *Kingship and the Gods,* pp. 42–51, 157–158.

17. H. Frankfort, *Kingship and the Gods,* pp. 85–88, Chap. 13.

18. H. Frankfort, *Kingship and the Gods,* Chap 13.

19. H. Frankfort, *Kingship and the Gods,* pp. 297–299.

20. G. Widengren, "The King and the Tree of Life in Ancient Near Eastern Religion."

21. T. Jacobsen.

22. H. Frankfort, *Kingship and the Gods,* p. 237; A. L. Oppenheim, "Babylonian and Assyrian Historical Texts," in J. B. Pritchard (Ed.), *Ancient Near Eastern Texts Relating to the Old Testament* (Princeton: Princeton University Press, 1955), p. 265.

23. T. H. Gaster, p. 24.

24. J. Campbell, "Oriental Mythology," *The Masks of God,* Vol. 2 (New York: Viking Press, 1962), Chap. 2.

25. H. L. Ginsberg, p. 129–142.

26. H. L. Ginsberg, p. 135: e. II AB (vii), lines 25–41.

27. J. W. Perry, *The Far Side of Madness,* Chap. 10.

28. C. G. Jung, *Collected Works,* Vol. 5: *Symbols of Transformation,* Bollingen Series 20 (New York: Pantheon, 1956).

29. T. Jacobsen; H. Frankfort, *Kingship and the Gods,* p. 51.

30. H. Frankfort, *Cylinder Seals,* p. 115, Plate XX, e.

31. F. M. Cornford, *From Religion to Philosophy* (New York: Harper & Row, 1957), pp. 108–110; H. W. Fairman, "The Kingship Rituals of Egypt," p. 76.

32. J. H. Breasted, *Development of Religion and Thought in Ancient Egypt* (New York: Harper & Row, 1959). (Originally published 1912.) Breasted traces the concept of immortality from the Old Kingdom, when the Pharaoh had the sole prerogative to an immortal soul, to its later democratized forms.

33. J. W. Perry, *Lord of the Four Quarters,* pp. 205–208, citing M. Granet, *Chinese Civilization,* trans. by K. E. Innes (New York: Knopf, 1930), p. 47.

Section 7. The Union of Opposites

1. E. O. James, *Myth and Ritual in the Ancient Near East,* pp. 125–128, and *The Cult of the Mother Goddess* (New York: Barnes & Noble, 1959), pp. 78–83.

2. S. Mowinckel, pp. 62, 75, 103.

3. G. Widengren, "Early Hebrew Myths and Their Interpretation," pp. 178–183.

4. R. Schärf, "The Image of the Marriage Between God and Israel," *Spring,* 1950, 70–89.

5. A. Bentzen, p. 17.

6. Psalm 45:1–2, 5–11, 13, 14–15, King James Version, arranged in verse form by J. W. Perry. See G. Widengren, "Early Hebrew Myths and Their Interpretations," pp. 176–199, discussing the sacred marriage.

7. H. W. Fairman, "The Kingship Rituals of Egypt," pp. 86–91.

8. S. A. B. Mercer, *Horus Royal God of Egypt* (Grafton: Society of Oriental Research, 1942) pp. 90–91; H. Frankfort, *Kingship and the Gods,* pp. 171 ff. For Frankfort's discussion of incestuous unions, see pp. 168 ff., 177 ff., fn. 81 on p. 387.

9. H. Frankfort, *Kingship and the Gods,* pp. 295–298, 330–331.

10. G. Widengren, "The King and the Tree of Life in Ancient Near Eastern Religion."

11. H. L. Ginsberg, "Ugaritic Myths, Epics, and Legends," IV AB, ii, lines 13–18, p. 142.

12. H. L. Ginsberg, IV AB, ii, lines 24–25.

13. H. L. Ginsberg, IV AB, ii, lines 31–35.

14. T. H. Gaster, p. 33.

15. J. W. Perry, *Lord of the Four Quarters,* p. 29.

Section 8. New Birth

1. Psalm 118:15–19, 22–23, trans. by A. R. Johnson in *Sacral Kingship in Ancient Israel,* pp. 117–118.

2. A. Bentzen, pp. 20–24; S. Mowinckel, pp. 62–69.

3. Psalm 2:1–8, trans. by A. R. Johnson in *Sacral Kingship in Ancient Israel,* pp. 119–120.

4. S. Mowinckel, p. 75.

5. Psalm 110:1–7, trans. by A. R. Johnson in *Sacral Kingship in Ancient Israel,* pp. 121–122.

6. R. Anthes, pp. 69–72.

7. A. M. Blackman; H. Frankfort, *Kingship and the Gods,* Chap. 2.

8. J. A. Wilson, "Egyptian Myths, Tales, and Mortuary Texts," in J. B. Pritchard (Ed.), *Ancient Near Eastern Texts Relating to the Old Testament;* see "The Contest of Horus and Seth for the Rule," pp. 14–17.

9. E. O. James, *The Cult of the Mother Goddess,* Chap. 1; J. Mellaart, *Earliest Civilizations of the Near East* (New York: McGraw-Hill, 1965), Chap. 7.

10. H. Frankfort, *Kingship and the Gods,* pp. 19–32.

11. H. Frankfort, *Kingship and the Gods,* pp. 286–294.

12. E. A. Speiser, Tablet I, lines 78–107.

13. H. L. Ginsberg, IV AB, ii, lines 32–38.

14. H. Güterbock, "Hittite Mythology," in S. N. Kramer, (Ed.), *Mythologies of the Ancient World,* pp. 155–175; E. O. James, *The Ancient Gods* (New York: Putnam, 1960), Chap. 1.

15. H. Frankfort, *Kingship and the Gods,* pp. 168–175.

16. H. Frankfort, *Kingship and the Gods,* p. 170, quoting *Pyramid Texts,* 1028–1030.

Section 9. The Renewed Society

1. S. Mowinckel, *He That Cometh,* p. 139.

2. S. Mowinckel, p. 143.

3. S. Mowinckel, p. 143.

4. A. R. Johnson, *Sacral Kingship in Ancient Israel,* Chap. 1; S. Mowinckel, Chap. 3, Sec. 2.

5. A. R. Johnson, *Sacral Kingship in Ancient Israel,* pp. 3–14.

6. G. Widengren, "Early Hebrew Myths and Their Interpretation," pp. 167–168.

7. Psalm 89:13–14, trans. by A. R. Johnson in *Sacral Kingship in Ancient Israel,* p. 100.

8. Psalm 68:10–11, trans. by A. R. Johnson in *Sacral Kingship in Ancient Israel,* p. 70–71.

9. A. R. Johnson, *Sacral Kingship in Ancient Israel,* pp. 24–25.

10. Psalm 89:34–37, trans. by A. R. Johnson in *Sacral Kingship in Ancient Israel,* pp. 25–26.

11. Psalm 72:1–7, trans. by A. R. Johnson in *Sacral Kingship in Ancient Israel,* pp. 7–8.

12. Psalm 72:13–14, 16–17, trans. by A. R. Johnson in *Sacral Kingship in Ancient Israel,* pp. 10–11.

13. Psalm 46:8–10, trans. by A. R. Johnson in *Sacral Kingship in Ancient Israel,* pp. 85–86.

14. H. Frankfort, *Kingship and the Gods,* Chap. 4.

15. H. Frankfort, *Kingship and the Gods,* p. 51–52; J. A. Wilson, *The Culture of Ancient Egypt* (Chicago: University of Chicago Press, 1960), pp. 48–49.

16. H. Frankfort, *Kingship and the Gods,* pp. 133–135.

17. H. Frankfort, *Kingship and the Gods,* p. 149.

18. H. Frankfort, *Kingship and the Gods,* p. 150.

19. H. Frankfort, *Kingship and the Gods,* p. 277.

20. H. Frankfort, *Kingship and the Gods,* pp. 278, 309–310.

21. H. Frankfort, *Kingship and the Gods,* pp. 331–332.

22. H. Frankfort, *Kingship and the Gods,* pp. 332–333.

23. J. W. Perry, "Image, Complex and Transference in Schizophrenia," in A. Burton (Ed.), *Psychotherapy of the Psychoses* (New York: Basic Books, 1961).

Section 10. The Quadrated World

1. T. H. Gaster, *Thespis,* p. 24.

2. J. Campbell, *The Masks of God,* Chap. 2.

3. G. Widengren, "Early Hebrew Myths and Their Interpretation," pp. 164–169.

4. S. A. B. Mercer, *An Egyptian Grammar,* Oriental Research Series, no. 1 (London: Luzac, 1929).

5. J. B. Pritchard, *The Ancient Near East* (Princeton: Princeton University Press, 1958), Plate 144.

6. Reproduced in J. W. Perry, *Lord of the Four Quarters,* Plate 2 A.

7. H. P. L'Orange, *Studies on the Iconography of Cosmic Kingship in the Ancient World* (Oslo: Instituttet for Sammenlignende Kulturforskning, 1953), Plates 1, 2, and 3.

8. A. L. Basham, *The Wonder That Was India* (New York: Grove Press, 1954), pp. 198–205: See Plate *XI* A, Figure *XV*, and reference to the Kautiliya Arthasastra, *LI*. 29, which gives instructions for the proper layout of a new city (Mauryan Dynasty, fourth century B.C.).

9. H. P. L'Orange, Plates 6, 7, and 9.

10. Plutarch, "Romulus," in *Plutarch's Lives*, Vol. 1, trans. by A. H. Clough (Boston: Little, Brown, 1881), pp. 50–51.

11. S. v. R. Cammann, "Suggested Origin of the Tibetan Mandala Paintings," *Art Quarterly*, 1950, (Spring), 106–119.

12. J. W. Perry, *The Self in Psychotic Process* (Berkeley: University of California Press, 1953) gives a full description of this case.

Chapter 6. From Monarch to Messiah

1. J. W. Perry, *Lord of the Four Quarters: Myths of the Royal Father* (New York: Braziller, 1966).

2. M. I. Dimont, *Jews, Gods and History* (New York: Simon & Schuster, 1962).

3. S. Mowinckel, *He That Cometh* (New York: Abingdon, 1954), Chap. 2.

4. J. Klausner, *The Messianic Idea in Israel* (New York: Macmillan, 1955), p. 41.

5. Amos 5:16, 18, trans. by J. Klausner, p. 39.

6. J. Klausner, p. 38.

7. J. Klausner, p. 46.

8. Hosea 13:13, in King James Version.

9. Hosea 2:1–2, trans. by J. Klausner, p. 47.

10. Hosea 2:16–17, trans. by J. Klausner, p. 48.

11. A. Bentzen, *King and Messiah* (London, Lutterworth, 1965), pp. 64–71, 52.

12. J. W. Perry, *Lord of the Four Quarters*, pp. 16–18.

13. J. Klausner, p. 49.

14. Hosea 2:19, trans. by J. Klausner, p. 49.

15. Hosea 2:18, trans. by J. Klausner, p. 50.

16. S. Mowinckel, Chaps. 4, 5.

17. S. Mowinckel, pp. 104–118.

18. Isaiah 9:6–7, trans. by S. Mowinckel, p. 104–106.

19. Isaiah 9:2, trans. by S. Mowinckel, p. 102.

20. S. Mowinckel, pp. 62, 75, 103.

21. Psalm 110:3, in King James Version.

22. S. Mowinckel, pp. 117–119.

23. Isaiah 7:14–15, trans. by S. Mowinckel, pp. 110–111.

24. A. R. Johnson, *Sacral Kingship in Ancient Israel* (Cardiff: University of Wales Press, 1955), Chap. 1.

25. Isaiah 11:1–5, in R. B. Chamberlin and others (Eds.), *The Dartmouth Bible* (Boston, Houghton Mifflin, 1961) pp. 565–566.

26. S. Mowinckel, pp. 119–122.

27. Zechariah 6:12–13, in King James Version; see also 3:8.

28. S. Mowinckel, pp. 104–108.

29. A. Bentzen, pp. 17–18, 40–46, 64–67. G. Widengren, "Early Hebrew Myths and Their Interpretation," in S. H. Hooke (Ed.), *Myth, Ritual and Kingship* (Oxford, Clarendon, 1958) pp. 164–169; S. Mowinckel, pp. 183–185.

30. S. Mowinckel, pp. 165–169, 184ff.

31. Micah 5:2, in King James Version.

32. Micah 5:3, in King James Version.

33. Micah 5:7, in King James Version.

34. H. H. Guthrie, *Israel's Sacred Songs* (New York: Seabury Press, 1966), Chap. 1; G. Hebert, *When Israel Came out of Egypt* (Richmond, Va.: John Knox Press, 1961), Chap. 4; S. Mowinckel, p. 133ff.

35. S. Mowinckel, p. 139.

36. S. Mowinckel, p. 141.

37. J. Klausner, pp. 160–163.

38. Isaiah 51:7, in R. B. Chamberlin and others (Eds.), *The Dartmouth Bible,* p. 678

39. J. Klausner, p. 180ff.

40. Isaiah 24:1, 20–21, 23, in R. B. Chamberlin and others (Eds.), *The Dartmouth Bible,* 569–570.

41. Isaiah 27:1, in King James Version.

42. Isaiah 25:8–9, in King James Version.

43. Isaiah 26:1–2, in King James Version.

44. Isaiah 26:17, in King James Version.

45. Isaiah 26:19, in King James Version.

46. Isaiah 51:4,6, in King James Version.

47. Isaiah 65:17–18, in King James Version.

48. See T. H. Gaster, *Thespis: Ritual, Myth and Drama in the Ancient Near East* (Garden City, N.Y.: Doubleday, 1961), p. 183, for a comparative account of the image of the world center; E. Burrows, "Some Cosmological Patterns in Babylonian Religion." in S. H. Hooke (Ed.), *The Labyrinth* (New York: Macmillan, 1935), pp. 46–57; S. Mowinckel, pp. 146, 270.

49. Isaiah 55:3, in King James Version; see also S. Mowinckel, p. 165.

50. Jeremiah 23:4, trans. by S. Mowinckel, p. 167.

51. Jeremiah 30:21, trans. by S. Mowinckel, p. 180.

52. Jeremiah 30:9, trans. by J. Klausner, p. 101.

53. J. Klausner, p. 115.

54. Jeremiah 31:33, trans. by J. Klausner, p. 98.

55. A. R. Johnson, Chap. 1.

56. J. Klausner, pp. 126, 132, citing Ezekiel 45:1–25 and 46:1–24; S. Mowinckel, pp. 168–169, 146.

57. Zechariah 9:9–10, trans. by J. Klausner, p. 203.
58. S. Mowinckel, p. 176.
59. Zechariah 14:9, trans. by J. Klausner, p. 205.
60. Zechariah 12:5–6, 9, trans. by J. Klausner, p. 204.
61. Joel 2:28–29, trans. by J. Klausner, p. 209.
62. A. Bentzen, p. 48ff; S. Mowinckel, pp. 187, 257.
63. S. Mowinckel, p. 219ff.
64. S. Mowinckel, pp. 215–218, citing the work of Nyberg on "corporate personality" and its embodiment in the ancestor; J. Pedersen, *Israel, Its Life and Culture* (London: Oxford University Press, 1934); J. Klausner, p. 157, 161–163; A. Bentzen, p. 50.
65. I. Engnell, *Studies in Divine Kingship in the Ancient Near East* Uppsala, Sweden: Almquist & Wiksells, 1943); G. Widengren. See A. Bentzen, pp. 61–67, and S. Mowinckel, pp. 22, 456, for a criticism of Engnell's and Widengren's conclusions.
66. S. Mowinckel, pp. 221–225.
67. Isaiah 42:1, 6, trans. by S. Mowinckel, pp. 189–190. The First Servant Song is Isaiah 42:1–4 (or 1–7).
68. Isaiah 49:1, 3, trans. by S. Mowinckel, pp. 191–193. The Second Servant Song is Isaiah 49:1–6 (or 1–9).
69. S. Mowinckel, pp. 462–463.
70. Isaiah 50:5–6, trans. by S. Mowinckel, pp. 193–196. The Third Servant Song is Isaiah 50:4–11 (or 4–9).
71. Isaiah 53:3–4,5,8–9, trans. by S. Mowinckel, pp. 196–205, The Fourth Servant Song is Isaiah 52:13 to 53:12. Mowinckel's translation deviates markedly from the King James Version.
72. Isaiah 53:11, trans. by S. Mowinckel, p. 198.
73. Isaiah 53:12, trans. by S. Mowinckel, p. 198.
74. S. Mowinckel, pp. 302, 368, 420–437.
75. 1 Enoch, *Book of Enoch* (Los Angeles: Work of the Chariot, 1970), reprinted from R. H. Charles (Ed.), *The Apocrypha and Pseudepigrapha of the Old Testament,* Vol. 3 (Oxford: Clarendon, 1913). This 1 Enoch is the "Ethiopic Book." 2 Esdras, in M. Komroff (Ed.), *The Apocrypha,* (New York: Tudor, 1936), p. 29ff.; S. Mowinckel, Chap. 10, analyzes the literature on the Son of Man motif.
76. S. Mowinckel, pp. 346, 424ff.
77. 1 Enoch 39 in "The First Parable" and 1 Enoch 70–71 in "The Third Parable"; in R. H. Charles (Ed.), pp. 210, 235 resp.
78. 2 Esdras 13 and 14, in M. Komroff (Ed.), pp. 62–65, 47 resp.; Daniel 7:13 contains the earliest mention of the Son of Man appearing thus riding the clouds; see S. Mowinckel, *He That Cometh,* pp. 348–353. 1 Enoch 51, 52, 62 (on the Judgment), in R. H. Charles (Ed.), pp. 218–220, 227–230.
79. 2 Esdras 7, in M. Komroff (Ed.), p. 47.
80. 1 Enoch 45–52 in "The Second Parable," and 1 Enoch 93–101

in "The Apocalypse of Weeks," in R. H. Charles (Ed.) pp. 213–220, 262–265, resp.; see S. Mowinckel, pp. 403–410 for a clarification of the obscure relations between the "Interim Kingdom" and "The Last Things."

81. J. H. Breasted, *The Development of Religion and Thought in Ancient Egypt* (New York: Harper & Row, 1959). (Originally published 1912.)

82. J. H. Breasted, *The Dawn of Conscience* (New York: Scribner's, 1933).

83. J. H. Breasted, *The Dawn of Conscience,* Chap. 10.

84. J. A. Wilson, "The Admonitions of Ipu-wer," in "Egyptian Oracles and Prophecies," in J. B. Pritchard (Ed.), *Ancient Near Eastern Texts Relating to the Old Testament* (Princeton: Princeton University Press, 1955), p. 443.

85. J. Duchesne-Guillemin, *The Hymns of Zarathustra* (Boston: Beacon Press, 1963).

86. M. J. Dresden, "Mythology of Ancient Iran," in S. N. Kramer (Ed.), *Mythologies of the Ancient World,* (Garden City, N.Y.: Doubleday, 1961), p. 344.

87. S. Mowinckel, pp. 302, 423.

88. A. Bentzen, p. 48ff.

89. J. W. Perry, *The Self in Psychotic Process* (Berkeley: University of California Press, 1953), pp. 20–21.

90. J. W. Perry, *The Self in Psychotic Process,* p. 22.

91. Thomas 95:17–19, in A. Guilleaumont and others, *The Gospel According to Thomas* (New York: Harper & Row, 1959); see also Thomas 82:14.

Bibliography

ALBRIGHT, W. F. *The Archeology of Palestine.* Baltimore: Penguin, 1960.

ANTHES, R. "Mythology in Ancient Egypt." In S. N. Kramer (Ed.), *Mythologies of the Ancient World.* Garden City, N.Y.: Doubleday, 1961.

ARIETI, S. *Interpretation of Schizophrenia.* New York: Basic Books, 1955.

BARNES, M., AND BURKE, J. *Mary Barnes: Two Accounts of a Journey Through Madness.* New York: Harcourt Brace Jovanovich, 1971.

BASHAM, A. L. *The Wonder That Was India.* New York: Grove Press, 1951.

BATESON, G. *Naven.* Stanford, Calif.: Stanford University Press, 1958.

BATESON, G., AND OTHERS. "Towards a Theory of Schizophrenia." *Behavioral Sciences,* 1956, *1,* 251–264.

BAYNES, H. G. *Mythology of the Soul.* London: Methuen, 1949.

BENTZEN, A. *King and Messiah.* London: Lutterworth, 1955.

BIRKELAND, H. *The Evildoers in the Book of Psalms.* Oslo: Det Norske Videnskaps–Akademi i Oslo, 1955.

BLACKMAN, A. M. "Myth and Ritual in Ancient Egypt." In S. H. Hooke (Ed.), *Myth and Ritual.* London: Oxford Press, 1933.

BOISEN, A. T. *The Exploration of the Inner World.* Chicago: Willet, Clark, 1936.

BREASTED, J. H. *The Dawn of Conscience.* New York: Scribner's, 1933.

BREASTED, J. H. *Development of Religion and Thought in Ancient Egypt.* New York: Harper & Row, 1959. (Originally published 1912.)

BURROWS, F. E. "Some Cosmological Patterns in Babylonian Religion." In S. H. Hooke (Ed.), *The Labyrinth.* New York: Macmillan, 1935.

CAMMANN, S. V. R. "Suggested Origin of the Tibetan Mandala Paintings." *Art Quarterly*, 1950, Spring, 106–119.

CAMPBELL, J. "Oriental Mythology." In *The Masks of God.* Vol. 2. New York: Viking Press, 1962.

CHAMBERLIN, R. B., AND OTHERS (Eds.) *The Dartmouth Bible.* Boston: Houghton Mifflin, 1961.

CHARLES, R. H. (Ed.) *The Apocrypha and Pseudepigrapha of the Old Testament.* Oxford: Clarendon, 1913.

CONFORD, F. M. *From Religion to Philosophy.* New York: Harper & Row, 1957.

d'ALVIELLA, G. "Initiation." In J. Hastings (Ed.), *Encyclopedia of Religion and Ethics,* Vol. 8. New York: Scribner's, 1911.

DE LANGHE, R. "Myth, Ritual and Kingship in the Ras Shamra Tablets." In S. H. Hooke (Ed.), *Myth, Ritual and Kingship.* Oxford: Clarendon, 1958.

DIMONT, M. I. *Jews, Gods and History.* New York: Simon & Schuster, 1962.

DRESDEN, M. J. "Mythology of Ancient Iran." In S. N. Kramer (Ed.), *Mythologies of the Ancient World.* Garden City, N.Y.: Doubleday, 1961.

DUCHESNE-GUILLEMIN, J. *The Hymns of Zarathustra.* Boston: Beacon Press, 1963.

ELIADE, M. *The Myth of the Eternal Return.* Bollingen Series 46. New York: Pantheon, 1954.

ENGNELL, I. *Studies on Divine Kingship in the Ancient Near East.* Uppsala, Sweden: Almquist & Wiksells, 1943.

FAIRMAN, H. W. "The Kingship Rituals of Egypt." In S. H. Hooke (Ed.), *Myth, Ritual and Kingship.* Oxford: Clarendon, 1958.

FEDERN, P. *Ego Psychology and the Psychoses.* New York: Basic Books, 1952.

FORDHAM, M. "The Origins of the Ego in Childhood." In M. Fordham (Ed.), *New Developments in Analytical Psychology.* London: Routledge & Kegan Paul, 1955.

FORDHAM, M. *The Life of Childhood.* London: Routledge & Kegan Paul, 1944.

FOUCAULT, M. *Madness and Civilization.* (R. Howard, Trans.) New York: Pantheon, 1955.

FRANKFORT, H. *Cylinder Seals: A Documentary on the Art and Religion of the Ancient Near East.* London: Macmillan, 1939.

FRANKFORT, H. *Kingship and the Gods.* Chicago: University of Chicago Press, 1939.

FRAZER, J. G. "Adonis, Attis, Osiris." In *The Golden Bough.* Pt. 4, Vol. 2. 1906 London: Macmillan, reprint, 1919.

FRAZER, J. G. "Balder the Beautiful." In *The Golden Bough.* Pt. 7, Vol. 2. 1913. London: Macmillan, reprint, 1919.

FREUD, S. "Psychoanalytic Notes Upon an Autobiographical Account of a Case of Paranoia." In *Collected Papers.* Vol. 3. London: Hogarth, 1950.

FROMM-REICHMANN, F. "Notes on the Development and Treatment of Schizophrenics by Psychoanalytic Therapy." *Psychiatry*, 1948, *11*, 263–272.

GASTER, T. H. *Thespis: Ritual, Myth and Drama in the Ancient Near East.* Garden City, N.Y.: Doubleday, 1961.

GINSBERG, H. L. "Ugaritic Myths, Epics and Legends." In J. B. Pritchard (Ed.), *Ancient Near Eastern Texts Relating to the Old Testament.* Princeton: Princeton University Press, 1955.

GORDON, C. H. "Canaanite Mythology." In S. N. Kramer (Ed.), *Mythologies of the Ancient World.* Garden City, N.Y.: Doubleday, 1961.

GRANET, M. *Chinese Civilization.* (K. E. Innes, Trans.) New York: Knopf, 1930.

GROF, S. *Realms of the Human Unconscious.* New York: Viking Press, 1975.

GRØNBECH, V. *The Culture of the Teutons.* Vol. 2. London: Oxford University Press, 1931.

GUILLEAUMONT, A., AND OTHERS. *The Gospel According to Thomas.* New York: Harper & Row, 1959.

GUNKEL, H. *Schöpfung und Chaos.* Göttingen, West Germany: Vandenhoeck & Ruprecht, 1895.

GÜTERBOCK, H. "Hittite Mythology." In S. N. Kramer (Ed.), *Mythologies of the Ancient World.* Garden City, N.Y.: Doubleday, 1961.

GUTHRIE, H. H. *Israel's Sacred Songs.* New York: Seabury Press, 1966.

HALLIDAY, W. R. "A Note on Herodotus VI.83 and the Hybristika." *Annual of the British School of Athens,* 1909–1910, *16,* 212.

HARDING, M. E. *Woman's Mysteries.* New York: Pantheon, 1955.

HARRISON, J. *Themis.* Cambridge, England: Cambridge University Press, 1927.

HEBERT, G. *When Israel Came Out of Egypt.* Richmond, Va.: John Knox Press, 1961.

HENDERSON, J. L. *Thresholds of Initiation.* Middletown, Conn.: Wesleyan University Press, 1967.

HOCART, A. M. *Kingship.* London: Oxford University Press, 1927.

HOOKE, S. H. *The Labyrinth.* London: Macmillan, 1935.

HOOKE, S. H. *Myth and Ritual.* London: Oxford University Press, 1933.

HOOKE, S. H. "The Myth and Ritual Patterns of the Ancient East." *Myth and Ritual.* London: Oxford University Press, 1933.

HOOKE, S. H. *Myth, Ritual and Kingship.* Oxford: Clarendon, 1958.

HOROWITZ, M. *Image Formation and Cognition.* New York: Appleton-Century-Crofts, 1970.

JACKSON, D., AND OTHERS. "Psychiatrist's Conception of the Schizophrenogenic Parent." *AMA Archives of Neurology and Psychiatry,* 1958, *79.*

JACOBSEN, T. "Mesopotamia." In H. Frankfort (Ed.), *Before Philosophy.* London: Penguin, 1949.

JAMES, E. O. *The Ancient Gods.* New York: Putnam's, 1960.

JAMES, E. O. *Christian Myth and Ritual.* New York: World Publishing Co., 1965. (Originally published 1937.)

JAMES, E. O. *The Cult of the Mother Goddess.* New York: Barnes & Noble, 1959.

JAMES, E. O. *Myth and Ritual in the Ancient Near East.* New York: Praeger, 1958.

JAMES, E. O. *Seasonal Feasts and Festivals.* New York: Barnes & Noble, 1961.

JOHNSON, A. R. "The Role of the King in the Jerusalem Cultus." In S. H. Hooke (Ed.), *The Labyrinth.* London: Macmillan, 1935.

JOHNSON, A. R. *Sacral Kingship in Ancient Israel.* Cardiff: University of Wales, Press, 1955.

JUNG, C. G. "Analytical Psychology and Education." In *Collected Works.* Vol. 17: *The Development of Personality.* Bollingen Series 20. New York: Pantheon, 1954.

JUNG, C. G. *Analytical Psychology: Its Theory and Practice.* The Tavistock Lectures. New York: Pantheon, 1968.

JUNG, C. G. *The Archetypes and the Collective Unconscious.* Vol. 9 of *Collected Works.* Bollingen Series 20. New York: Pantheon 1959.

JUNG, C. G. "The Association Method." In *Collected Works.* Vol. 2: *Experimental Researches.* Vol. 2 of *Collected Works,* Bollingen Series 20. Princeton: Princeton University Press, 1973.

JUNG, C. G. "Commentary on the Secret of the Golden Flower." In *Collected Works.* Vol. 13: *Alchemical Studies.* Bollingen Series 20. New York: Pantheon, 1971.

JUNG, C. G. "Concerning Mandala Symbolism." In *Collected Works.* Vol. 9: *The Archetypes and the Collective Unconscious.* Bollingen Series 20. New York: Pantheon, 1960.

JUNG, C. G. "Conscious, Unconscious, and Individuation." In *Collected Works.* Vol. 9: *The Archetypes and the Collective Unconscious.* Bollingen Series 20. New York: Pantheon, 1959.

JUNG, C. G. "General Aspects of Dream Psychology." In *Collected Works.* Vol. 18: *The Structure and Dynamics of the Psyche.* Bollingen Series 20. New York: Pantheon, 1960.

JUNG, C. G. "Instinct and the Unconscious." In *Collected Works.* Vol. 18: *The Structure and Dynamics of the Psyche.* Bollingen Series 20. New York: Pantheon, 1960.

JUNG, C. G. "Mind and Earth." In *Collected Works.* Vol. 10: *Civilization in Transition.* Bollingen Series 20. New York: Pantheon, 1963.

JUNG, C. G. *Mysterium Coniunctionis.* Vol. 14 of *Collected Works.* Bollingen Series 20. New York: Pantheon, 1963.

JUNG, C. G. "On Psychic Energy." In *Collected Works.* Vol. 18: *The Structure and Dynamics of the Psyche.* Bollingen Series 20. New York: Pantheon, 1960.

JUNG, C. G. "On the Importance of the Unconscious in Psychopathology." In *Collected Works.* Vol. 3: *The Psychogenesis of Mental Disease.* Bollingen Series 20. New York: Pantheon, 1960.

JUNG, C. G. "On the Psychogenesis of Schizophrenia." In *Collected Works.* Vol. 3: *The Psychogenesis of Mental Disease.* Bollingen Series 20. New York: Pantheon, 1960.

JUNG, C. G. "The Phenomenology of the Spirit in Fairytales." In *Collected Works.* Vol. 9: *The Archetypes and the Collective Unconscious.* Bollingen Series 20. New York: Pantheon, 1959.

JUNG, C. G. *Psychological Types.* New York: Harcourt Brace Jovanovich, 1926.

JUNG, C. G. "A Psychological View of Conscience." In *Collected Works.* Vol. 10: *Civilization in Transition.* Bollingen Series 20. New York: Pantheon, 1964.

JUNG, C. G. *Psychology and Alchemy.* Vol. 12 of *Collected Works.* Bollingen Series 20. New York: Pantheon, 1953.

JUNG, C. G. "The Psychology of Dementia Praecox." In *Collected Works.* Vol. 3: *The Psychogenesis of Mental Disease.* Bollingen Series 20. New York: Pantheon, 1960.

JUNG, C. G. "The Psychology of the Unconscious." In *Collected Works.* Vol. 7: *Two Essays on Analytical Psychology.* Bollingen Series 20. New York: Pantheon, 1953.

JUNG, C. G. "Recent Thoughts on Schizophrenia." In *Collected Works.* Vol. 3: *The Psychogenesis of Mental Disease.* Bollingen Series 20. New York: Pantheon, 1960.

JUNG, C. G. "The Relations Between the Ego and the Unconscious." In *Collected Works.* Vol. 7: *Two Essays on Analytical Psychology.* Bollingen Series 20. New York: Pantheon, 1953.

JUNG, C. G. "A Review of the Complex Theory." In *Collected Works.* Vol. 18: *The Structure and Dynamics of the Psyche.* Bollingen Series 20. New York: Pantheon, 1959.

JUNG, C. G. "Schizophrenia." In *Collected Works.* Vol. 3: *The Psychogenesis of Mental Disease.* Bollingen Series 20. New York: Pantheon, 1960.

JUNG, C. G. "Spirit and Life." In *Collected Works.* Vol. 18: *The Structure and Dynamics of the Psyche.* Bollingen Series 20. New York: Pantheon, 1960.

JUNG, C. G. "The Structure of the Psyche." In *Collected Works.* Vol. 18: *The Structure and Dynamics of the Psyche.* Bollingen Series 20. New York: Pantheon, 1960.

JUNG, C. G. *Symbols of Transformation.* (R. F. C. Hull, Trans.) Vol. 5 of *Collected Works.* Bollingen Series 20. New York: Pantheon, 1956.

KAUFMANN, M. R. "Religious Delusions in Schizophrenia." *International Journal of Psychoanalysis.* 1939, *20.*

KLAUSNER, J. *The Messianic Idea in Israel.* New York: Macmillan, 1955.

KOGAN, I. M. "Weltuntergangserlebnis and Wiedergeburtsphantasie bei einem Schizophrenen." *Internationale Zeitschrift für Psychoanalyse,* 1932, *18,* 86–104.

KOMROFF, M. (Ed.) *The Apocrypha.* New York: Tudor, 1936.

KRAMER, S. N. *Sumerian Mythology.* New York: Harper & Row, 1961.

KRAMER, S. N. "Sumerian Myths and Epic Tales." In J. B. Pritchard (Ed.), *Ancient Near Eastern Texts Relating to the Old Testament.* Princeton: Princeton University Press, 1955.

KRAMER, S. N. *Mythologies of the Ancient World.* Garden City, N.Y.: Doubleday, 1961.

LAING, R. D. *The Politics of Experience.* New York: Pantheon, 1967.

LAING, R. D., AND ESTERSON, A. *Sanity, Madness, and the Family.* Baltimore: Pelican Books, 1970.

LEVY, G. R. *The Gate of Horn.* London: Faber & Faber, 1948.

L'ORANGE, H. P. *Studies on the Iconography of Cosmic Kingship in the Ancient World.* Oslo: Instituttet for Sammenlignende Kulturforskning, 1953.

MELLAART, J. *Earliest Civilizations of the Near East.* New York: McGraw-Hill, 1965.

MERCER, S. A. B. *An Egyptian Grammar for Beginners.* Oriental Research Series, no. 1. London: Luzac, 1929.

MERCER, S. A. B. *Horus Royal God of Egypt.* Grafton, Mass.: Society of Oriental Research, 1942.

METMAN, P. "The Ego in Schizophrenia." *Journal of Analytical Psychology,* 1956, *1,* 161–176; and, 1957, *2,* 51–70.

MOWINCKEL, S. *He That Cometh.* (G. W. Anderson, Trans.) New York: Abingdon, 1954.

MURRAY, G. "Excursus on the Ritual Forms Preserved in Greek Tragedy." In J. Harrison, *Themis.* Cambridge, England: Cambridge University Press, 1927.

NEUMANN, E. *The Great Mother.* Bollingen Series 47. New York: Pantheon, 1955.

NEUMANN, E. *The Origins and History of Consciousness.* Bollingen Series 42. New York: Pantheon, 1954.

PEDERSEN, J. *Israel, Its Life and Culture.* London: Oxford University Press, 1934.

PERRY, J. W. "Acute Catatonic Schizophrenia." *Journal of Analytical Psychology,* 1957, *2,* 137–152.

PERRY, J. W. "Emotions and Object Relations." *Journal of Analytical Psychology,* 1970, *15,* 1–12.

PERRY, J. W. *The Far Side of Madness.* Englewood Cliffs, N.J.: Prentice-Hall, 1974.

PERRY, J. W. "Image, Complex, and Transference in Schizophrenia." In A. Burton (Ed.), *Psychotherapy of the Psychoses.* New York: Basic Books, 1961.

PERRY, J. W. *Lord of the Four Quarters: Myths of the Royal Father.* New York: Braziller, 1966.

PERRY, J. W. "Reconstitutive Process in the Psychopathology of the Self." *Annals of the New York Academy of Sciences,* 1962, *96,* 853–876.

PERRY, J. W. *The Self in Psychotic Process.* Berkeley: University of California Press, 1953.

PERRY, J. W. "Societal Implications of the Renewal Process." *Spring,* 1971, 153–167.

PLUTARCH. "Romulus." In A. H. Clough (Trans.), *Plutarch's Lives,* Vol. 1. Boston: Little, Brown, 1881.

PRITCHARD, J. B. *Ancient Near Eastern Texts Relating to the Old Testament.* Princeton: Princeton University Press, 1955.

PRITCHARD, J. B. *The Ancient Near East.* Princeton: Princeton University Press, 1958.

ROSENBAUM, C. P. *The Meaning of Madness.* New York: Science House, 1970.

SACHS, A. "Akkadian Rituals." In J. B. Pritchard (Ed.), *Ancient Near Eastern Texts Relating to the Old Testament.* Princeton: Princeton University Press, 1955.

SANTAYANA, G. *Poems.* New York: Scribner's, 1923.

SCHÄRF, R. "The Image of the Marriage Between God and Israel." *Spring,* 1950, 70–89.

SCHEFF, T. J. *Being Mentally Ill.* Chicago: Aldine Press, 1966.

SECHEHAYE, M. *Symbolic Realization.* New York: International Universities Press, 1957.

SMITH, W. R. *The Religion of the Semites.* New York: Meridian Books, 1956. (Originally Published 1901.)

SPEISER, E. A. "Akkadian Myths and Epics." In J. B. Pritchard (Ed.), *Ancient Near Eastern Texts Relating to the Old Testament.* Princeton: Princeton University Press, 1955.

SPRING, W. A. "Observations on World Destruction Fantasies." *Psychoanalytic Quarterly,* 1939, *8,* 363–376.

STORCH, A. "The Primitive Archaic Forms of Inner Experience and Thought in Schizophrenia." *Association for Research in Nervous and Mental Disease.* New York: Funk & Wagnalls, 1924.

SULLIVAN, H. S. "Schizophrenia: Its Conservative and Malignant Features." *Schizophrenia as a Human Process.* New York: Norton, 1962.

VAILLANT, G. C. *The Aztecs of Mexico.* Baltimore: Penguin Books, 1953. (Originally published 1941.)

VAN GENNEP, A. *The Rites of Passage.* Chicago: University of Chicago Press, 1960.

VON DOMARUS, E. "The Specific Laws of Logic in Schizophrenia." In J. S. Kasanin (Ed.), *Language and Thought in Schizophrenia.* Berkeley: University of California Press, 1944.

VON FRANZ, M. L. *The Problem of the Puer Aeternus.* New York: Spring Publications, 1970.

WHITMONT, E. C. *The Symbolic Quest.* New York: Putnam, 1969.

WICKES, F. *The Inner World of Childhood.* New York: Farrar, Straus & Giroux, 1927.

WIDENGREN, G. "Early Hebrew Myths and Their Interpretation." In S. H. Hooke (Ed.), *Myth, Ritual and Kingship.* Oxford: Clarendon, 1958.

WIDENGREN, G. "The King and the Tree of Life in Ancient Near Eastern Religion." In *Uppsala Universitets Ārsskrift.* Vol. 4. Uppsala, Sweden: Lundequisttika Bodhendeln, 1951.

WILSON, J. A. "The Admonitions of Ipu-wer." In J. B. Pritchard (Ed.), *Ancient Near Eastern Texts Relating to the Old Testament.* Princeton: Princeton University Press, 1955.

WILSON, J. A. *The Culture of Ancient Egypt.* Chicago: University of Chicago Press, 1960.

WILSON, J. A. "Egyptian Myths, Tales, and Mortuary Texts." In J. B. Pritchard (Ed.), *Ancient Near Eastern Texts Relating to the Old Testament.* Princeton: Princeton University Press, 1955.

WYNNE, L., AND OTHERS. "Pseudomutuality in the Family Relations of Schizophrenics." *Psychiatry,* 1958, *21,* 205.

Index

A

Affect image: archetypal image as, 28; concept of, 18–19
Agnew Project, 3
Ambivalence, 49–50
Anger, 50–51
Anima, concept of, 26
Animus, of mother, 33–34, 44–45, 48–49, 54, 68–70, 126
Apotheosis: background of image of, 132–133; in Canaan, 133; in case protocols, 134–136, 203, 206, 207, 209, 210, 211, 213, 214, 215, 216, 217, 219, 221–222; cultural, 134, 135, 137; in Egypt, 84, 132, 136, 137; heroic, 134, 135, 136; in Israel, 90–91, 127–132; in Mesopotamia, 86–87, 133, 136–137; political, 134–135; in psychic form, 134–138; religious, 134, 135; ritual form of, 127–138.
Archetypal image: concept of, 26; personal level related to, 67–68. *See also* Affect image
Archetype: central, 39–41, 62, 68–70; in chronically regressive personality,

Archetype (Continued)
47, 48–49, 50, 51, 54–55, 56; defined, 26
ARIETI, S., 9, 245
Autonomous psyche, unconscious as, 27–28
Autonomous shift, 49

B

BARNES, M., 10, 245
BATESON, G., 34, 245
BAYNES, H. G., 7, 245
Beginnings. *See* Return to beginnings
Birth, new: background of image of, 146–148; in Canaan, 148; in case protocols, 149–150, 203–204, 206, 207–208, 209, 211, 212, 213, 214, 216, 217–218, 219, 221; in Egypt, 84, 146–147; in Israel, 91, 144–146; in Mesopotamia, 87, 147–148; in psychic form, 148–150; ritual form of, 144–150
BOISEN, A. T., 7, 12, 245
BREASTED, J. H., 187, 245
BURKE, J., 10, 245
BURTON, A., 2

C

CAMPBELL, J., 133, 159, 246
Canaan, myth and ritual in, 88, 94, 101, 116–117, 123, 133, 141–142, 148
Case 1, 95–97, 109, 162–163, 190–191, 202–204
Case 2, 134–136, 161, 204–206
Case 3, 80, 149–150, 161–162, 206–208
Case 4, 56–60, 62–78, 80, 108–109, 117–118, 162, 208–209
Case 5, 102–103, 162, 209–211
Case 6, 81, 125–126, 162, 211–212
Case 7, 157–158, 212–213
Case 8, 142, 213–215
Case 9, 81, 124–125, 215–216
Case 10, 31, 109, 156–157, 216–218
Case 11, 81, 218–219
Case 12, 81, 118, 219–221
Center: background of image of, 94; in Canaan, 94; in case protocols, 95–97, 203, 204, 207, 208, 210, 211, 212, 220; in Egypt, 83, 94; in Israel, 89, 93–94; in Mesopotamia, 85, 94; in psychic form, 95–97; renewal of, 193–200; ritual form of, 92–97
Central archetype, 39–41, 62, 68–70
Central injury: concept of, 41, 45; results of, 45–56, 62
Centrality, myth and ritual of, 2
Complex: in chronically regressive personality, 45, 46, 47–48, 49, 50, 56; concept of, 26–27; roots of, 31–32
Consciousness: evolution of, 194–195; level of, lowered, 47–48
Cosmic conflict: in acute psychotic regression, 63–65; background of image of, 115–117; in Canaan, 116–117; in case protocols, 117–118, 203, 205, 207, 208–209, 210, 211, 212–213, 214, 215, 217, 218, 220; in Egypt, 83–84, 115–116; interpretation of, 70–72; in Israel, 90, 111–115; in Mesopotamia, 86, 116; personal aspects of, 72–73; in psychic form, 117–122; ritual form of, 111–122; symbolic geography of, 119–120
Cultural canon, return to beginnings related to, 110

D

Death: background of image of, 100–101; in Canaan, 101; in case protocols, 102–103, 203, 204–205, 207, 208, 210, 211, 214, 215, 216, 217, 218, 219–220; in Egypt, 83, 100; in Israel, 89–90, 98–100; in Mesopotamia, 85–86, 100; in psychic form, 101–103; ritual form of, 97–103
Delusions: amplification of, 65–66; interpretation of, 67–78; myths compared with, 66–67; system of, in acute psychotic regression, 63–67
Diabasis: principles of, 4–6; project at, 197–199
Double bind, self-image related to, 34

E

Ego: concept of, 23–24, 38; prepsychotic, 44; in schizophrenia, 43–44; weakness of, 48–49
Egypt, myth and ritual in, 82–85, 94, 100, 107, 115–116, 123, 132, 136, 137, 140, 146–147, 154–155, 160, 186–188
ELIADE, M., 108, 110, 246
Emotional psyche, 27–28
Emotions: development of, 24–29; development of, and self-image, 23–41; feelings distinguished from, 45; images related to, 25; in psychotic episode, 17–18
Eros, power related to, 51–52

F

Feelings: concept of, 45; withholding of, 44–46, 49–51, 58–59
FOUCAULT, M., 14, 246
FREUD, S., 8, 122, 246
FROMM-REICHMANN, F., 9, 247

G

GASTER, T. H., 80, 122, 123, 133, 159, 247
GROF, S., 10, 247
Guilt, 53–55, 59

H

HARRISON, J., 80, 247
Healing: external factors in, 13–17; internal factors in, 17–22; in psychotic episodes, 11–22
HOROWITZ, M., 9, 247
Hyperphrenia, 10

I

Injury, central, 41, 45–56, 62
Israel, myth and ritual in, 88–91, 93–94, 98–100, 104–106, 111–115, 122–123, 127–132, 138–140, 144–146, 152–154, 159–160, 166–188

J

JUNG, C. G., 7, 12, 25, 47, 52, 55, 62, 120, 135, 136, 248–249
Jung Institute, 2

K

KLAUSNER, J., 169, 176, 249

L

Labeling, and psychotic episodes, 12–15
LAING, R. D., 12, 250
LEVENE, H., 4
Logos: mastery and power drives in, 74; modality of, 51

M

McLean Hospital, 2
Marriage, sacred. *See* Sacred marriage
Mesopotamia, myth and ritual in, 85–88, 94, 100, 107–108, 116, 123, 133, 136–137, 140–141, 147–148, 155–156, 160
Messiah: background of image of, 186–188; Christian renderings of, 188–189; democratization of, 175–182; in Egypt, 186–188; in Iran, 188; in Israel, 166–188; in myth and ritual, 165–191; in psychic form, 190–191;
Messiah (Continued)
as servant of lord, 182–185; as son of man, 185–186
Monarch: restoration of idea of, 168–175; transformation of, to messiah, 165–175
Mother, *animus* of: and central archetype, 68–70; chronically regressive personality related to, 44–45, 48–49, 54; concept of, 33–34; and reversal of opposites, 126
Mother bond: compounding of, 46–47; in schizophrenia, 44–45, 56–58; and self-image, 32–38
MOWINCKEL, S., 151, 170, 171, 175–176, 250
Myths: delusions compared with, 66–67; importance of, 91–92, 194–195; ritual and culture related to, 79–80

N

NEUMANN, E., 56, 250
Northeast Community Mental Health Service (San Francisco), 4

O

Opposites, clash of. *See* Cosmic conflict
Opposites, reversal of: background of image of, 123–124; in Canaan, 123; in case protocols, 124–126, 203, 206, 207, 209, 210, 212, 213, 214, 215, 217, 219, 220; in Egypt, 84, 123; in Israel, 90, 122–123; in Mesopotamia, 86, 123; in psychic form, 124–127; ritual form of, 122–127
Opposites, union of. *See* Sacred marriage

P

Paranoid anxiety: in acute psychotic regression, 73–75; enemy in, role of, 120–121
Parental expectations, and self-image, 35–37
Personal experience, archetypal image and, 67–68
Personality, chronically regressive: case of, 56–60; components of, 43–60; defined, 10

Personality, prepsychotic, case of, 56–60
Power, eros related to, 51–52
Prepsychotic state: case of, 62–78; characteristics of, 62
Psychoanalysis, trends in, 8
Psychotic episode: dramatic performance in, 80–81; emotions in, 17–18; healing factors in, 11–22; labeling and, 12–15; nurturance for, 15–16; reorganization of self through, 61–62; self-image in, 19–22; symbolism and, 6–7, 17, 18–22

Q

Quadrated world: background of image of, 160–161; in case protocols, 161–163, 204, 206, 208, 209, 211, 212, 213, 218, 221; in Egypt, 85, 160; in Israel, 91, 159–160; in Mesopotamia, 88, 160; in psychic form, 161–164; ritual form of, 159–164

R

Rebirth. *See* Birth, new
Regression, acute psychotic: defined, 10; example of, 61–78; resolution in, 75–78
Regression, chronic. *See* Personality, chronically regressive
Renewal: of the center, 193–200; concept of, 11–13; process of, 196–197; ritual drama of, 79–164
Renewed society. *See* Society, renewed
Return to beginnings: background of image of, 107–108; in case protocols, 108–109, 203, 205, 207, 208, 210, 211, 212, 214, 215, 216–217, 218–219, 220; in Egypt, 83, 107; in Israel, 90, 104–106; in Mesopotamia, 86, 107–108; in psychic form, 108–111; ritual form of, 103–111
Reversal. *See* Opposites, reversal of
Ritual, in renewal, role of, 79–164. *See also* Myths

S

Sacred marriage: background of image of, 140–142; in Canaan, 141–142; in case protocols, 142, 203, 206, 207, 209, 210, 212, 213, 214, 217, 219, 221; in Egypt, 84, 140; in Israel, 91, 138–140; in Mesopotamia, 87, 140–141; in psychic form, 142–143; ritual form of, 138–144
SANTAYANA, G., 1, 251
SCHEFF, T., 12–13, 251
Schizoid, chronic, 10
Schizophrenia: catatonic, 52, 56, 63; ego in, 43–44; mother bond in, 44–45, 56–58; residential setting for, 3–6; self-image in, 62; term of, 10
SECHEHAYE, M., 9–10, 12, 251
Self-image: and emotional development, 23–41; genesis of, 31–32; importance of, 29–41; and mother bond, 32–38; parental expectations and, 35–37; personal, concept of, 62; in schizophrenia, 62; transformation of, 19–22, 38–41
SILVERMAN, J., 3
SMITH, W. R., 79, 251
Society, renewed: background of image of, 154–156; in case protocols, 156–158; 204, 206, 208, 209, 211, 212, 213, 214, 216, 218, 221; in Egypt, 84–85, 154–155; in Israel, 91, 152–154; in Mesopotamia, 87–88, 155–156; in psychic form, 156–158; ritual form of, 150–158
SULLIVAN, H. S., 9, 12, 251
Symbolic imagery, emotion and, 25
Symbolism: interpretations of, 8–9; and psychotic episodes, 6–7, 17, 18–22

T

Thinking, 52–53, 59
Time, sense of, 55–56, 59–60

U

Unconscious: complexes in, 26–27; personal and collective, 28

W

WATTS, A., 2
Worcester State Hospital, 12